RIGHTLY DIVID THE WORD

Things That Differ

"Rightly dividing the word of truth." (2 Tim. 2:15)

"And they shall teach my people the difference." (Ezek. 44:23)

William S. Penfold

N. John Jeyanandam

P. K. Abraham

JOHN RITCHIE LTD

CHRISTIAN PUBLICATIONS

40 Beansburn, Kilmarnock, Scotland

Rightly Dividing the Word – Things that Differ.

First Indian Edition: May 1995, and Reprint June 1996

This Edition: 2006
ISBN 1 904064 32 9

PREFACE

"For ever, O Lord, Thy word is settled in heaven", "For the Word of the Lord is right" and is very pure, and true from the beginning. The Word is the saying of His righteousness (Ps. 33:4, 119:89, 123, 140 & 160). The Lord Jesus is "The Word of God" (Rev. 19:13) and passages like John 1:1-3, 14, Hebrew 4:12, 13 and 1 John 1:1 identify the Word of God with the Lord Himself. Thus, the Holy Scriptures deserve diligent and careful study, and claim holy respect. His people, therefore, should handle God's Word with care, and it is our responsibility to interpret and teach it with fear, in order to maintain its integrity and the purity of its doctrinal truths. We are exhorted to "rightly divide the Word of Truth" (2 Tim. 2:15) and having thus learned, we are not to "wrest ... the Scriptures", to our own destruction (2 Pet. 3:16).

These tabulated summaries, with notes, have been carefully and prayerfully prepared with a view to enable readers of God's Word, to *distinguish* truths, which may otherwise pass unnoticed or remain confused. Although brief in many cases, a few vital truths are presented in more detail, and with helpful Charts. These Papers contrast distinctions and compare similarities, and bring truth to light.

Our earlier desire to reprint sound doctrinal books, now out of print, and to attempt to have them translated into some of the Indian languages, was finally abandoned in favour of the principle of placing truths *side by side*, using comparison and contrast to show essential distinctions. The outcome, here presented, covers over 40 Study Papers of inter-related subjects, for the edification and building up of His people.

The purpose of this book is to elevate and bring honour and glory to the Lord Jesus Christ and the Holy Scripture, the Written Word of God; and to clarify any doubts and uncertainties one may have. It is firmly believed, that this book will educate young believers and re-assure others. In these post modern days, when the revealed divine truths are denied, apostasy increases and every man seems to believe and do that which is right in his own eyes, we are sure the truths high lighted here will build assurance and hope.

It is the compilers' intention, if the Lord will, that these papers, should be accurately translated into the main languages of India, and in a few of the languages of Africa and Europe, where His people do not have access to the now available abundant variety of sound doctrinal teaching in the English language.

Should these Papers clear misunderstandings and confusions and stimulate a desire for a deeper study of Holy Writ, the compilers will consider their objectives attained.

William S. Penfold
N John Jeyanandam
P K Abraham

FOREWORD

The re-printing of this very helpful compilation not only reflects the desire of the sole surviving contributor, Mr John Jeyanandam, to make the work available to rising generations, but also the desire of the publishers to preserve the original intention of the brethren involved to honour our Lord Jesus Christ and highlight the importance of having an accurate understanding of the Holy Scriptures. The truth of Scripture is under attack from many quarters, with perceived difficulties being used to undermine the confidence of many believers, particularly younger believers; hence the need to make available a work of this nature. There has been neither the desire nor the need on the part of the publishers to review or revise the material. It is therefore our prayer that this work will find its way into the hands and hearts of a younger generation and be used by the Lord to encourage a careful and thoughtful study of the Holy Scriptures, leading to "rightly dividing the word of truth".

John Ritchie Ltd.

April 2006

CONTENTS

CHARTS

The Church Which Is His Body and the Church of God At

The word 'church', in our K J Version, is not a translation of the Greek word "*ekklesia*", which is a compound word derived from the preposition '*ek*' (out of) and the noun, '*klesis*' (a calling). The literal sense of the word is, "a called-out company". The correct rendering of this word, therefore, would be "Assembly" or "Gathering". In fact it is used only for the New Testament thought of the Assembly of saints, with the two exceptions, in Acts 7:38, for the congregation of Israel; and again in Acts 19:32, 39, 41 for a heathen mob at Ephesus.

This word is used in the N T, in three different ways:

1. The *whole company of* the redeemed throughout the present age, the company of which Christ said, "I will build My church" (Matt. 16:18). This is further described as, "the church which is His body" (Eph. 1:22; 5:23). We find the word is used in the same way in other passages like Eph. 3:10; 5:25, 29, 32; Col. 1:18, 24; Heb. 12:23.

2. In the *singular number,* the church is limited to local gatherings as "the church which is at Jerusalem" (Acts 8:1; 11:22), or at Antioch (Acts 13:1), at Ephesus (Acts 20:17), at Cenchrea (Rom. 16:1), at Corinth (I Cor. 1:2) at Thessalonica (I Thess. 1:1) and generally (I Tim 3: 5, 15).

3. In the *plural form,* with reference to several local churches in an area or district. The churches of Judaea (I Thess. 2:14; Acts 9:31), of Galatia (I Cor. 16:1; Gal. 1:2), of Asia (I Cor. 16:19), and of Macedonia (2 Cor. 8:1). More generally, it sometimes includes all the assemblies of God, as 'other churches' in 2 Cor. 11:8; 'the care of all the churches' in 2 Cor. 11:28; and 'the churches of God' in 2 Thess. 1:4.

From the above, we find its application is *two-fold:*

1. As the whole company of the redeemed believers throughout the present age, and

2. As a local company of believers gathering at a particular place and time.

The Lord's first reference of this word in Matt. 16:18 refer to the whole company, *the church which is His body* and His second reference in Matt. 18:17 is to its *local aspect.* Remarkably enough in the OT also, we may discover a similar two-fold sense "congregation" and "assembly" as to its Jewish context. The two commonly used Hebrew words are:

"Edah" - from a root which means, "to appoint".

"Qahal" - "an assembly called together".

The former is used to designate the *whole nation* of Israel, whether gathered or not (Num. 1:2; 20:1). The latter word always refers to a *specific gathering*, often as linked with a particular time or place. (Deut. 9:10; Judges 21:8).

In the following tabulation, the clear distinctions of these two N T applications are brought out.

The Church which is His body. Eph. 1:23	The Church of God at... I Cor. 1:2
The Lord Jesus Christ builds it. (Mat. 16:18)	The believers build it through the operation of the Holy Spirit. (I Cor. 3:6,10)
Gathered out from the world. (Acts 15:14)	Gathered to Christ Jesus the Lord. (I Cor. 1:1-3, 5:4)
Began on the day of Pentecost. (Acts 2)	Begins locally by spiritual planting of individual believers (1 Cor. 3:6)
It is His (one) Body. (Eph. 1:22, 23; 2:16; 1 Cor. 12:12, 13)	It is a company, locally expressing the Body of Christ, (1 Cor. 1:1-3; 12:27)
It is a revelation of truth (Eph. 3:3-5)	It is a practical aspect of truth (I Tim. 3:15)
It is entered at conversion and is a *standing* in Christ, as opposed to a *state* of life. All were baptized in the Spirit at Pentecost. (I Cor. 12:13)	Entered by reception, "In the Lord". (Acts. 9:26-29; Rom. 16:2)
No difference of sex (Gal. 3:28)	Differences of sex exist. (I Cor. 14:34-35; I Tim. 2:8-15)
No unsaved are in it (John 10:27, 28; Eph. 5:25-27)	Unsaved may be present (I Cor. 14:24)
Nothing false can enter. (Eph. 5:25-27)	'Wolves' can enter. (Acts 20:29)
Cannot be excommunicated. (Eph. 5:29-30; Rom. 8:38, 39)	Assembly excommunicates (I Cor. 5:13)
The Lord disciplines. (Heb. 12:5, 6)	The assembly disciplines (Matt. 18:17)
God cares for it. (Heb. 12:5, 6)	The Elders care for it. (I Tim. 3:5)
The Lord nourisheth and cherisheth it. (Eph. 5:29)	The Elders feed it. (I Pet. 5:2)

The Church which is His body. Eph. 1:23	The Church of God at... I Cor. 1:2
Perfect unity exists. (Eph. 2:16-19; 4:4-6; 4:16)	**Divisions and schisms can creep in (1 Cor. 3:1-4; 12:25)**
Satan cannot prevail against it. (Matt. 16:18)	**Satan can corrupt it (2 Cor. 11:1-3)**
To be presented faultless. (Eph. 5:27)	**Can be removed in judgment. (Rev. 2:5)**

Though some similarities seem to appear in the following Scriptural descriptions, as to the use of the word '**church**', the clear distinctions between the *two aspects* as differentiated above are evident and they should be maintained.

The Church which is His Body	The Local Assembly
Is called "the Church" (Eph. 1:22)	**Is called "Church of God" (thus called 13 times in NT)**
Called the Church which is His Body (Eph. 1:23; I Cor. 12:12)	**Called "Body of Christ", (I Cor. 12:27) but never as "The Body".**
"A holy Temple" (Eph. 2:21)	**"Temple of God" (I Cor. 3:16) "House of God" (I Tim. 3:15) "Ye (Ephesians) are – a habitation of God" (Eph. 2:22)**
"One fold" (Jn. 10:16) (Gr. "POIMNE" meaning 'flock')	**A 'flock' (Acts 20:28) (Gr. "POIMNION" meaning 'Little flock')**
Will be revealed in a coming day as a 'bride'. (Rev. 21:2)	**Is "as a chaste virgin" (2 Cor. 11:2)**

The following are the names given in the Word of God for the Believers:

1. "Christians" Acts 11:26; 26:28; I Pet. 4:16
2. "Believers" Acts 5:14; 1 Tim. 4:12
3. "Brethren" Gal. 1:2; Eph. 6:23; Col. 1:2; 4:15
4. "Saints" Rom. 1:7; I Cor. 1:2 etc.
5. "Disciples" Acts 11:26

All these simply gather together, unto the name of our Lord Jesus Christ (Matt. 18:20)

There is no federation or circle of fellowship or union of churches; however, fellowship exists among various local assemblies based on the "sharing in common" of truth (I Cor. 7:17; 11:16).

Assemblies have no earthly centre of authority or organizational hierarchy. Each assembly is independently responsible to the Lord. (Rev. chs. 1-3)

The Unscriptural Uses of the Word "Church".

The word 'church' is being used in a number of varied senses, as indicated below. We

We should be careful to avoid such expressions as they are unscriptural. The true and clear sense with which this word 'church' is used in the Word of God, should be clearly understood. The terminology such as these, encourage either Ecumenism or Exclusivism:

1. For a building consecrated or used for religious meetings or a meeting place.

2. "The church on earth", "The Body on earth", "The Local Body". Scripture never divides Body in this way between those already with Christ in heaven and those left on earth.

3. "The early Church", "the Church of the 20th Century" etc. thus distinguishing according to the times.

4. It is not Scriptural to categorize a number of Christians or companies or Churches together and call them by their area, or of a certain land, (e.g. 'The Church of England', "The Church of South India') or language, (e.g. 'Tamil Church', 'Malayalam Assembly') or doctrine (e.g. 'Baptist Church', 'Pentecostal Church') or name of a person (e.g. 'Lutheran Church', 'Azad Memorial Church') etc.

The accuracy, with which the Holy Scripture defines these terms, indicates that the use of loose terminology such as given below should be avoided:

The Visible Church,   The Church on earth

The Early Church,   The body on earth

The Local Body,   The universal Church, etc.

Descriptive Name	Implications	References
Church of God	Origin and Ownership	Acts 20:28; I Cor. 1:2;
Churches of saints	Composition	I Cor. 14:33;
Churches of Christ	Lordship & Enrichment, or Sovereignty and Headship.	Rom. 16:16;
Church of the Living God.	Character	I Tim. 3:15
Churches of the Gentiles	Derivation	Rom. 16:4
Church in their / his house	Location	Philemon 2; Col 4:15; I Cor. 16:19
Church which is at Cenchrea	Location - Town	Rom. 16:1
Church of the Thessalonians	Local Composition	I Thess. 1:1
Churches of Asia	Area Limitation	I Cor. 16:19

The Assembly
as A Building, as A Body and as A Flock

A thoughtful reader of the New Testament will observe that the Holy Spirit has used several metaphors for the Church, of which, "The Building", "The Body" and "The Flock" are prominent. It must be carefully noted that even in these metaphors, the *two* aspects of the Church, viz. the local aspect (the church at...) and the total aspect (the church which is His body) are clearly distinguished, as brought out in this tabulation :

COMPLETE ASPECT	LOCAL ASPECT
BUILDING: (Ephesians 2:21) "In whom (Jesus Christ Himself being the Chief Corner Stone) ALL the building fitly framed together groweth unto a holy temple in the Lord." 'All' believers from the day of Pentecost till the rapture make up the *whole* Holy Temple in the Lord. (Think of the Holiest of all covered with Gold, indicating a habitation for the Lord)	*BUILDING:* (Ephesians 2:22) "In whom YE also are builded together for a habitation of God through the Spirit." 'YE' limiting to the assembly at Ephesus (v.22), as a habitation of God through the Holy Spirit. This shows that it is necessary for the believers to give the Holy Spirit the freedom without preconceived programmes that He may act with complete liberty and grant preeminence and prerogative to exalt Christ in the midst.

COMPLETE ASPECT	LOCAL ASPECT
BODY: (1 Cor. 12:12) "For as the body is one, and hath many members . . . of that one body." This picture of a human body (up to verse 26) describes the different parts of the body with their various functions. The exception to this is v.13, which describes how the body (Church) came into being, "For (also) by one Spirit are we ALL (emphatic) baptised into one body".	*BODY: (I Cor. 12:27)* "Now ye are *the* body of Christ, and members in particular." Notice the word *'the'* italicised, is not in the Greek. We have to consider the implication of its omission in the original which reads as 'Now ye are body of Christ'. It is clear that the body of Christ was not made up of Corinthians alone. But in their local emphasis they were to show all the *characteristics* of the one body described in the previous verses.
FLOCK: (John 10:16) "Other sheep I have which are not of this fold (Israel). Them (emphatic) also I must bring and they shall hear my voice and there shall be one Flock (a 'Fold') and one Shepherd." The 'other sheep' are Gentiles, the truth of which Peter finally grasped through the vision of the sheet knit at the four corners with the living creatures (Acts 10:11), which he explains in Acts 11:6. The four corners emphasize gentiles from all over the earth.	*FLOCK: (Acts 20:28)* "Take heed therefore unto yourselves, and to all the flock (meaning 'little flock') over which the Holy Spirit hath made you overseers, to feed the Church of God, which He hath purchased with his own blood". Elders are personally responsible for feeding the sheep, not to do by proxy or by any alternative methods. (1 Pet. 5:2). The margin 'little flock' clearly, differentiates the local shepherd's responsibility from the 'one flock' of which the Lord is the 'good' or "beautiful shepherd".

The Over-All – Total Aspect of the Above Similitudes

The Building

The Lord is building His church (Matt. 16:18), whereas believers are building according to the pattern left to them by the Apostles and Prophets. This building work will be in accord with, and *not* contrary to, the doctrine of the Apostles and Prophets (Eph. 2:20), which they laid as a foundation for others to build upon (I Cor. 3:10). This *construction work* is what is compared to two kinds of materials – Gold, Silver and Precious Stones or Wood, Hay and Stubble, as found in 1 Cor.

3:12. (Please see "God's Building" Paper No. 01:03).

The Body

Although the baptism in the Spirit (Luke 3:16; John 14:17; Acts 1:5, 8), took place in Acts 2, it is not specifically mentioned there. The Holy Spirit coming upon the disciples and filling them is of course clearly seen in Acts 2:1-4, and we see Peter specifically describing this later in Acts 11:15-16.

On reflection, what would you expect if "the baptism in the Spirit" had been mentioned in Acts 2? Surely we should view things as fulfilled to the *whole* body. Every member from Pentecost to the Rapture, *all* having been given to the Son in eternity past (John 17:2), and baptised in the Spirit – the Holy Spirit rested upon them – thus the promise being fulfilled. "For by one Spirit are we *all* baptised into *one* body" (I Cor. 12:13)

The One Flock

The "one flock" (John 10:16) signifies that Christ's flock of sheep extends beyond the confines of the Jewish nation.

The stress on the "one flock" emphasises the unifying voice of the Great Shepherd (Heb. 13:20), which would break down all the barriers to the ultimate "one flock" of Christ's sheep.

The sense conveyed is of a **spiritual unity**, which exists in spite of any thing to the contrary.

John 10:19 records "There was a *division* therefore again". Indeed there is an enemy whose plans thrive on it.

Conclusion

Bringing the three metaphoric words 'Building', 'Body' and 'Flock' together, we note the two distinctions as to their *'total'* and the *'local'* aspects and the following conclusions are drawn :

The TOTAL position is not something for which *we* are responsible.

The LOCAL position in each case is *our* responsibility.

The Building: No wood, hay or stubble (I Cor. 3:12) would provide a habitation of God. *How* we build, even upon the foundation of Jesus Christ, so that God may be pleased to dwell among us, is what matters. "The church of the living God, the pillar and ground of the truth" (I Tim. 3:15). The alternative situation is also possible, that is, the Lord standing *outside* (Rev. 3:20).

The Body: The many members – all interdependent – is the burden of the figure of "A Body". In other words, care one for another; mutual consideration, humility and esteeming the other better than one's self are necessary to avoid schism. Division in a body is unthinkable. (1 Cor. 12)

The Flock: Under-shepherds must feed their flock, watching over it all the time. Frequent bringing in of brethren from outside for ministry is wrong. Should local responsibility be shelved the sheep become alienated. (I Pet. 5:2).

NOTE: This paper should be considered along side that entitled "The Church which is His Body and the Church of God At". (Paper No. 01-01)

God's Building

In symbolic language, the Apostle Paul speaks regarding the construction of God's Building here on earth and the significance of our part in this important work (I Cor. 3:9-18). It should be noted that in the *dispensational aspect of* God's Building, referred to in Ephesians 2:21-22, it is the Holy Spirit Who is the Builder, and there *is positively no defective* workmanship in its construction; but in I Corinthians 3, it is the *local aspect* of the Church, and the labours of the believers that are in view. Consequently faulty work is evidenced.

The materials are differentiated below:

Gold, Silver & Precious Stones	Wood, Hay and Stubble
1. Cost: **Very expensive, valuable and precious**	1. Cost: **Very cheap and common: Once they had life.**
2. Character: **Man cannot manufacture them – Durable.**	2. Character: **Products of earth, not durable.**
3. Construction: **Part of compact creation, comparatively small but precious, difficult to mine.**	3. Construction: **Fast growth, big and bulky but comparatively valueless.**
4. Durability: **Withstands fire. Comes out shining (v 14).**	4. Durability: **Completely destroyed by fire, "saved: yet so as through fire", (v. 15)**

Conclusion:

Two vital aspects regarding this passage should be borne in mind:

1. What I Cor. 3:12 says is, that *our spiritual work* is compared to two different kinds of *materials,* and it raises an important question as to whether our work will withstand the fire of God. Note, that the word *'work'* is used four times in this passage, and that we are building with the spiritual equivalent of these materials.

2. I Cor. 3:10 says that *we* are building *upon* the foundation already laid down by the Apostles (Eph. 2:20), i.e. the *doctrinal foundation* of the church, laid by the Apostle Paul "as a wise master builder". Our work upon this foundation should be of the Spirit and not of the flesh. Our work, however honest, sincere, and sacrificial, if not built *upon that foundation* laid by the Apostle, it will be of the inferior nature of wood, hay and stubble.

These two aspects of the building should be clearly distinguished: *The Holy Spirit builds* upon the foundation of the Lord Jesus Christ, with the building materials, which are the redeemed believers, the living stones (Eph. 2:21, 22; I Peter 2:5). However, *as believers, we are now building* upon that foundation of the Apostles and the Prophets – the doctrinal truth laid by them – and *how* we "build thereupon" that is, *our works,* is the criteria. The objective of our work is described in Eph. 4:12-13.

The Difference between the Lord's Table and the Lord's Supper

The Lord's Table (1 Cor. 10:14-22)	The Lord's Supper (1 Cor. 11:23-34)
The symbols, cup and bread (Note the order) are the same, but the implication is *saint-ward, and the order of institution reversed.*	The symbols, bread and cup are the same but their implication is *God-ward.*
The emphasis here is on *fellowship,* the basis of which is the death of Christ, involving the shedding of blood. Hence, the cup, the symbol of the blood is mentioned *first* (1 Cor. 10:16)	The practice here of a local assembly is in *obedience* to the Lord's desire (request). Hence the order mentioned is the historic one as instituted by the Lord. (The cup in Luke 22:17 is the last cup of the Passover supper).
Speaks of the *oneness* of the believers as one bread and yet also of fellowship.	Speaks of *remembrance* of the Blesser, not of our blessings – "in remembrance of me".
Not limited to time, place or circumstance.	Limited to time and place, the whole assembly gathering on the Lord's Day, in one place (1 Cor. 11: 23-26; Acts 20: 7).
Signifies the *daily fellowship* that individual believers have with God and in abiding and in communing with the Lord Jesus.	It is *obedience* to the behest "Remember Me", and gives a collective expression in priesthood in effectively offering up Christ to the Father.
The cup and bread represents personal spiritual fellowship of the Lord's people.	The symbols are just the means to the remembrance of, and to show, the Lord's death till He come.
Speaks of the fellowship we have with the Lord and fellowship with the saints through His precious Blood.	Speaks of His life, death, resurrection and ascension, in remembrance of the Lord on the first day of the week (Heb. 13: 15)

The Lord's Table (1 Cor. 10:14-22)	The Lord's Supper (1 Cor. 11:23-34)
Because fellowship with the Lord, (into which we are received) is not by men, no man can put any one out of this fellowship. However participation with the table of demons automatically disqualifies (1 Cor. 10:21; 1 John 1:3).	Moral and spiritual defilement disqualifies. Disqualification may arise through ignorance of the scriptural principles of gathering (involving inter denominationalism). Assembly excommunicates for moral sin (1 Cor. 5:11) and for damnable heresies. (1 Tim.1: 19, 20)

Note:

(1) John 6:56-63 relates to the New Birth and does not relate to the Lord's table or the supper.

(2) 1 Cor. 11:29 "The Lord's body", is the Lord's own body and 1 Cor. 12: 27 "Body of Christ" is a description of the believers at Corinth. They are not the same.

Please also refer Paper No: 01 - 07

Priests, Bishops and Deacons

The priesthood of all believers in Christ and the work of bishops and deacons are important subjects in the New Testament. This paper outlines the Scriptural patterns and explains the spiritual aspects of these different functions.

The Correct Scriptural Pattern as against the Corrupt Practices in Christendom:

In Apostolic times, the words for bishops, priests and deacons had clear and unmistakable meanings. They were never intended to support hierarchical systems, which created different levels of power and authority in the Churches. It was the introduction of these unscriptural practices, which brought about the division of clergy and laity.

The Church is not an organisation but an organism. It is a living thing, and if it lives it grows, and like the body of a man, it nourishes and protects itself, in virtue of the power of its *life* which is Christ Himself. So in a church, bishops and deacons are necessary to its well-being. Hand and foot serve the body, they do not control it; but the head does. Bishops and deacons *serve* the Church, they do not control it – it is the Lord, the Spirit that controls. "Not as lords over God's heritage." (I Pet. 5:3).

"The Bishops and Deacons" are viewed as forming part of the assembly. In Philippians 1:1, separate mention of them is to indicate their place and service within the company of the saints. There are no hierarchical overtones in these two words as accepted and practised in Christendom. In Christendom we find one bishop over many churches; while in the N T we have a number of bishops as members of one local church.

Priests, Bishops and Deacons Defined:

In the Scripture the terms priests, bishops (overseers) and deacons are not *degrees* in a hierarchy, but describe the *character* of the service rendered in a church. They often are seen simultaneously in the same individual, but spring from different sanctions:

1. Priesthood arises from *spiritual new-birth,* and the offering of Christ, as the true burnt-offering, to God.

2. Overseership arises from *spiritual character,* and with gifts, thus becoming an example to the flock.

3. Deaconship arises from *spiritual gifts,* thus serving the flock, holding the mystery of the faith in a pure conscience. (I Tim. 3:9).

In the churches, it is the *character* of the bishop or deacon that counts. It is not an office but a *work.* He must be a man of God, and be *among* the people of God, to stand in front of the flock that he may lead them by *example* as well as by *precept*. He is to be *seen* as well as *heard*. As for his function, the Good Samaritan provides the type. He 'took care' of his neighbour, the man who needed him, to bind up the wounded, to comfort the distressed, to succour those who have fallen into the hands of the enemy – that is the service and ministry of the bishop. And he should be apt to teach. The deacon should excel in teaching, having earned a place of trust amongst the Lord's people (I Tim. 3:10).

The Lord Himself is the perfect embodiment of the type. He came "not to be served but to serve, (not to be deaconed but to deacon) and to give His life a ransom for many" (Mark 10:45). Having spent various periods of time, building up and ministering to several churches, the apostle Paul illustrates the true character of a deacon and a bishop. To the Thessalonians he became *nurse (mother)* and *brother and father* (I Thess. 2:7-12).

Priests

Nowhere in the Scripture, do we find any trace of a type of Priesthood as an office, amongst the saints of the church, as we find in Christendom today. The priestly office is but a human arrangement borrowed from Judaism and Paganism, like the rest of the sacerdotal system.

All heart – believers in the Lord Jesus Christ, without distinction of age or sex are priests, and as to high priest, there is only one, Jesus Christ, the Son of God our great High Priest (Heb. 4:14; 8:1) and there are no vice-high-priests.

All believers are priests, *holy* as to the divine purpose, *royal* as to their priestly dignity. (I Peter 2:5, 9).

Priestly Ministry

All true believers in Christ, as living stones, are built up into a spiritual house. As a holy priesthood, they offer up spiritual sac-

rifices, well pleasing and acceptable to God by Jesus Christ. (I Peter 2:5).

The Word of God categorises these ministries as 'sacrifices' acceptable to God. In the exercise of his ministry as a sacrificing priest, every believer-priest offers sacrifices as detailed in the following N T Scriptures:

1. *Presenting ourselves* and our bodies as a living sacrifice acceptable to God (Rom. 12:1).

2. Sacrifices *of praise to God,* the fruit of our lips. (Heb.13:15).

3. *Giving our material* substances to God, as an acceptable sacrifice. (Phil. 4:18).

4. The sacrifices *of good works,* "to do good" which is well pleasing to God. (Heb. 13:16).

5. And to communicate (Heb. 13:16) (give to others in cash or kind) which has the same commendation 'pleasure to God'.

Priesthood is one of the most precious privileges of the people of God, and let no man or system rob us of it, by depriving in any manner as to the offering up ot spiritual sacrifices to God.

Gift is distinct from priesthood. A believer may not be gifted to preach or to teach, but he as a priest will enjoy Christ and tell the Father so. Christ has made him for that purpose. (Heb. 13:15).

The priesthood of Israel was selective, typical of Christ and earthly; but that of the believer in Christ, in contrast, is irrespective of nationality, it is spiritual, and is operating in the heavenlies.

If Christ is really present as High Priest in the assembly, it is presumptuous for any man to come between and take Christ's place. For one man to presume to take pre-eminence and dictate who shall take part and when, and how, is to ignore Him, Who is the "High Priest over the House of God". (Heb. 10:21-23). And it is the Holy Spirit who takes the things of Christ and reveals them to us. (John 16:15)

Bishops

The word 'Bishops' (episkopos) is translated 'overseers' in Acts 20:28; I Tim. 3:2 and Titus 1:7. But overseer and elder is the same person (Acts 20:17, 28; I Pet 5:1-2). The word "oversight" (episkopeo) (I Pet 5:2) does not imply the entering upon such a responsibility or into that office, but the *fulfilment* of its ministry. It is not a matter of assuming a position, but of the *discharge* of the duties, in "Taking the oversight or overseeing" which is a verbal noun.

The word 'elder' describes the *maturity* of the person, his spiritual experience and understanding, while the word 'overseer' indicates the character of the work. The former referring to the *man* and the latter to his *function* or work.

Elder: As 'elders' they are charged with *guiding* the flock. While some weight of years is in this word, it carries also the meaning of "maturity of spiritual experience". It is good for a local church to be blessed with older men of God, men of experience with God, having learned much in the school of God.

Overseers: This is the ministry of *guarding* the flock, and *watching* over them. This ministry was to be wholehearted and willing and "not by constraint", nor of the lust for profit. Love of gain and money (base gain) for spiritual service was never to be the motive and must have no part in the ministry of elders. (I Pet. 5:2).

Overseers as Shepherds: The work of the shepherds is the responsibility to feed and tend the flock of God. Their ministry was a *giving one*. They were to act as pastors in the local church (Eph. 4:11). They are in fact under-shepherds as Christ is the Chief-Shepherd (I Pet. 5:4). The Lord had charged Peter, an apostle, to shepherd and feed the flock, both sheep and lambs (John 21:1-17), which charge Peter also commits to faithful men. (I Pet. 5:1, 2)

The shepherds, spiritual leaders of Israel in the days of Ezekiel (Ezk. 34:1-4, 8-10) had a solemn five-fold indictment levelled against them: They *fleeced* the flock for their own comfort (v3); They *fed not* the flock because of laziness (v8); They *fed on* the flock (v10); They failed to *guard* the flock (v8); They felt no responsibility to *care* for the flock (v4). They showed a loveless *neglect:* let every shepherd be warned.

Plurality of Elders:

In the local church, plurality of elders is a safeguard against various dangers. Exhortation is given to the elders (plural) (Acts 20:17; Phil. 1:1; I Tim. 5:17; Titus 1:5; I Pet. 5:1). Peter takes his place among the elders as a fellow-elder. He did not take a position as an apostle or prelate above them as having a special office.

1. Plurality preserves against error: A body of elders seeking the mind and will of God together is less likely to fall into error, or to allow it, than one man ruling and making his own judgement. In the multitude of counsellors there is safety. (Pro. 11:14)

2. Plurality preserves from ill-balanced ministry: It is unscriptural to think that all the gifts can reside in one man. It is the variety of gifts in the elders that provide the well balanced diet of spiritual good required for health and development of all the flock of God, lambs I and sheep. Continual importation of gift from outside of the assembly is not sanctioned in the word of God.

14

3. *Plurality preserves from giving undue place or glory to one man:* Christendom seeks to honour its leaders with special titles, ranks and robes, to mark them out as distinct from others. This divides the brotherhood into different ranks, which thing the Lord hates (Mat. 23:5-11; Rev. 2:6, 15). Who made thee to differ, O man?

4. *Plurality preserves* from *the danger of human domination:* Diotrephes (3 John 9-10), was a man who loved that place of pre-eminence. There is no charge of doctrinal error, of moral failure, lack of zeal, gift or industry levelled against him. His error of casting out arose from perverted love, the love "to have the pre-eminence". There is only One in the Church who can say "I am the first" (Rev. 1:17).

5. *Plurality preserves from disintegration in times of persecution:* Where God's people have gathered around one man and depend on him for their spiritual good and direction, when that man is taken away suddenly, the sheep will wander and be scattered like a flock without a shepherd. The government and care of the flock is delegated to a body of elders who will give account of their stewardship, in a coming day (Heb. 13:17).

Elders are being raised by the work of the Holy Spirit (Acts 20:28). They are recognised by their spiritual care and overseeing, evidencing by their work, that they are doing that very thing. They are being recognised according as they give evidence of their divine qualifications. (I Tim. 3:1-7; Titus 1:6-9; I Pet. 5:2).

We are to be careful of the phrase "to rule" (I Tim. 3:4, 5; 5:17 KJV), "To rule" is a poor translation, for "to stand before". (Strong No. 4291). 'Rule' of Hebrews 13:7, 17 & 24, is Strong No. 2233 and means "to lead by example". As a father stands before his children, in leading, in guiding and therefore drawing out the trust and faith in him,

so is an elder standing before an assembly. They will need to trust him to lead them aright.

The functions of the elders are "to stand before", that is to guide (I Tim. 3:4-5; 5:17); to teach (1 Tim. 5:17); to guard the body of revealed truth from perversions and errors (Titus 1:9), and also to guard from the "grievous wolves" entering among His people (Acts 20:29); and to oversee as a shepherd his flock (John 21:16; Acts 20:28; Heb. 13:17; I Pet. 5:2).

Deacons

The deacons are those men gifted by the Lord for the service of ministry of God's word and its teaching within the assembly.

The word 'deacon' (Diakonos) is used thirty times in the NT and is translated 'servant' or 'minister', simply meaning one who renders service among the saints, whether in secular things or spiritual. The qualifications of the deacons are stated in I Tim. 3:8-13. These qualities are of a similar standard to those required of elders.

The deacon has at least two separate spheres of service, one *spiritual:* and the other *secular,* for both of which, he has to be one like Stephen, full of the Holy Spirit. (Acts 6:3; 7:55). The first as gifted and trained by the Holy Spirit and the second as recognised by the assembly (I Tim. 3:10; Acts 6:3).

1. The *secular side* can be seen in Acts 6:2-24; Rom. 16:1; 2 Cor. 8:4, 19. It is a physical, material, administrative service, for the benefit of the company of saints, by men acceptable and responsible to that company (Acts 6:5).

2. The *spiritual work* is indicated in Acts 6:8; 8:40, as found in the life of Stephen and Philip (Acts Ch 7 & 8).

Phebe is called "a servant (deaconess) of the church" (Rom. 16:1), and would be acknowledged as one by whom definite acts of service, consistent with her sex, were carried out and acknowledged by the church. Within the material and physical sphere would be the works of mercy, the care of the sick, the hospitality within the home etc; and within the spiritual realm would be the teaching of the younger women, and in respect of the teaching and care of children etc. (Titus 2:4,5).

It must not be thought then, that the work of the deacon is only in the secular sphere, nor that it is inferior to that of the bishops or elders as found in ecclesiastical circles. It is not a probationary step. What is meant by I Tim. 3:13 is "They that have served (used the office of a deacon) well acquire to themselves (not a good degree for promotion, but) a *good standing* place", a person who can be trusted with God's truth (the faith in a good conscience), against the day of judgement (I Cor. 3:13,14): It is not a step to promotion.

The following tabulation summarises the points of comparison and contrast between Priests, Elders and Deacons:

The Difference between Priests, Elders and Deacons

PRIESTS (All born-again believers)	ELDERS (Same word as Bishops & Overseers)	DEACONS (Servants)
1. *All* born-again believers are priests, and a Holy Priesthood (I Peter 2:3-5). *All* are kings and priests to God and shall reign on earth (Rev. 1:6 and 5:10).	*Manifest* themselves by a shepherd's heart through example in: 1. Character, 2. Doctrine and 3. Work (I Tim. 3:1-7)	They *Manifest* themselves by holding the mystery of the faith in a pure conscience. (I Tim. 3:9) and by teaching the assembly.
2. Priesthood depends on *sonship*. We are God's sons, and of Christ's priesthood. (Heb. 5:5, 6)	Dependent upon their fatherly *character* made evident: "Not many fathers". (I Cor. 4:15; cf I Thess 2:7,8).	Dependent upon their *acceptability*: They must be proved as to their holding the faith (I Tim. 3:10).
3. Divinely *constituted* and not dependent on ecclesiastical ordination and or recognition.	Dependent upon being: 1. Blameless (not faultless) (I Tim. 3:2) 2. Apt to teach: able to meet all the needs of the sheep/lambs by the use of the scripture, and 3. Hospitable.	Dependent also upon acceptability in service to the assembly in teaching-by which they earn for themselves a good degree *or position of trust,* among the saints (I Tim. 3:13).

PRIESTS (All born-again believers)	ELDERS (Same word as Bishops & Overseers)	DEACONS (Servants)
4. Priests are (constituted) made by God. This is not one of the gifts. The person *himself* is the priest.	*Gifted* to fulfil the work of caring for the sheep as a shepherd, in leading by example, love, feeding, and by tending the local flock (Acts 20:28)	*Gifted* to fulfil the need for teaching in the assembly through which they gain great boldness in the faith (I Tim. 3:13).
5. Priesthood should be *exercised* continuously (Heb. 13:15) through Christ, and manifested by: 1. Fruit of our lips, (praise) 2. Doing good, (service) and 3. Communicating, (giving); all these are through the Spirit's guidance.	Their service is amongst the flock (I Pet. 5:2), in homes of the sheep and lambs, visiting the sick (James 5:14) and comforting them; and also "given to hospitality" (I Tim. 3:2) in their own homes.	Their *service* is in and for the assembly but, contrary to current practice, must involve the teaching of the assembly also, because of I Tim. 3:9, 10 and 13, Unless the mystery of the faith were publicly taught, they would not be proved, nor gain boldness.
6. Demands that a priest must have his hands *full* of the sacrifice (Christ) (Lev. 8:27), through abiding in Christ (John 15). No priest was to appear before God *empty*.	Demands constant *preparation of heart* and life (I Tim. 3:2)	Demands that the servant wait upon his ministry (Rom. 12:7) by studying to show himself approved (2 Tim. 2:15) and *wholly giving* himself.
7. For *all* believers irrespective of *sex* – but public expression is limited to *"the men"* (I Tim. 2:8)	Belongs, (ultimately) to shepherds (I Tim.3:1, 2) with experience	In a general sense to all the gifted brothers and also to sisters with certain limitation as to a woman's status (I Cor. 14:34; I Tim. 2:12; Rom. 16:1).

17

Explanation and Amplifications:

1. BISHOPS (Greek 'Episcopos') ELDERS (Greek 'Presbuteros') and OVERSEERS (Greek 'Episkopos') all apply to the *same* person and describe the *same* ministry .The word 'Bishop' in English is an imported ecclesiastical term. "Office of a Bishop" is also an ecclesiastical term but is only one word in Greek, meaning 'service'. (I Tim. 3:1).

    'Elders', – means men of maturity.

    'Overseers' – means men who watch-over.

2. DEACONS: (Greek 'Diakonos') – means 'servant'. He is a person who acts, or waits on service. Greek 'Doulos' means a 'Bond Servant' (I Tim. 3:10). "Use the office of a Deacon", an ecclesiastical term, but is only one word in Greek, which means: "to serve".

3. All the above mentioned terms (viz. Priests, Elders and Deacons) are therefore NOT TITLES for individuals. It is not for a personal prestige which would introduce pre-eminence. We are *all* members *one of another* avoiding monopoly and self-elevation. (I Cor. 12:17-27).

4. The recognition of such persons must, therefore, be through their *work* and *character,* so that what *he does* indicates what *he is,* before God.

5. The *indiscriminate* use of the word "the oversight" implies a committee of authority. This word (noun) does not appear in the Word of God. The correct use of "oversight" is only as a verb or verbal-noun, and the English word "eldership" expresses it correctly, as to its *work aspect* and not as *an office.*

18

The Mystery

The word 'Mystery' (Gr. 'Musterion'), in the New Testament does not carry the idea of a secret or mysterious element but is a revelation of the plans of God, incapable of discovery by mere reason and natural apprehension, hitherto un-revealed, or withheld but now divinely revealed or divulged by God. It is made known in a *manner* and at a *time* appointed by God, to the Apostles and Prophets (Eph. 3:5) illuminated by His Spirit. Ordinarily, 'mystery' is something *withheld* or an *un-revealed* knowledge, but in the NT significance, it refers to truth *revealed*.

This mystery is a hidden wisdom and was kept secret from before the world began. It was hidden in God, but now revealed according to the commandment of God, unto the obedience of faith. It contains a supernatural element, and is spiritually discerned as taught by the Spirit. It is not discoverable by human wisdom. (Rom. 16:25, 26; I Cor. 2:7).

The following are the New Testament or Church mysteries, of which the first two are designated as *"great* Mysteries":

1.   The mystery of Godliness which traces from the incarnation of Christ, to His reception into Glory (I Tim. 3:16).

2.   The mystery of Christ and the Church is described as a man leaving his father and mother and cleaving to his wife, to become one flesh (Eph. 5:32).

3.   The mystery of God and of Christ, involving Christ as the fullness of the Godhead in bodily form (Col. 2:2, 9; I Cor. 2:7).

4.   The mystery among the Gentiles, "Christ in you the hope of Glory" (Col. 1:26, 27).

5.   The mystery of the Church, the body of Christ, being a union of both Jews and Gentiles in equality (an abomination under the OT dispensational status). (Eph. 3:1-11; 6:19; Col. 4:3).

6.   The mystery of the resurrection of the dead and the translation of the living N T saints, at the consummation of the Church (I Cor. 15:51, 52; I Thess. 4:14-18).

7.   The mystery of Israel's stumbling to blindness, her condition during the present Gospel or Church age and her full and final restoration (Rom. 11:25, 26).

8.   The mystery of iniquity and the spirit of disobedience to God (2 Thess. 2:7).

Even though Israel possessed better advantages (Rom. 3:1-2) and were entrusted with many good things (Rom. 9:3-5) these mysteries (revealed secrets) all given to Paul for the Church, are incomparable outshining of divine grace, beyond any truth entrusted to Israel.

Was it the Bread that was Broken or The Lord's Body?

(1 Corinthians 11:24)

A problem seems to exist in the record in I Corinthians 11:24, which in the AV reads:

"And when He had given thanks, He *break* it, and said, 'take, eat: this is My body, which is *broken* for you: this do in remembrance of Me'."

The word "this do" appears to be a command as much as anything. The word *'this'* in connection with "this is my body", refers to the *bread,* and not to His *body.* His body was not broken, though He was smitten, scourged, buffeted, crowned with thorns and nailed to the cross. The soldiers did break the legs of the other two, who were crucified with Him, but not those of Jesus, for "a bone of Him shall not be broken" (John 19:36; Ex 12:46; Num 9:12; Ps 34:20). Therefore, that "which is *broken*", refers to the act of *breaking the bread or loaf.* It is the bread that was broken by the Lord.

Herein lays a difference between the *Lord* acting at His supper, and the manner in which *we* should act. The Lord Jesus, and He alone, *broke the bread,* and thereafter passed it on to His disciples, making it available to them. "When He had given thanks, He *break* it (the bread) and gave it to the disciples". Ec-clesiastical priesthood has adapted to itself, the place of the Lord, in distributing the bread by breaking it on behalf of the individuals (or individual wafers), and also administering the cup, and thus set aside the importance of "in remembrance of me". It is certainly our prerogative to give thanks, not only for the bread and the cup, but for the Lord's redemptive work on the cross. Giving thanks is an honour left to the *individual believer* present at the supper. This eliminates the need for any one person, by appointment or otherwise, to take upon himself the responsibility to *break* the bread and give it to other members present. What bears the weight of importance is that each of the members present breaks the loaf, each individual for himself, and partakes in it, which is the actual REMEMBRANCE OF ME.

A comparison of the four accounts of the Lord's Supper, is given below, with the allocated serial numbers (not verse numbers) to each action, in connection with the Lord's Supper, which will be found helpful in aligning these four records.

Note: Please also refer to "The Difference between the Lord's Table and the Lord's Supper" Paper No: 01-04.

Sl. No.	MATTHEW (26: 26-27)	Sl. No.	MARK (14: 22-24)	Sl. No.	LUKE (22: 19-20)	Sl. No.	PAUL (1 Cor. 11: 23-26)
						0	That the Lord Jesus the same night in which he was betrayed
1	And as they were eating, Jesus,	1	And as they did eat, Jesus	1	. . .	1	. . .
2	took bread,	2	took bread,	2	And he took bread ,	2	took bread:
3	and blessed it (ευλογησας)	3	and blessed, (ευλογησας)	3	and gave thanks, (ευχαριστησας)	3	and when He had given thanks, (ευχαριστησας)
4	and brake it	4	and brake it,	4	and brake it,	4	He brake it,
5	and gave it to the disciples,	5	and gave to them,	5	and gave unto them,	5	. . .
6	and said,	6	and said,	6	saying,	6	and said,
7	"Take, eat;	7	"Take, eat:	7	. . .	7	"Take, eat:
8	this is my body".	8	this is my body."	8	"This is my body	8	this is my body,
9	. . .	9	. . .	9	which is given for you:	9	which is broken for you:
10	. . .	10	. . .	10	this do in remembrance of me."	10	this do in remembrance of me."
11	. . .	11	. . .	11	Likewise also	11	After the same manner also
12	And He took	12	And He took	12	. . .	12	. . .
13	the cup,	13	the cup,	13	the cup	13	He took the cup,
14	. . .	14	. . .	14	after supper,	14	when He had supped,
15	and gave thanks,	15	and when he had given thanks,	15	. . .	15	. . .

16	and gave it to them,	16	He gave it to them :	16	...	16	...
17	saying, "Drink ye all of it;	17	and they all drank of it.	17	...	17	...
18	...	18	And he said unto them,	18	saying,	18	saying,
19	...	19	...	19	"This cup	19	"This cup
20	For this is my blood of the new testament,	20	"This is my blood of the new testament,	20	is the new testament in my blood,	20	is the new testament in my blood:
21	which is shed for many	21	which is shed for many".	21	...	21	...
22	for the remission of sins."	22		22	...	22	...
23	...	23		23	which is shed for you."	23	...
24	...	24		24	...	24	this do ye, as oft as ye drink it, in remembrance of me."
						0	For as often as ye eat this bread, and drink this cup. ye do shew the Lord's death, till He come.

Note: Greek 'eulogeo' (Strong - 2127), used In Matt. 26:26 and in Mark 14:22 literally means, "to speak well of" signifying, "to praise (or bless), to celebrate with praises".

Greek 'eucharisteo' (Strong - 2168) used in Luke 22:19 and in 1 Cor. 11:24 means, "to express gratitude" or "to give thanks".

Greek 'klao' (Strong - 2806) means, "to break, to break off pieces". Other passages used: Matt. 14:19; 15:36; Mark 6:41; Luke 24:30; Acts 20:7; 1 Cor. 10:16 also in John 19:32 & 33.

Spiritual Gifts

The expression "Pentecostalism" represents to the mind special characteristics and practices, which confuse or even baffle, being supposedly based on the truth of the Word of God.

It must not be denied that the Holy Spirit did give special endowments and gifts in order to prove that God was indeed speaking through the sign-gifts there by establishing the new truth concerning Christ and the resurrection and so convince mainly Jews, and also Gentiles (Acts 10:46).

The tabulation on page No 27, entitled "Spiritual Gifts" (I Cor. 12:1), is so laid out to show the manner in which the transitional sign-gifts were superseded or ceased completely – as did the tongues-gift.

In the following notes, this truth has been developed. The purpose of these notes is to clarify the importance of the attached tabulation and to distinguish between "transitory gifts" and those that remain and are permanent.

Explanation

Much confusion exists in Pentecostal circles and groups associated with charismatic tendencies and characteristics, in respect of the Acts of the Apostles, but particularly in regard to the claims arising from Mark 16:14-20 and Joel's prophecy quoted in Acts 2. The Irving Brothers were mainly responsible in the late 19th century for the rise of Pentecostalism. Previous to this no confusion had existed in respect of these passages.

I. The instructions contained in Mark 16:14-20 are restricted to the Apostles only.

> v. 14 the eleven, ('them' is in italics in AV, that is, not given in the Greek Text)
>
> v. 15 Ye
>
> v. 19 them
>
> v. 20 they ('them' is in italics in AV)

II. Signs were to "follow them that believe", i.e. of His disciples in verse 14 marked by 'unbelief'. (Follow = Strong - 3877, means "attend as a result") which were described as:

1. Casting out devils – currently used by Pentecostals on those coming within their power.

2. Speak with new tongues – new to the speakers.

3. Take up serpents – Pentecostals dare not do this or rarely mention it.

4. Drink any deadly thing – Pentecostals are unwilling to try this!

5. Lay hands on the sick – Pentecostals readily do this, but the failure of heal-

ing is attributed to unbelief on the part of the receiver.

III. Verse 20 states, "the Lord... confirming the word with signs following" – what the Lord said to His *Apostles* in verse 18, is recorded as having been fulfilled.

IV. In commenting on Heb 1:1, 2, on the progress and completion of the revelation of God's word, the writer goes on in Heb 2:3, with a warning of the possibility of anything other than judgement falling upon those who neglect so great salvation, which in 2:3 and 4, he describes as witnessed beyond any doubt or question:

1. *First* spoken by none less than the Lord.

2. *Confirmed* (Past tense) to the Hebrews (Jews), – a completed act.

3. By *them* that heard Him – the Apostles (Mark 16:14-18).

V. God had borne witness to His word through the Apostles, with signs and wonders and divers miracles and gifts of the Holy Spirit (I Cor. 12:7-11), since the Jews, in unbelief required a sign (1 Cor. 1:22-24).

VI. A further evidence of discontinuance is that the Apostles with the Prophets completed their 'commission', (and of course had fallen asleep), having laid the foundation, an accomplished work (Eph. 2:20). (Note how verses 21 & 22 read).

VII. It should be apparent that the gifts in Mark 16 were to the Apostles only and were for convincing the Jews so that all that was required of the Apostles in Mark 16:17-18, had (as shown in Heb. 2:4) been accomplished.

Note carefully Mark 16:20, which confirms that only Apostles were in view. We need to consider how "those signs shall *follow*" ("attend as a result" Strong - 3877) "them that believe".

1. Cast out demons: Only the Apostles are shown in scripture as accomplishing this.

2. Speak with new tongues (new to them), the sign was in the Apostles (Acts 2). The sign was in them that believed (Act 10:46, 19:6) additionally glorified God (10:46) and prophesied (19:6), as evidences essential to convince the Jews.

3. Take up serpents – We have Acts 28:4, 5 only for this: – sign in the Apostle.

4. Drink any deadly thing – No scriptural fulfilment for this.

5. Lay hands on the sick – Only possible inclusion in Acts 9:34, but no hands were laid on Aeneas in Acts 9:34.

Hebrew 2:4 attest as fully completed the commissioning of the twelve apostles, confirming with signs following, as given in Mark 16:14 - 20.

VIII. The details of Joel's prophecy in Acts 2 were in no way fulfilled at Pentecost. Joel records a visit of the Spirit in *judgement* (Acts 2:16). "This is *that*", to take place before the great and notable day of the Lord (Acts 2:20). Admittedly judgement was due to the Jews who "by wicked (Roman) hands have crucified and slain" Jesus of Nazareth. But instead, grace had been manifested as in Acts 2:33, because Jesus had been exalted and glorified to God's right hand and had shed forth *this*, (i.e.) blessing. To summarise:

Acts 2:16 "This is *that*" Spirit's visitation in judgement mentioned by Joel,

Acts 2:33 this is this, "Shed forth *this*" the Spirits visitation at Pentecost, in unmerited grace and blessing.

(A full treatment of this subject, as combined with "Prophecy, and Tongues" appears in a separate tabulation Paper No 02-02.)

IX. Those signs lapsed having been fulfilled, as to the Jews; and as to the Gentiles after such incidents as by Paul at Ephesus (Acts 19:11), (consider 2 Cor. 12:12, the signs of an Apostle).

The "new tongues" of Mark 16:17 were quite an inferior gift (I Cor. 14:28), and last in the list by *significance, value and prominence.*

X. Why insist, as does Pentecostalism, on the blunt outdated instrument of tongues, when God has provided an instrument "Sharper than any two edged sword dividing asunder bone and marrow, soul and spirit" (Heb. 4:12), an instrument, so spiritually powerful as to need fully supersede the wonders, signs and miracles. Signs did not apparently bring the same conviction of sin, as does the word of God, which is the Sword of the Spirit (Eph. 6:17).

This great truth of the power of the Word of God is hardly stressed today, because we do not believe it to be quick and powerful, and that which the Spirit of God uses to accomplish HIS WILL. The proliferation of various versions, particularly the N.I.V. partly accounts for this.

XI. The Assemblies were planted and were developing in the early years, partly as a result of the signs of Mark 16, and of the sign gifts exercised at Corinth, as found in I Corinthians chapters 12 to 14, when the Apostles and Prophets were *laying the foundation* of the Church doctrine (I Cor. 3:10 & Eph. 2:20).

XII Columns 1 and 3 in our Tabulation, stress the *gifts* given by the Spirit, to the individual believer, but columns 2 and 4 show that the person *himself was* the gift given by the risen Lord (Eph. 4:10,11, I Cor. 12:5).

Using I Cor. 12:4-7, the columns have been noted as (Item No: 4):

> Column 1 – The manifestation of the Spirit (vv 4 & 7).
>
> Columns 2 & 3 – The operation of God (v6).
>
> Column 4 – The administration of the risen Lord (v5).

The evidence in support of these three divisions, – yet the *same* Spirit, are:-

Column 1. The Manifestation of the Spirit

Philip : The Spirit said unto Philip (Acts 8:29).

The Spirit caught away Philip (Acts 8:39).

Peter : The Spirit said unto him (Peter) "Behold three men seek..." (Acts 10:19).

The Spirit bade me go with them (Acts 11:12).

Paul & Others : The Holy Spirit said "Separate me Barnabas and Saul for the work where unto I have called them" (Acts 13:2).

So then being sent forth by the Holy Spirit (Acts 13:4).

Were forbidden by the Holy Spirit (Acts 16:6).

But the Spirit suffered them not. (Acts 16:7).

Columns 2 & 3: The Operation of God

The Assemblies at Philippi, at Thessalonica and at Corinth were brought into being in quite different ways and with very different believers, as follows:

Philippi : Lydia: A woman who worshipped God (Acts 16:14).

The keeper of the prison and his household:

They believed God (Acts 16:34).

Thessalonica: Turned to God from idols to serve the living and true God (I Thess. 1:9).

Corinth : Church of God at Corinth (I Cor. 1:7).

God is faithful by whom ye were called into the fellowship (I Cor. 1:9).

It is the "salvation of God" diverted from preaching to Jews, which gave the Gentiles an opportunity to be saved (Acts 28:28).

Column 4: The Administration of the risen Lord

Stephen : Lord Jesus, receive my spirit (Acts 7:59).

Lord, lay not this sin to their charge. (Acts 7:60).

Paul : Who art thou, Lord (Acts 9:5).

The Lord, even Jesus that appeared (Acts 9:17)

Then spake the Lord to Paul, "Be not afraid..." (Acts 18:9).

The Lord stood by him and said.... (Acts 23:11).

Peter : But Peter said, "Not so Lord..." (Acts 10:14).

The angel of the Lord came upon him (Acts 12:7).

How the Lord had brought him out of the prison (Acts 12:17).

XIII. The list of gifts given in I Cor. 12:8-11: (Column 1 Item No 7 in the tabulation).

The Greek word 'heteros', (Strong - 2087 meaning "another of a *different* kind") in verses 9 and 11, differentiate the Greek word 'allos' (Strong - 243 meaning "one of the *same* kind"), thus making three divisions of these nine gifts into 2 + 5 + 2. (Both these words are rendered as 'another' in AV. Please refer J N Darby's translation).

XIV. Pastors and Teachers: (Column 4 item 7(4) in the tabulation)

The A V (Textus Receptus version of Eph. 4:11), gives only four mentions of the word 'some' (Strong – 3588). The Greek word, '*kai*' (Strong - 2532) meaning 'and' or 'even'. This could indicate only four different types of gifted men and therefore the Pastor-Teacher is just *one* man. Whilst this appears to be the correct interpretation, personified in Timothy, Titus, Sylvanus, Epaphroditus and the like, involving a period of residence among the saints, nevertheless in present day circumstances, it could hardly be said that the teacher carried out the work also of a pastor. He might well have done so, had he been able to stay for a longer period. (His presence being regarded by the assembly as needful and the teacher-pastor being exercised to do so.) Nevertheless we should not lower the standard of God's word on account of changed conditions. The maximum benefit would accrue from an exercised servant who was a pastor-teacher, who "treadeth out the corn" in the local assembly.

Categories of Spiritual Gifts

These spiritual gifts may be put into three groups, of both as to TIME and CHARACTER:

Gifts: as to Time

1. FOUNDATIONAL – Apostles and Prophets – (including Prophecy). Therefore, are temporary in nature (Eph. 2:20, 1 Cor. 12:29)

2. TRANSITIONAL – Revelatory gifts: Knowledge & Tongues – Therefore, "it shall vanish away" and "They shall cease". (I Cor. 13:8).

3. CONTINUAL – Evangelists, Pastors even/and Teachers – Therefore, will be manifest throughout the entire church age.

Gifts: as to Character

1. THAT REVEAL – Wisdom, Knowledge, Prophecy, are all *revelatory gifts,* through which God revealed His mind, and gave instruction *until* His mind was fully known in the Scriptures which were completed.

2. THAT ARE SIGNS – Faith, Healing, Miracles, Discernment, Tongues, Interpretation are all *sign gifts,* giving proof that the revelations thus given are all of God, carrying His authority and sovereignty.

3. THAT EDIFY – Others are *edifying gifts.* They are of an edifying, constructing and perfecting nature, which continued and are still needed today.

Spiritual Gifts

	Column 1	Column 2	Column 3	Column 4
1	I Cor. 12:4-11	I Cor. 12: 28 -31	Rom. 12 : 3 – 8	Eph. 4:4- 13
2	AD 59	AD 59	AD 60	AD 64
3	Gifts are *spiritual enablements* given to believers by the Holy Spirit for the functioning of the assembly.	*Gifted men* given to the Local assembly for the transitional period up to the completion of the word of God.	List of *activities* of gifted believers which, except for Prophecy, apply today.	Gifts are *men*, given by the glorified Christ, for the building up of the Body, the Church.
4	Manifestation of the spirit I Cor. 12:4, 7	Operation of God I Cor. 12:6	Operation of God I Cor. 12:6	Administration of the risen Lord I Cor. 12:5
5	Giver: The same Holy spirit	Giver: God has set them	Giver: God	Giver: The ascended Lord Jesus Christ

	Column 1	Column 2	Column 3	Column 4
6	Recipient: Individual believers	Recipient: Local assembly	Recipient: Many members in one body	Recipient: The churches of the saints
7	List: 1. Wisdom* 2. Knowledge* 3. Faith* 4. Healing* 5. Miracles* 6. Prophecy* 7. Discernment* 8. Tongues* 9. Interpreting*	List : 1. Apostles* 2. Prophets* 3. Teachers 4. Miracles* 5. Healings* 6. Helps 7. Governments 8. Tongues*	List: 1. Prophecy* 2. Service (Ministry) 3. Teaching 4. Exhortations 5. Giving 6. Rule 7. Showing Mercy	List : 1. Apostles* 2. Prophets* 3. Evangelists 4. Pastors and/ even Teachers

Remarks

This tabulation is necessarily divided into four columns, as the gifts are detailed in the Scripture. They give expression to,

(1) *Revelatory gifts* that would be during the period of the Apostles and Prophets,

(2) *Sign gifts,* that were transitional and

(3) *Edifying gifts* that will continue throughout the church age.

• These columns are given in the *order of dates,* when these Epistles were written (Item No. 2). The observant reader will notice that, as the date of the year's progress, as shown in each column in the tabulation, the miraculous gifts-drop out. Therefore the list in Romans corresponds to the gifts that exist today, except Prophecy.

• The transitional gifts have been appropriately marked with an asterisk (*).

• The words 'firstly', 'secondarily', 'thirdly' and "after that" in I Cor. 12:28-31, (column 2. Item No.7) indicate their place of importance, tongues being *least.*

• Tongues: "Do *all* speak with tongues?" (I Cor. 12:30) clearly reveals that the teaching, "speaking in tongues is evidence for salvation or evidence for receiving the Holy Spirit", is an error.

• Apostles and Prophets, (column 4 Item No.7), gifts which were foundational (Eph. 2:20), were to LAPSE, once the Scriptures were completed. When the far more powerful Word of God, which can discern even the thoughts and intents of the heart (Heb 4:12), was complete, the remaining part – gift of Prophecy and Knowledge (I Cor.

13:8, 9), were superseded, and other miraculous sign - gifts were LAPSED.

• Upon His return to heaven, the victorious Lord Jesus Christ gave GIFTS (Charisma) and MINISTRATIONS (Diakenos):

'Charisma' – A gift involving grace, on the part of God as the Donor, as used in: His free bestowal upon sinners (Rom.5:15, 16; 6:23). His endowments upon believers by the operation of the Holy Spirit (Rom. 12:6; I Cor. 12:4, 9, 28, 30, 31; I Tim. 4:14; 2 Tim. 1:6; I Pet 4:10). Imparted through human instructions (Rom .1:11).

'Diakonia' – The office and work of a 'diakonos', or servant, involving service or ministry, as used in :

The Service of the Lord Jesus (Luke 22:27).

of domestic duties (Luke 10:40)

of spiritual ministration as used:

of apostolic ministry (Acts 1:17, 25; 12:25; 21:19; Rom. 11:13).

of the service of believers (Acts 6:1; Rom. 12:7; I Cor. 12:5; Eph. 4:12).

of the ministry of the Holy Spirit (2 Cor. 3:8).

of the ministry of angels (Heb. 1:14)

of the general ministry of a servant of the Lord in preaching and teaching. (Acts 20:24; 2 Cor. 4:1; 6:3; 11:8).

The Gifts of Prophecy and of Tongues Compared

The gift of prophecy and the gift of tongues are singled out, and compared and contrasted in the 14th Chapter of First Corinthians, which may be observed as under:

PROPHECY	TONGUES
1. It is profitable to the assembly for edification, exhortation and comfort (v.3).	Unless interpreted it has no value to the individual who does the speaking (v.3 & 11), or to the assembly (v.5, 13 & 16). Also prophesying or revelation or teaching in tongues, but without interpretation brings no edification (v.6).
2. It is profitable for the unbelievers (unsaved) and for the unlearned (who are saved) (v.24).	The absence of an interpreter would adversely affect or hinder the unbelievers, although it may be edifying to the speaker (v.22 & 23), but would create only uncertainty (v.9). With no interpreter, edifying oneself (understanding) would be out of place (v.14, 15).
3. Prophecy enables the unlearned, the saved, (v.16) to evidence his *understanding* by giving assent in his vocal 'Amen'. The word 'unlearned' is a category, of people rather than a separate place to sit (as the AV word 'occupies' seem to imply).	Tongues came as a surprise to the unbeliever; but prophecy creates understanding resulting in his acknowledgement of God's presence in the gathering. (v.25)

PROPHECY	TONGUES
4. Prophecy generates *understanding*. Hence the exhortation, "in understanding be *men*" (v. 20).	Tongues appeared to create malice possibly in vying for the *spectacular* like *children* would (v. 20).
5. Teaching others, although just in five words with understanding, is MORE profitable (v. 19).	Talking and teaching, though in 10,000 words in a tongue, is NOT profitable. Five words with understanding are best.
6. Although the gifted N.T prophet has now been replaced by the Word of God, nevertheless, the order in v. 29-32 should be followed in the conduct of a gathering, left open to the Spirit of God, to guide the gifted brethren.	*Five restrictions* are placed on tongues: (1) Only two or three at the most and that (2) by course, that is one at a time, and that too (3) only if an interpreter is present. (4) The speaker must be self-controlled and able to keep silence (5) Brethren only should speak in the assembly, not sisters (v. 27-34).
7. Believers were exhorted to desire (covet) this gift of prophecy (v. 39).	Forbid not to speak in tongues, but with *decency* and *orderliness* – by arrangement – should be maintained (v. 39-40).

NOTE: The word 'unlearned' appearing in vv. 16 and 23, (item No. 3 under "Prophecy", in the above tabulation) is the translation of the Greek word 'idiotes', usually taken to mean a private person or an unskilled one. J N Darby in his translation puts it nicely, "simple (Christian)" v. 16, and "simple (person)" v. 23. This word also occurs in Acts 4:13, where it is rendered 'ignorant', possibly referring to a lack of professional training, and in 2 Cor. 11:6, and is translated 'rude', probably unskilled in oratory, or simple in speech.

Tongues

Tongues particularly was a poor instrument and was not given to *all* (I Cor. 12:30). The order of I Cor. 12:28, is *not sequential* but according to *diminishing values*. This is proved by I Cor. 12:31, which says "covet earnestly the best gifts", in the sense *of better in value* (Strong - 2909: "More vigour, greater advantage and additional nobility"). Only as the gifts are of diminishing value, can there be any sense in recommending, to covet earnestly those that are best.

This is confirmed by the reasoning at the end of the tongues dissertation in I Cor. 14:39, where "coveting earnestly" applies to and singles out the best gift of prophecy. What follows "And forbid not to speak with tongues", effectively highlights the inferiority of the gift of tongues. So why be concerned to use the latter?

Prophecy

New Testament prophets were *different* to Old Testament prophets. The Old Testament prophets *foretold the future* and where this vision ceased the people perished (Pro. 29:18); and the prophets were to be blamed (Lament. 2:14). New Testament prophets, on the other hand, *forth-told truth* for the need that then existed in order to fill the gap, because the New Testament was either not revealed and or not written.

All should know and appreciate the wonderful power in the Word of God, which replaces prophecy, bringing conviction of sin to unbelievers as also to believers, as well as comfort and consolation.

The Word of God

The gift of prophecy has been superseded by the word of God, which provides complete revelation of all that God has for us and desires us to know. Tongues, however, came to an *abrupt end* (the meaning of the Greek word 'PAUO' translated 'cease' in I Cor. 13:8). In view of Revelation 22:18, persons who take to themselves the title of a New Testament prophet and speak in terms of "Thus saith the Lord", must therefore, be suspect.

No gift, whatever its name, was ever proved to be *better* than the Word of God. This powerful weapon of the Holy Spirit in being able to divide asunder soul and spirit, joints and marrow (Heb 4:12) (recall Felix in Acts 24:25) is a discerner of the thoughts and intents of the heart, RIGHTLY and NECESSARILY SUPERSEDES these two gifts (tongues and prophecy) and also the gift of knowledge (I Cor. 13:8).

Love

Love is the surpassingly excellent way, without which a gifted person is nothing, and is not profited. Hence, this exhortation "Follow after love" (v. 1).

The danger at Corinth, not to speak of elsewhere, was of using the gifts bereft of love, for which there is no substitute – the *more excellent way* (I Cor. 12:31) – which equally applies to the teaching and preaching of the Word of God to saint and sinner. Its absence speaks for itself, being similar to a temple-bell or tinkling cymbal. *All* could have this surpassingly excellent **gift of love**. It was unrestricted, unlike all the other gifts, which were restricted and every believer could possess it.

Conclusion

"Forbid not to speak with tongues. Let all things be done decently and in order" (I Cor. 14:39,40), is an instruction given to the Church at Corinth at a time when the gift of tongues was in vogue, *before* it came to an abrupt end, "they shall cease" (I Cor. 13:8). Now, during *the present church age*, the principle of *'decency'* and *'orderliness'* should continue to govern *all* the gatherings of the saints (assembly gatherings).

Remarks

At this point, we may mention that those translating these papers from a Bible in Hindi, Oriya, Nepali, Bengali, Tamil and Malayalam and may be other translations, and also those reading these various languages, will meet with some difficulty: The verse I Cor. 12:28, in the above mentioned translations, gives a 'first', 'second', 'third' which expresses *sequential order*, whereas the King James Authorised Version gives as 'first', 'secondarily', 'thirdly', 'after that', and 'then', all words indicating *values* only.

I Cor. 12:31 says, "But, covet the *better* (margin) gifts". (In the Tamil Bible, this has a very expressive meaning "more important"). This clearly confirms that the *value order* is what is meant here. That there are 'superior' and 'inferior' gifts is thus clearly brought out in these passages

32

Babel and the Day of Pentecost
Facts Contrasted

GENESIS 11	ACTS 2
One language and one speech (v. 1)	All with one accord in one place. All speaking Aramaic/Greek.
A building of satanic deception and confusion.	A house filled with a rushing mighty wind.
Man – made brick (not stones)	God-created "living stones" (1 Pet. 1:5)
Imagination of human minds (v. 6) standing in front of a God of revelation, to introduce sun-worship. A mighty hunter before (in front of, therefore obscuring) the Lord. Beginning of his kingdom was Babel = confusion (Gen 10:9, 10).	Revelation in the Gospel. Christ to sit on His throne. (Acts 2:30-33). But confounds, because every man heard them speaking his own dialect. (v. 6) (Note - Not tongue).
Low dead-level of the plain of Shinar.	An upper-room (Acts 1:13, 2:1).
The Lord came down from heaven (v. 5)	A sound from heaven (v. 2).
To see what men build.	To draw attention to what the Lord was building.
Resulting in the imposition of idolatrous sun-worship and its unrestrainedly sin (v. 6)	Results in the gift of GRACE in salvation to 3,000 souls.
Defied God's control over them through revelation (v. 4).	Tarried at Jerusalem (Luke 24:49) in *obedience* to the Lord's command, in prayer and supplication (Acts 1:14).

GENESIS 11	ACTS 2
Man ascended the tower of Babel, but God descended to confound their tongue.	The Lord ascended into Heaven and the Holy Spirit descended. (John 16:7)
Babel's sin *scattered* them (v. 8).	The Spirit of God *united* them in one accord (Acts 2:46)
Contusion of tongues: Not of a random, but a systematic distribution of clear, intelligent languages.	Although they could speak one with another in Greek, they heard a variety of tongues, even of dialects v. 7. But the Apostles spoke the same "the wonderful works of God" (v. 11).
Whereupon the people were *scattered* and divided into nations, tongues, lands and families (10:5, 20, 31, 32).	Greek speaking Jews of the Dispersion "Diaspora" from far flung nations and lands were *united* together by doctrine and practice (v. 42).
A city and tower built of clay by the children of men.	A holy habitation of God, builded together through the Spirit (Eph. 2:22).
They had slime (bitumen) for mortar.	Fitly framed together through the Holy Spirit (Eph. 2:21, 22).
Man wanted to make a name for himself.	The exalted Lord has given His Bride, His name (Rev. 21:9). True believers desire only exaltation of 'His' name.

Tongues:
A Sign of God's Judgement

"In the law it is written, 'With men of other tongues and other lips will I speak unto this people: and yet for all that will they not hear me, saith the Lord'. Wherefore tongues are for a sign, not to them that believe, but to them that believe not: but prophesying serveth not for them that believe not, but for them which believe" (I Cor. 14:21-22). In this passage, the apostle quotes the prophecy of Isaiah 28:11, 12. He quotes part of the verse that is relevant to the gift of tongues. Isaiah refers to Israel as "this people" and they are quoted in I Cor. 14:21 as such and their unbelief is referred to in the words, "Yet they will not hear". Thus the Apostle concludes that tongues are a sign not to them that believe but to them that believe not, a clear reference to the nation of Israel – those who would not hearken to God's words (The Corinthian saints were made up of both Jews and Gentiles).

The prophecy of Isaiah is an echo of an earlier prophecy given by Moses as recorded in Deuteronomy 28:49. The prophecy of Isaiah had its immediate reference to the invasion of the land by the Assyrians, which took place in the fourteenth year of Hezekiah (Isa. 36:1), whereas Deuteronomy 28:49 and Jeremiah 5:15 refer to the captivity of Judah in Babylon.

Hearing these foreign tongues of Assyria and Babylon spoken by such invaders or captors of Israel, was definitely not a sign of blessing upon them, but rather a sign of God's displeasure, and of judgement, as His longsuffering had come to an end (Jer. 7:16).

The apostle Peter on the day of Pentecost speaking by the Holy Spirit in using Joel's prophecy confirms that God's longsuffering had come to an end. Peter, therefore urged his hearers to "save themselves from this untoward generation" (Acts 2:40).

The principle of tongues as a punishment to His people in the Old Testament was carried over into the New Testament. The pattern of God's dealings with His chosen people the Israelites to discipline them, as far as tongues are concerned, is fourfold:

1. God had a message for the people.

2. The people refuse to listen.

3. God causes tongues to be heard as a proof of His judgement.

4. God thereafter scatters the disobedient people, among the Gentiles.

The following tabulation reveals the similarity of each visitation of the judgement of God, as recorded in the Scripture. Hearing and speaking the foreign idolatrous tongues, in the place of the more expressive language, the Hebrew in which they received their laws and commandments, is indeed a judgement of God on them.

God has a message for the people	The people refuse to listen	God causes tongues to be heard, as a proof of His judgement	To be followed by dispersion
Be fruitful and multiply and fill the earth (Gen 9:1,7)	But they built a tower, "Lest we be scattered abroad over the face of the whole earth" (Gen 11:4)	Come, let us go down and confound their language (Gen 11:7)	So the Lord scattered them abroad upon the face of the earth (Gen 11:8, 9). This would be before the days of Peleg (Gen 10:25).
If thou shall return (Deut. 11:26-28)	If thou wilt not hearken (Deut.28:15)	The Lord shall bring a nation against thee from far... a nation whose tongue thou shall not understand (Deut. 28:49)	The Lord shall scatter thee among all people from one end of the earth unto the other (Deut. 28:64, 65).
If Israel would return unto Me, (Jer. 4:1), then Psalms 81:8-16 will result. If Israel had walked in His ways, God would have subdued their enemies.	But they have refused to receive correction, they have made their faces harder than rock, they have refused to return. (Jer. 5:3)	I will bring a nation upon you from afar... a nation whose language thou knowest not, neither understandest what they say. (Jer. 5:15)	Like as ye have forsaken Me... So shall ye serve strangers in a land that is not yours? (Jer. 5:19)
This is the rest wherewith ye may cause the weary to rest and this is the refreshing. (Isa. 28:12)	Yet they would not hear (Isa. 28:12). Un-godly Jews were mocking God's message through Isaiah, as mere repetition (Isa. 28:9, 10).	For with stammering lips and another tongue will he speak to this people? (Isa. 28:11)	That they might go and fall backward, and be broken and snared and taken. (Isa. 28:13)
Come unto me and I will give you rest (Matt 11:28)	O Jerusalem, Jerusalem, thou that killest the prophets and stonest them which are sent unto thee, how oft would I have gathered thy children together and ye would not (Matt 23:37).	Began to speak with other tongues as the Spirit gave them utterance (Acts 2:4). Gentiles* in Acts 10: 45, 46 and the disciples of John in Acts 19:6 confirm by tongues that God has left Israel to unbelief. * See Note.	Behold your house is left unto you desolate (Matt. 23:38). Verily I say unto you there shall not be left here one stone upon another that shall not be thrown down (Matt. 24:2). Ye judge yourselves unworthy of everlasting life, lo we turn to the Gentiles (see Acts 13:44-52).

Note: * (Item No 5 Column 3)

On account of the judgemental character of tongues, when the house of Cornelius received the Gospel and were saved, it was reported that, "The gentiles had also received the word of God" (Acts 11:1) without reference to tongues at all.

When we consider the above four principles as brought out in this tabulation, it should be understood why Peter initially launched into Joel 2:28-32, describing God's judgement, before "the great and notable day of the Lord", when the Lord will return and the Holy Spirit will be poured forth, (Ezek. 36:26) then Israel will call upon the Lord to be saved. Their salvation is typified in the valley of dry bones, when breath will come into them, and they shall live (Ezek. 37:10, 14) and also when the new covenant is mediated to Israel, as in Hebrew 8:10-12, and in Jer. 31:31-34.

The absence of *foreign tongues* in the land of Israel, during Millennium will be a clear sign to the nation of Israel, that they are enjoying the blessings of God, as in Isaiah 33:17, 19: "Thine eyes shall see the King in His beauty" and "Thou shall not see a *fierce people, a people of deeper speech,* than thou canst perceive; *of a stammering tongue, that thou canst not understand"*. "The tongue of the stammerers shall be ready to speak plainly" (Isa. 32:4), will be one of the blessings of the Millennium to His people, a restored and converted Israel. Even five cities in Egypt will then speak the language of Israel (Isa. 19:18).

None of Joel Chapter 2 could be fulfilled on the day or Pentecost. So, while Acts 2:16 says *"this is that,* which was spoken by the prophet Joel"*, notwithstanding, God was gracious to those who repented, in giving them the Holy Spirit; "He hath *shed forth this"* (Acts 2:33). Nevertheless the OT pattern persisted, because Israel as a Nation refused to repent of crucifying the Son of God and ultimately were scattered among the Gentiles. Then Paul and Barnabas waxed bold and said: "It was necessary that the word of God

should *first* have been spoken to you (Jews); but seeing ye put from you (Jews) and judge yourselves unworthy of everlasting life, lo, *we turn to the Gentiles"* (Acts 13:46).

It would be possible to clearly picture this, in the parable of the fig tree (Israel in unbelief), planted in the vineyard (Luke 13:6-8). This vineyard is the house of Israel (Isa. 5:7). During our Lord's three years of His glorious earthly ministry, He was constantly seeking fruit from Israel (the fig tree, out of Chaldea – Jer. 24:5-6), but found none. However, the dresser of the vineyard sought another year of grace of the Lord and a period of grace was mercifully extended to the Jewish Nation ("I shall dig about it, and dung it"). But their barrenness in unbelief and disobedience continued unabated in that they counselled against the Apostles (Acts 5:27-41), stoned Stephen (Acts 7), killed James and sought for Peter (Acts 12:3). In unbelief and envy they spoke against the Gospel contradicting and blaspheming (Acts 13:46). Thus what the Lord predicted of their Jerusalem Temple, *"Your* house" (Mat. 23:38) no more *"My* house of prayer" (Mat. 21:13) is left unto you desolate and "there shall not be left one stone upon another" (Mat. 24:2) was literally fulfilled in AD 70 ("Then after that thou shall cut it down" Luke 13:8). The Nation is still in dispersion scattered throughout the world, hearing foreign tongues bereft of the Hebrew, the channel of their OT revelation of God.

Thus the principle of tongues as a punishment to His people was carried over into the NT period. The Corinthians hankered after speaking in *tongues* and the argument presented by the apostle Paul in I Cor. 14:21, 22 shows *tongues as a sign of Judgement* and *least in value,* the least of all the gifts (the last one listed), instead of the "more excellent way" (I Cor. 12:31).

When Israel was set aside, the sign gift of tongues (which were intelligible and not gibberish) necessarily ceased (I Cor. 13:8).

Israel and the Church

A thoughtful reader of the Word of God will observe that the whole character of God's dealings with the Church has been *different* from that with Israel. It is made abundantly plain in the Scripture, that the Church is NOT an extension of the OT Israel, but a wholly NEW entity. Our Lord Himself said, "I *will* (future) build *My* church" The OT saints do have a distinct place of their own (Heb. 11:13-16). However, the Church is a unique, divine masterpiece. The Church which is His body, inseparably united with its Head, the Lord Jesus Christ (Eph. 4:16), "is the bride of the Lamb" (Rev. 21:9). Hebrews 12:23 makes the distinction between 'the spirits of just men made perfect' (the OT saints), and "the church of the firstborn (the N T church)".

The Israel

Regarding the nation Israel, Deuteronomy 4:34 states: "Hath God assayed to go and take Him a nation from the midst of another nation". The Lord of hosts did this in bringing His vine out of Egypt (Ps. 80:8; Isa. 5:1-7). After Israel was established in their land, blessings of an earthly character were promised to them, on condition of their obedience.

Israel's blessings as a Nation, were to be *material* (Deut. 28:1-14), but this blessing would come upon them only if they would hearken diligently and observe to do all that

God commanded them (Deut. 28:1,2). History proves that Israel failed to obey; the result was that instead of blessing, the predicted curse in Deut 28:15, came upon them, until they were destroyed as a nation (Deut. 28:20,45).

The warnings to Israel could not have been plainer (Deut. 28:15, 58-63). If they disobeyed, they would be excluded from the land, and scattered among the nations (v. 64), and finally they would be sold as slaves (Deut. 28:68). All these were confirmed by history.

The reader should carefully go through Deuteronomy Chapter 28 to 30:5, where two things are finally predicted of Israel:

(i) If those scattered disobedient Jews in the midst of the different nations, where they still remain to this day, *call to mind* the terms of the blessings and cursings.

(ii) And if they *return and obey* with all their heart,

then the Lord will turn their captivity, and will have compassion on them. Then will God return and gather them back to the land from which they had been scattered. There was an actual physical scattering by God, and the same passage of God's word states, that there will be a divine re-gathering to the same land, even the land promised to Abraham, Isaac and Jacob (Deut. 30:5).

Israel is God's treasure hid in the field (earth) (Matt. 13:44) and they are His earthly people. Because of Israel's idolatry and failure as God's *earthly* people, He gave the government to the Gentiles. So the "times of the Gentiles" (Luke 21:24) began with Nebuchadnezzar's reign, as we find in Daniel chapter two. *(Please see "The Times of the Gentiles" Paper No. 04-02).*

This "times of the Gentiles" will end with the Stone smashing the whole image as found in Daniel chapter two. This Stone cut out without hands, is Israel's Messiah, who will step into time with His *heavenly* people, the bride (Mat. 24:30; Rev. 19:14-16), to save His *earthly* people Jews, His elect (Isa. 45:4; 65:9) from extinction (Mat. 24:22).

The last three feasts of Jehovah (Lev. Ch. 23) are to be fulfilled then. They are *yet future:*

(i) The feast of trumpets (Lev. 23:24), for the in-gathering of Israel (as-above).

(ii) The Day of Atonement (Lev. 23:27) followed by the judgement of the living nations (Matt. 25:31-46). This judgement will turn entirely on how the Gentiles will treat "my brethren" the Jews, during this great tribulation period.

(iii) This will be followed by the feast of tabernacles. It may also be viewed in its heavenly aspect as "the marriage supper of the Lamb" (Rev. 19:9), but for earth the commencement of the millennial rule of Christ.

This programme of God's dealings with unfaithful Israel, concerns:

(i) The earth – the land of Israel in particular.

(ii) The fulfilment of all the OT prophecies from Isaiah to Malachi. Nothing in any of these prophetical books refers to the Church which remained as a *mystery,* until God revealed it to the Apostle Paul (Eph. 3:4-8).

(iii) The Church is therefore not in prophecy, but was a *revelation* through Paul, and is dealt with *only* in the N T.

(iv) Israel should be *watching* for their *Messiah* (Son of Man) (Matt. 24:36-44; 25:13; Mark 13:33-37) but the Church is waiting for their *Lord* (the Bridegroom) – "His Son" (I Cor. 1:7; I Thess. 1:10; 2 Thess. 3:5) (Please note this difference between *watch* and *wait*).

The counterpart to Deuteronomy Chapters 28 to 31, in the N T, is the epistle to Romans:

Romans Ch. 9 Israel in the PAST – Jehovah's vineyard (Isa. 5:1-7).

Romans Ch. 10 Israel in the PRESENT – Blindness and unbelief – in the fig tree (Jer. 24:5) now planted in the vineyard (Luke 13:6).

Romans Ch. 11 Israel in the FUTURE – Their final recovery (Hos. 3:5; Acts 15:16).

These three chapters reach a beautiful climax in Romans 11:15:

"For if the casting away of them (see Deut. 28:20,45) be the reconciling of the world, what shall the receiving of them be, but life from the dead?"

The valley of dry bones of Ezekiel Chapter 37 is indicative of Israel's national revival and reconciliation. "Son of man, these bones are the *whole house of Israel*" (v. 11). When the Spirit of God changes their hearts of stone, (Hebrews 8:10-12), Deut. 30:1-5 will be realised, and they will enter into their promised land during Millennium.

The Contrast – Old and New

It will be plain that God's dealing with Israel, as seen above, is quite different from that of the Church, which as our Lord proclaimed, "I will build my church", and which came into being on the day of Pentecost (Acts Ch. 2) after His ascension.

Should the contrast between Israel and the Church as to their origin, calling, promises, worship, principles of conduct and future destiny be clear, it would be seen how misleading it is, to apply to the Church those scriptures which relate to Israel, and vice-versa. The dispensational truths relating to the "Fullness of times" and "The grace of God" (Eph. 1:10; 3:2), should therefore, not be mistaken for the covenants and promises given to Israel as a Nation in the OT.

Much confusion has resulted from the inability among the Lord's people to differentiate Scripture, as to whether they may apply to Israel or to the Church, to their spiritual detriment.

This third section of **Rightly Dividing** study papers, seeks to remedy this deficiency. The basic information is diverse, involving both history and prophecy. Comparisons and contrasts on the various aspects of this absorbing subject have necessitated an analysis under various sub-titles. With those sub-titles, it has been possible to add papers on the various shades of differences between Israel and the Church, which may be spiritually discerned.

While we may all appreciate that there is a difference between the *Law* and *Grace* (John 1:17), (Refer Paper No: 03-04) do we appreciate that the following also involve differences; indeed between *Israel* and the *Church?* For instance:

Related to Israel	Related to Church
Old Bottles (Judaism) (Matt. 9:17)	New Bottles (The Gospel) (Matt. 9:17)
Day of the Lord (Joel 1:15; 2:1, 11, 31)	The Day of Christ (I Cor. 1:8, 5:5; Phil. 1:6, 10)
Son of Man (Matt. 19:28; 24:30)	Son of God (Matt. 26:63; Rom.1:4; Gal. 2:20)
House of Israel (Acts 2:36)	Bride, the Lamb's wife (Rev. 21:9)
Great Tribulation (Matt. 24:21)	Tribulation (John 16:33)
Watch (Matt. 24:43)	Wait (I Thess. 1:10)
Jew, Gentile (I Cor. 10:32)	The Church (I Cor. 10:32)
The King (Matt. 2:2)	The Lord (John 13:13, 14)

Did not the Lord draw attention to the difference in the *order* and *significance* of words, when He reversed the order of His names and said in John 13:13, 14 "Ye call *me Master and Lord*, for so I am. If I then *your Lord and Master*, have washed your feet..." He was gently reproving His disciples for using words (of great significance) in the wrong order. What would He say to us, should we make such mistakes and think we were in the feast of Tabernacles, as did Peter in Luke 9:33?

So, for this and other reasons, differences often unnoticed have been highlighted in these papers, under the general subject "Israel and the Church", which may avoid Christians falling into the current error of "Bringing in the Kingdom", or "Bringing back the King". These tabulation–summaries, appearing in these papers should assist us to grasp the orderly beauty and symmetry of the Word of God, which otherwise, may appear to the unlearned as a mere confusion of inharmonious and conflicting ideas.

Israel and the Church – Contrasted

ISRAEL Past (Rom Ch.9), Present (Rom Ch. 10) and Future (Rom Ch. 11)	CHURCH (Ephesians 3:5)
The Children of Israel (Ex. 6:13).	The Children of *God* (Rom. 8:16).
Sons *of Abraham* (John 8:39).	Sons of God (I John 3:1).
An *earthly* people (Gen.15:18-21, 22:18).	*A heavenly* people (I Pet.2:10; Heb. 3:1).
Multiplied as the *sand* of the seashore, (Rom. 9:27 Gen. 13:16; 22:17; Hosea 1:10).	Multiplied as the *stars of* the heaven (Gen 15:5); Much people in heaven (Rev.5: 11).
A nation from the midst of another *nation,* (Egypt) (Deut. 4:34).	A people taken out from the *Gentiles,* for His name (Acts 15:14).
Formed *from* the foundation of the world. (Matt. 13:35; 25:34)	Foreordained from *before* the foundation of the world (John 17:24; Eph. 1:4).
A *treasure* hid in the field (earth) (Matt. 13:44).	The *pearl* of great price (Matt. 13:46).
The 'This *fold*' (John. 10:16) is Israel from which the disciples were led out.	The *one flock* (John 10:16; Gal. 3:28).
The choicest *vine* that brought-forth wild grapes, (Isa. 5:2) replanted as an unbelieving *fig tree* (Luke 13:6).	The branches to bring forth much fruit, *abiding* in the true Vine (Jesus Christ), and that the fruit should remain, (John 15:5, 16).
The elect of *earth.* (Isa. 45:4, 65:9)	The elect of *heaven* (Rom. 8:33, Col. 3:12)
The House *of Jacob* (Luke. 1:32, 33)	The house *of God* (I Tim. 3:15).
Christ sitting on the Throne of David (Luke 1:32)	Christ occupying, the Father's Throne (Rev. 3:21).
Relationship being one of *Covenant,* inheriting the promises given to Abraham (Gen. 15:18-21).	Relationship, one of Spiritual *Birth* and joint heirs with Christ (Rom. 8:17).
An *earthly* regeneration (Matt. 19:28, Ezekiel 37:10). Refers to the re-creation of the social order and renewal of the earth, when His kingdom will come (Isa. 11:6-9; Jer. 31:33, 34; Ezek. 36:26-28). (This regeneration is yet to take place, when Christ will come to reign.)	A *spiritual* regeneration (Titus 3:5). Refers to the Christian's new birth of being born of the Spirit (John 1:12; 3:5; Rom. 8:15, 16)

ISRAEL Past (Rom ch.9), Present (Rom ch. 10) and Future (Rom ch. 11)	CHURCH (Ephesians 3:5)
Relates to the earth, is *earthly,* unique amongst the nations. (Deut. 7:6; 26:19)	Relates to heavenly places, is *heavenly,* unique in oneness with Christ (Eph. 1:22, 23).
Involves a Nation and Christ the *King* of the Jews (Matt. 2:2; 19:28) yet to acknowledge Christ as their *King.*	Involves Christ "the **head** over all, to the church" (Eph. 1:22). (AV 'things' and "to be" is in italics and not found in the Greek, so to be ignored). We are to acknowledge Christ as the *Head* (Eph. 5:24).
Israelites will be the *friend* of the Bridegroom, i.e. Christ (John. 3:29), as like the five wise and ready virgins, (Matt. 25:10).	The Church will be *the Bride* of the Lamb, the Bride of the Bridegroom (John. 3:29, Rev. 19:7).
The Nation of Israel is an *unfaithful wife,* who will be forgiven and restored (Hos. Chs. 1-3, 2:1-17,23; Ezek. Ch.16, Isa. 54:1-10).	The Church is represented as a *chaste virgin* being prepared for the marriage (II Cor. 11:2) and is the Bride of Christ (Eph. 5:28-32).
The *fall* of Israel (Rom 11:11).	The *salvation* of the Church (Rom. 11:11).
Some branches of Israel were *broken off* (Rom. 11:17).	The wild olive tree *grafted* in (Rom. 11:17).
Temple destroyed, not one stone left upon another (Matt. 24:2). Another temple at Jerusalem yet to be built, (Rev. 11:2) which will also be destroyed (Dan. 9:26). A *material* temple.	The Church will be built as a holy temple, with living stones (Eph. 2:21, 22; I Pet. 2:4-6). "I will build my church" (Matt. 16:18). A *spiritual temple.*
To go through Tribulation in the latter days which is yet future (Deut. 4:30) A time of trouble out of which they will be delivered (Dan. 12:1)	Not appointed to wrath (I Thess. 5:9). The wrath mentioned in this verse is NOT the judgement at the great white throne (Rev. 20:11). *But* the wrath of God at Armageddon (Rev. 14:19-20), which is yet future.
The time of Jacob's trouble (Jer. 30:7)	The time of felicity and rejoicing (Rev. 19:7).
The *Day of the Lord* (Isa. 2:12; 13:6, 9; Jer. 46:10 Mal. 4:5). It is connected with judgment.	*The Day of Christ.* (I Cor. 1:8, 5:5, Phil. 1:6). It relates to the reward and blessing at His coming.
The faithful remnant going into the millennium will rule over many things (Matt. 24:47; 25:21).	In the millennium, the 12 Apostles will rule over the saved Israel (Matt. 19:28). The church will reign on the earth (Rev. 5:10) and judge angels (I Cor. 6:3).

Some Expressions that Require Elucidation

Problems are generated by such expressions, some of which appear in the Word of God and are used erroneously, since they are taken out of context.

1. Amillennialism

Amillennialism means No-Millennium, that is to say, there is no future for the people of Israel, in the land promised to Abraham, Isaac and Jacob. This would mean that God has *broken* His covenant with Abraham, (Gen. 13:15, 16; 15:18-21; 17:6-8). This teaching contradicts the faithfulness of the unchanging covenant – keeping – God. "The faithful God, which keepeth covenant" (Deut. 7:9).

An Amillennialist will contend that all the promises to Abraham are fulfilled in the Church, they being only spiritual. One Scripture, apart from many more, should reveal the error of such wrong teaching. God said to Jacob in Genesis 28:13, "The *land* where on *thou* liest, to *thee* will I give it, and to thy *seed*". Each of those two promises (*land* and *seed*) are yet *future* and *literal*. (Heb. 11:13, 14).

Symbolism in Scripture does not necessarily make the matter spiritual as opposed to actual and real. Consider Hosea 6:2: "After *two days* He will revive us. In the *third day* He will raise us up, and we shall live in His sight". The suggested interpretation here is of *two millennia* (2000 years) of grace while the church is gathered, and the *third day*, the Millennium of the feast of Tabernacles, for Israel in their land again, and the Lord reigning as their King and David risen and reigning as His servant, being their prince forever (Ezekiel 37:24).

2. The Israel of God

The use of this description "The Israel of God", (Gal. 6:16) in connection with prophecy, is to take it out of context. It is inserted in the Epistle to the Galatians, as the final proof that salvation is an act of grace, not of circumcision or of un-circumcision; but a new creature (Gal. 6:15). Hence, this could not be taken to assert that the NT Church of Christ is the new Israel of God or a continuation of the old Israel (Rom. 11:25, 26).

3. The Nation of Israel Becomes a Holy Nation

Again if the Scripture said this, we would have no problem. In fact this "Holy Nation" of I Peter 2:9, was *"not a people"*, as the following verse (v.10) so clearly states. They were not a Nation of Israel and thus could not become what they never were. Therefore, the statement, "A Holy Nation", can only apply to the church, which is gathered out of the world, (Acts 15:14) *as altogether a new entity.* As we, the *NT saints* are a Holy Nation, which were not a people before, how can we (Church) become a nation with a Promised Land, King and kingdom etc. as the *old nation* of Israel had. Thus the NT church is not the Nation of Israel.

The Second Coming of Christ

TO every true Christian the second coming of Christ ought to be a precious as well as an exciting subject. We should be intensely interested in what scripture has to say with regard to this event for it will mark for us the most wonderful moment of our lives. It will be so because,

> We shall, in our glorified bodies, gaze upon Christ for the first time. He will be known of us by sight and no longer by faith.

> We shall reach the state of moral perfection for the first time. *The final* phase of our salvation will be effected, and in bodies changed and redeemed by power, we shall be both morally and physically like Christ, for "we shall see Him as He is" (I John 3:2).

> We shall experience complete satisfaction for the first time. Rejoicing eternally in the very presence of Christ, we shall be happy and fully satisfied.

The first coming of the Lord Jesus Christ to this very small but unique and important planet earth had its historical fulfilment. While His *second coming* lies still in the future. At his first advent Christ came as a Saviour to die sacrificially; at His second advent, He will return as King to reign universally. Moreover, each of these two advents is shown to be composed of two stages – a *secret phase* and a *public manifestation*. This was so at His first advent – secrecy surrounded His nativity; publicity marked His triumphal entry into Jerusalem, when Christ presented Himself officially as King to the nation of Israel. Similarly, Christ's Second Advent will be characterised by two distinct stages:

1. The resurrection of the dead and the rapture of the saints will constitute the first phase. This will be *private* meeting with His own. The rendezvous will be in the air. (I Thess. 4:16; 17).

2. The subsequent descent to the earth will form the second stage, when accompanied by glorified saints and angelic intelligences, the King of kings shall *publicly* set foot on the Mount of Olives (Zech 14:4).

The Old Testament abounds in references to this second stage of Christ's second coming, but the first stage (the resurrection of the dead and the rapture of the living saints) is not alluded to in any of its pages. Neither is this resurrection and rapture spoken of in any of the synoptic gospels (Matthew, Mark and Luke). Only in the fourth gospel, John's unique record is it directly mentioned. This fact in itself is remarkable, for Christ's title in relation to the rapture is "Son of God", which is the theme of John's Gospel (John 14:1-4). In this character, He comes *secretly* to bring blessing to His own. On the contrary, Christ's title associated with this second stage of the Second Advent – His coming in regal splendour – is "Son of Man" (Matt. 24:27; Mark 13:26; Luke 21:27; the synoptic gospels). As such, He will *come publicly* to judge His enemies and to rule the world.

The striking and remarkable details of the first stage of His second advent, the resurrection of the dead and the rapture of His people, were held by God as a mystery, but revealed to Apostles and Prophets in due time. (Eph. 3:5,7; Col. 1:25-27; I Cor. 15:51). We find them in Paul's writings viz, I Cor. 15:12-58 and I Thess. 4:13-18.

The first stage of Christ's second coming was a *mystery revealed,* while the second stage is the *theme of prophecy.*

The first is a descent, into the *air* only for the removal of His own, but the other is a descent to the *earth* as we read in Zech. 14:4. The first is characterised by *deepest affection*

for the objects of His Divine favour; and the other by terrible *desolating judgments* upon His enemies (Rev. 1:7).

The reader will compare the last chapter of the New Testament with the last chapter of the Old. In Revelation 22:16 we read, "I am the root and the offspring of David, and the *Bright and Morning Star".* But in Malachi 4:2,3 we have, "Unto you that fear My Name shall *the Sun of Righteousness* arise with healing in His wings; and ye shall go forth, and grow up as calves of the stall. And ye shall tread down the wicked, for they shall be ashes under the soles of your feet in the day that I shall do this, saith Jehovah of Hosts." Such are the different characters of hope set before the *heavenly* and the *earthly* people respectively. Who can fail to see that these Scriptures speak of two entirely different events? The morning star is visible before the sun, as every one knows.

The careful examination of the various passages relating to the Second Advent shows clearly that there are *no* similarities between these two phases. They stand in striking contrast in several important respects as the accompanying tabulation will reveal:

COMING FOR THE CHURCH	COMING TO ISRAEL
As the Lord Himself (Phil. 3:20; I Thess. 4:16)	As the Son of Man (Matt. 24:27-30)
New Testament mystery and not a subject of OT prophecy (I Cor. 15:51)	Foretold in the Old Testament over and over again (Dan. 7:13, Jude 14)
For the Church's rapture (I Thess. 4:17)	For Israel's deliverance (Isa. Chs. 61-66, Dan. 7:21-22)
For His saints (I Thess. 4:16-17)	*With* His saints (Zech. 14:5, Jude 14)
All believers taken to be with the Lord (I Thess. 4:17)	Some taken (removed) for judgement and others left behind to enter into the Kingdom (Luke 17:34-37)

COMING FOR THE CHURCH	COMING TO ISRAEL
Into the *air* (I Thess. 4:17)	To the *earth* (Zech. 14:4)
To receive the Church (John 14:3)	To execute vengeance on them those know not God (II Thess. 1:7-8)
As the Morning Star (Rev. 22:16)	As the Sun of Righteousness (Mal. 4:2)
All over in a moment, and *not seen* by the nations (I Cor. 15:52)	Christ *seen* by all, from all locations (Isa. 63:1, Matt. 24:30; Rev. 1:7)
Preceded by signs of moral degradation (II Tim. 3:1-5)	Preceded by material signs and moral degrada-tions (Joel 2:30, Matt. 24:29, 38)
Christians *await* (I Thess. 1:10)	Jewish remnant *watches* (Matt. 24:42-51)
The immediate hope of the Church and expected any time (John 21:22; Phil. 3:20) and will be followed by Daniel's 70th week.	Will follow Daniel's 70th week (Dan. 9:24-27; Rev. 13:5)
Followed by the judgement seat of Christ (II Cor. 5:10; Rom .14:10).	Followed by the judgement of Israel (Zech. 13:8, 9; Matt. 24:31) and the living nations (Zech. 14:12; Matt. 25:32)
Ushers in the tribulation (II Thess. Ch. 2; Rev 4:1; 5:1)	Ushers in the millennium (Dan. 2:44; Rev. Chs. 19, 20)

The Sabbath, The Lord's Day and Associated Matters, Contrasted

THE SABBATH	THE LORD'S DAY
The *seventh day* of the week (Ex. 16:26, 30).	*The first day* of the week. (John 20:1, 19)
The day of rest for the Creator (Gen. 2:2). (Not on account of exhaustion, Isa. 40:28, but an indication of satisfaction and completion (Ex. 20:11).	The day of Christ's resurrection, (The basis of our rest due to His finished work of redemption John 19:30) (John 20:1; Matt. 28:1).
Its observance was *obligatory* under Law (Ex. 20:8-11) and was a sign between God and Israel (Ex. 31:13, 16-17). Marked out what God could do for His earthly people.	Its observance is a *privilege* under grace, being made distinctive by the Lord's resurrection and His people being filled (Acts 2:1 & Lev. 23:10-15), it is appropriate for the local assembly to gather to 'break bread' (Acts 20:7).
Its observance marked out an earthly people, *Israel;*	Its observance distinguishes a heavenly people, gathered as *Churches.*
Its observance indicated what Israel *could do* for God. (Neh. 9:14)	Its observance signifies the enjoyment of what Christ is and *has done* for God. (The great Burnt-offering.)
Its observance, was celebrated by the offering of two lambs as a burnt offering for each of the morning and evening sacrifices (Num. 28:9,10), and by the reading of the Law of God (Deut. 31:11,12,13; Nehemiah 8:8,9).	Its observance, is marked by the Lord's Supper, ('breaking of bread') in remembrance of the Lord's death till He come. (Acts 20:7; I Cor. 11:23-26), and by the preaching of the word (Acts 20:7).
To be kept holy (Ex. 20:8).	No such command in the N.T. but we are exhorted to be holy in all the ways on *all the days.* (1 Pet 1:14; 2 Pet 3:11; Eph 1:4)
No work to be done (Ex. 20:10).	No such command in the N.T. but we should keep ourselves active in the Lord as on any other day (Col 2:16, 17).

THE SABBATH	THE LORD'S DAY
The daily sacrifice was killed and offered, although this involved work (Num. 28:3-8).	This obviously cannot apply, as OT sacrifices were shadows of CHRIST.
"In the end of the Sabbaths" (Matt. 28:1) *note plural* – indicating the end of a system – a Sabbath is after all a shadow of good things to come (Col. 2:17). (The words 'Sabbath' and 'week' are *in plural* in the Greek Text – Refer Newberry)	"As it began to dawn toward the first of the weeks" (Mat 28:1) – plural indicating the importance of another "Day", "the first" (day is in *italics*) of the weeks (plural). For the first three centuries after the resurrection the first day of the week was never confused with the Sabbath day.
Its meaning implies 'rest' (Ex. 20:11), although the literal meaning is "to desist or cease (from work)' not so much *rest* but ceasing *from activity*.	Its name: "the Lord's day". Because the Lord rose from among the dead on that day (Rev. 1:10). Howbeit, it is also the number for resurrection – also the eighth day.
"A Sabbath day's journey" (Acts 1:12) was a Rabbinical restriction imposing an approximate 2,000 cubits, limit to a journey on the Sabbath.	Obviously no such restriction can apply. Acts 20 deals with the journey problem and the Lord's Day, in very detailed particulars.

The observance of the Lord's Supper

In Acts Chapter 20, the actions of the Apostle Paul give guidance on this matter. He preached till midnight, as the Lord's Day (as with all days) commenced at 6 p.m. "And the evening and the morning, were the first day" (Gen. 1:5).

Paul had waited *seven* days to break bread with the disciples, which means he arrived in the forenoon of the previous Sunday, but only *after* the disciples had observed the Lord's Supper. From this apostolic action, once given as a pattern for others in the future, we can observe:

1. Paul's principles led him to break bread, as a function of a NT assembly, (here "disciples" is stressed appropriately). Otherwise:

i. he would have broken bread on-board the ship, or

ii. on arriving on the Sunday, using, "as often as ye do this …", he could have organized *another* gathering for breaking of bread, for himself and others who had or had not already participated.

2. Paul refrained from acting outside the understanding of the Lord's mind. It therefore follows that "as often as you do this …" is not to encourage believers to take part *several times* on the same Lord's day, but taking part *only once*; once every Lord's day. In Acts 20, Paul missed that privilege on the day he arrived at Troas, which was a Lord's Day. Thus we take instruction from Paul's action.

The Law and Grace

The precepts given in the Ten-Commandments under the Law, as compared to what is expected of believers now, during this age of grace:

God's Commandments to Israel Under Sinai	God's Spiritual Precepts and Commands Under Grace
1. "Thou shall have no other gods before me" (Ex. 20:3)	Believers under grace have clear and emphatic instruction: "Sanctify the Lord God in your hearts" (I Pet. 3:15), "Glorify God in your body, and in your spirit, which are God's." (I Cor. 6:20). Unceasing prayer and faithful service, as abiding in Christ, gives rise to constant, continuous, joyous, moment by moment dependence upon the exalted Lord Jesus Christ. (I Cor. 1:31).
2. "Thou shall not make unto thee any graven image." (Ex. 20:4)	"Little children, keep yourselves from idols" (I John 5:21) "Neither be ye idolaters" (I Cor. 10:7). The instructions to the believers go beyond the making of images or their worship; they involve putting anything in front of God and before Him in His service. For, covetousness in any form is considered as idolatry, for it consists of putting personal desires *ahead* of the love for God (Col. 3:5).
3. "Thou shall not take the Name of the Lord thy God in vain" (Ex. 20:7)	While this commandment is not repeated in those exact words, reverence for the *name* and *person* of God and for the Name of the Lord Jesus Christ is clearly expected of the believer. There is to be no irreverence when speaking of God, or using His Name, as also in our attitude and in our actions. (Beware of doing what even the disciples dared not. They NEVER addressed our LORD even *once*, as just "Jesus". So avoid this unscriptural modern trend.)

49

God's Commandments to Israel Under Sinai	God's Spiritual Precepts and Commands Under Grace
4. "Remember the Sabbath day to keep it holy" (Ex. 20:8) *(Please refer to "The Sabbath and the Lord's Day" Paper No 03-03)*	This is the one commandment not repeated to believers under grace. On the contrary, now believers are instructed not to regard one day above another (Rom. 14:5, 6; Gal. 4:9-11). Not just one special day but *every day* is to be lived in the spiritual fellowship and service of the Lord, to Whom we belong.
5. "Honour thy father and thy mother" (Ex. 20:12) ("in order that, thy days may be long upon the land-earth")	Obedience and honour to parents, is twice commanded in the NT. (Eph. 6:2, 3 and Col. 3:20). Under grace, children are to "Obey... for this is right," and "Children, obey... for this is pleasing unto the Lord".
6. "Thou shall not kill" (Ex. 20:13)	Compare I John 3:14, 15 and Matt. 5:21, 22.
7. "Thou shall not commit adultery" (Ex. 20:14).	Compare I Cor. 6:13-20; I Thess. 4:3 also Luke 16:18; Matt. 19:9.
8. "Thou shall not steal" (Ex. 20:15)	Compare I Thess. 4:6. (I Cor. 6:10, 11 coupled with Eph. 4:28 'Such were some of you').
9. "Thou shall not bear false witness (Lie)" (Ex. 20:16)	Compare Col. 3:9; Eph. 4:15, 25, Disobedience to this, will grieve the Holy Spirit (Eph. 4:30.) and lose communion with Him till restored by repentance.
10. "Thou shall not covet" (Ex. 20:17)	Compare Eph. 5:3; Col. 3:5; Heb. 13:5. (If disobedience persisted it would attract ex-communication. I Cor. 5:11).

Conclusion:

While God Jehovah brought Israel out of bondage in Egypt, establishing them as a nation, He commanded them in the wilderness, to build a sanctuary, "that He may *dwell among them*" (Ex. 25:8). As the Lord God, Who dwelt among them is Holy, (Lev. 11:44), so His people as a nation are to keep themselves Holy. So the Holy God gave them the commandments and the laws for them to keep and to obey.

Likewise, in a more intimate and realistic way, under this grace age, every believer is *indwelt by Christ,* (Rom. 8:9; I Cor. 6:19, 20; Gal. 4:6; Col. 1:27), and so we are obliged to keep ourselves Holy (I Pet 1:15, 16), in a far superior sense. This is the will of God concerning His people (I Thess. 4:3). Thus it is expected of every N T saint to "put off the old-man with his deeds" and "put on the new-man after the image of Him that created him" (Col. 3:9-17), and all his conduct in every respect is to be as "becometh saints" (Eph 5:1-3).

The Gospel of the Kingdom
and
The Gospel of Christ

In this paper, we shall explain and differentiate the Gospel of the Kingdom and the Gospel of Christ.

Gospel

The Greek word "*euangelion*" means 'good news' and the verb "*euangelizo*" means "to announce good tidings". Corresponding English words are evangel and evangelise (Note the word 'angel', firmly rooted in these words – since it means 'messenger'). Thus Gospel means 'good-news', and absolutely essential to man's salvation. In the New Testament it denotes the good tidings of the Kingdom of God and of salvation through Christ, to be received by faith, on the basis of His expiatory death, His burial, resurrection, and ascension to be received by faith.

The Gospel of the Kingdom

This is the good-news of God's purposes to establish on the earth the Kingdom of Christ, the seed of David according to the flesh (Rom. 1:3), in fulfilment of the Davidic Covenant (2 Sam. 7:16).

The Good news of this Kingdom was announced by the OT prophets (Isa. 9:6, 7),

and was proclaimed, beginning with the ministry of John the Baptist and carried on by our Lord (Matt. 9:35) and His twelve disciples (Matt. 10:5-16), but ended with the Jewish rejection of the Messiah. This kingdom Gospel was preached *only* to the Jews, the lost sheep of the house of Israel, but NOT to the Gentiles (Matt. 10:5, 6; 15:24). This Gospel will again be proclaimed after the consummation of the Church, during the great Tribulation period (Matt. 24:14); all of these are yet to take place.

Closely connected, although perhaps not identical in its emphasis with the Gospel of the Kingdom, is the EVERLASTING GOSPEL (Rev. 14:6-12), preached to all the earth-dwellers during the latter part of the Tribulation. Everlasting Gospel is described as the announcement of divine judgment upon the wicked in the coming great Tribulation and will be good news to the suffering believers as it heralds their coming deliverance and reward (Rev. 14:12), and those who "dwell on the earth" are exhorted to fear God and worship Him (Rev. 14:7). It would mean the everlasting nature of the judgment.

The Gospel of Grace

This is the good news that Jesus Christ died on the cross as a vicarious Sin-Bearer, for the sins of the world, and that He was buried and that He was raised from the dead for our justification (1 Cor. 15:3,4). All who believe on Him are justified and delivered from God's wrath and thus are reconciled to God by Christ (Rom. 5:9, 10).

This Gospel of grace, is preached throughout the present Grace Age, both to the Jews and to the Gentiles, beginning from Jerusalem, Judaea, Samaria and to the uttermost part of the earth – to all the world (Acts 1:8; Mark 16:15). This grace period is described in 2 Cor. 6:2 as "now is the *day* of salvation". The "now" covers the *day of grace,* a period which began with the first advent of Christ and will end with His coming in the air for the church. This period is characterised by God acting in longsuffering (2 Peter 3:25) with men and not dealing with them in His wrath, as He would deal with them later.

There are different terms used in the New Testament, to describe, this Gospel, the Good-News, which are listed below:

1. "The gospel of God" (Rom. 1:1), signifies its *source,* which originates in His love (John 3:16). The message was settled in heaven (Ps. 2:7-8) before the foundation of the world. (1 Cor. 2:7).

2. "The gospel of Christ" (2 Cor. 10:14), denotes its *subject*. Christ is the object of our faith.

3. "The gospel of the grace of God" (Acts 20:24), directs attention to its *unmerited favour,* and saves whom the Law condemns.

4. "The gospel of your salvation" (Eph. 1:13), specifies *its purpose* and is the "power of God unto salvation to every one that believeth" (Rom. 1:16).

5. "The gospel of peace" (Eph. 6:15), evidences the *inward peace.* It is the peace of reconciliation attained through Christ between the believing sinner and a Holy God. (Rom. 5:1). It is an inner protection and assurance in our spiritual warfare.

6. "The glorious gospel of Christ" (2 Cor. 4:4), so called as it *concerns Him* who is in the glory and Who is bringing many sons to glory (Heb 2:10).

7. "My (Paul's) gospel" (Rom. 2:16; 16:25; 2 Tim. 2:8), identifies its *human channel*. It was given to Paul by inspiration and revelation (Gal. 1:12; 1 Tim. 3:16; Eph. 3:1-3) and he was appointed as the minister of these mysteries (Acts 22:10; Eph. 3:7).

8. "The gospel which was preached of me (Paul)" (Gal. 1:11; 2:2), names the *message* Paul preached.

9. "Our gospel" (2 Cor. 4:3; 1 Thess. 1:5; 2 Thess. 2:14) shows its *commitment* to the recipients of grace, because it has been revealed to us by the Holy Spirit. Paul included himself with the assemblies, when he called the message *"our* gospel". We could not understand the gospel if it were not revealed to us by the Holy Spirit. The message has come to us in the sense that all truth is made known by God (Matt. 16:17; 2 Cor. 4:3, 6; Eph. 1:17-23; I John 2:20, 27).

10. "Another (another of a *different* sort) gospel, which is not another (another of the *same* kind)", (Gal. 1:6, 7; 2 Cor. 11:4), but consists of any sort of *denial or perversion* of the gospel of the grace of God, and that denies the full efficacy of God's *grace alone* to save, keep and perfect. The gospel message, which requires any sort of human merit and effort, is *'another'* gospel of a

different kind. That will be a gospel not of God, a gospel which preached Christ plus Law, a gospel which was not of grace alone.

11. "The Mystery of the gospel" (Eph. 6: 19), signifies that this Gospel was hitherto hid, but now *revealed* to the Apostles and Prophets by the Spirit (Eph. 3:4, 5) (*Please refer to Paper No.01-06 titled "The Mystery"*).

Conclusion

The word "GOSPEL", therefore, includes various aspects of the good news of divine revelation. The good news of the Gospel of grace, the Gospel of the coming Kingdom, and the Everlasting Gospel are all different, and they emphasise different aspects, according to their *dispensations*. The Gospel of grace is salvation for all men through *grace* alone, during this present church age, the Gospel of the Kingdom emphasises the anticipated presence of the King and His Kingdom in this world when God will fulfil His promise to Israel, and the Everlasting Gospel emphasises God's *judgement* upon the wicked during the great Tribulation period. However, *grace* is the basis for salvation in *all* the dispensations and is under *all* circumstances the only way of salvation from sin.

Note:

1. "Another gospel which is not another" (Gal. 1:6, 7). Two Greek words, with distinct different meanings are used here. The first '*heteros*', means another of a different kind, and the second '*allos*', another of the same kind. The first denotes qualitative difference and distinguishes one of two kinds. The second denotes a numerical difference and differentiates two of the same kind.

2. "The truth of the gospel" (Gal. 2:14), denotes the teaching concerning it, in contrast to its perversions.

Please refer to separate Tabulation titled: "Christ's Commission to the Apostles in respect of the Kingdom and the Church - Compared" (Paper No. 03-06)

Christ's Commission to the Apostles in Respect of The Kingdom and The Church Compared

Christ's Commission to His Disciples (Matt. 10:5-23)	Christ's Commission to the Church (Matt. 28:18-20; Lk. 24:46- 49; Acts 1:8)
Preachers: Heralds of Israel's King. (Matt. 10:9-14).	*Preachers:* Ambassadors for Christ. (2 Cor. 5:20).
Sphere of Service: Not in the way of the Gentiles, nor to the city of the Samaritans, but to Israel only (Matt. 10:5, 6).	*Sphere of Service:* To *all* nations, *'the entire* world' (Mk. 16:15; Lk. 24:47). The order is, first at Jerusalem, Judaea, Samaria and then unto the uttermost part of the earth (Acts 1:8).
Amongst Whom: The *lost sheep* of Israel only (Matt. 10:5-6; Compare with Luke 19:10). This word 'lost' also refers to Israel as a nation "That which was lost".	*Amongst Whom:* *All people* without distinction of Jew and Gentile. (1 Tim. 2:4; 2 Peter 3:9)
The Message: "The Gospel of the Kingdom" (Matt. 4:23). "Repent ye: for the kingdom of heaven is at hand". (Matt. 3:2).	*The Message:* The Gospel of Grace, (Rom. 1:16; 1 Cor. 15:1-4) "Baptising them . . . and teaching them to observe *all* things, whatsoever I have commanded you" (Matt. 28:20).
It's Authority: "Spirit of your Father Who speaketh in you" (Matt. 10:19, 20).	*It's Authority:* The Holy Spirit sent by the risen Lord will speak with authority and boldness (Acts 1:8; 4:8, 31; 7:55).

Christ's Commission to His Disciples (Matt. 10:5-23)	Christ's Commission to the Church (Matt. 28:18-20; Lk. 24:46- 49; Acts 1:8)
It's Operation: In kingdom miracles: "Heal the sick, cleanse the lepers, raise the dead, cast out devils" (Matt. 10:8). (Note this was a specific command to the Apostles).	*It's Operation:* "In baptising them in the name of the Father and of the Son and of the Holy Spirit" (Matt. 28:19). (Note carefully that there is *no command,* nor any indication to perform any miracles or healings.)
The Servants' Motivation: "Freely ye have received, freely give" (Matt. 10:8).	*The Servants' Motivation:* God's grace and love constrain us. (2 Cor. 5:14; 6; l).
Hearer's Response: To *receive* the message or to go into eternal judgment. (Matt. 10:14, 15).	*Hearer's Response:* To *believe* on the Lord Jesus Christ (Acts 16:31) or to go into eternal judgement and perdition (2 Pet. 3:7-9)
Result: Peace came upon the house that was worthy. (Compare this with what the Lord said to Zacchaeus, a son of Abraham. Luke 19:9).	*Result:* "Thou shall be saved and thy house" (Acts 16:31 of course only if they – thy house – also believe).
Guidance If Rejected: For those who do not receive you shake off the dust from your feet (Matt. 10:14).	*Guidance if Rejected:* Those who do not believe the Gospel: "They left and went to other places" "Salvation of God is sent unto the Gentiles and they will hear it" (Acts 17:13, 14; 28:28-31).
Preachers' Maintenance: God to provide; "The workman is worthy of his *meat*" (Matt. 10:10)	*Preachers' Maintenance:* 'The labourer is worthy of his *reward".* (I Tim. 5:18) "For His name's sake they went forth, taking nothing from the *Gentiles* (unsaved heathen)" (3 John 7) *"Taking"* means accepting from unbelievers as a policy and or appealing for funds.
Duration: *Until* Christ was rejected (as their King) and crucified by Israel. Again to be *resumed* after the rapture of the Church; during the first half of the tribulation period (Matt. 24:14), to be preached by 144,000 sealed servants of God from all the tribes of Israel. (Rev. Ch. 7)	*Duration:* Throughout the *Church Age,* from the day of Pentecost to the Rapture. "Lo, I am with you always even unto the end of the world (Age)" (Matt. 28:20), specifically indicating this Church Age only.

A Comparison between the Parables of the Great Supper and the Marriage of the King's Son

The Parable of the Great Supper (Luke 14: 16-24) *(From A Gentile Aspect)*	The Parable of the Marriage of the King's Son (Matt. 22: 2-14) *(From An Israel/Jewish Aspect)*
v. 17 *One* Servant	**v. 3 *Many* Servants**
Traces the progress of the Gospel of God's grace since the cross, through the one servant the Holy Spirit.	Traces the progress of God's dealings particularly with Israel (the Gentiles being a secondary consideration).
No mention	v. 3 May indicate O.T. prophets were the first servants.
No mention	v. 4 "Other Servants" preaching an enlarged message given in detail which involves killing an ox reminding of the Cross.
No mention of burning the City (obviously Jerusalem). But v. 21 reminds us of Jerusalem with its streets and lanes and v. 23 of the Gospel going out to Gentiles (Roman) highways and hedges (Jewish fields had landmarks not hedges) indicating the progress of the Gospel.	v. 7 "His armies" would be God using the Roman legions in AD 70, as He used Cyrus to re-gather Israel, "Cyrus, He is my shepherd" (Isa. 44:28) and Babylon "My battle-axe" (Jer. 51:20), and King of Babylon "my Servant" to punish Israel (Jer. 25:9)

The Parable of the Great Supper (Luke 14: 16-24) *(From A Gentile Aspect)*	The Parable of the Marriage of the King's Son (Matt. 22: 2-14) *(From An Israel/Jewish Aspect)*
v. 17 *One* Servant	v. 3 *Many* Servants
No mention – Since the Holy Spirit is the person who creates the new birth, "So is every one that is born of the spirit" (John 3:8)	v. 11 The many servants may be the reason for this 'mistake' (no wedding garment). Even Simon was, by mistake, baptised. (Acts 8: 20)
v. 24 None of these men that were bidden (unbelieving Israel) shall taste of my supper.	v. 13 The offender is cast into outer darkness. (As with the wicked servant in Matt. 24: 48-57)
Conclusion This parable reveals the smugness of the man in Luke 14:15 who obviously thought he would be eating in the Kingdom, i.e. Even those bidden Jews ('and bade many' v. 16) will not even bother to respond. It highlights indifference to the message by Jews and the transfer of advantage to Gentiles (which, of course, also arises in Matt. 22:10.)	**Conclusion** The parable, coming as it does between Christ's manifestation as "Son of Man" to and for the Jews (Matt. 24:30, 31) and the setting up of His throne in order to judge the living nations (Matt. 25:31-32), highlights *its Jewish application.*

The Difference between the Parables of the Pounds and of the Talents

Major points only are Differentiated

	The Parable of the Pounds (Luke 19:12-27)	The Parable of the Talents (Matthew 25: 14-30)
v. 12	To receive for himself a Millennial kingdom and to return.	Not mentioned.
v. 13	10 pounds: one pound each.	v. 15 5 Talents, 2 Talents and 1 Talent
v.13	Command : *Occupy* till I come,	No command.
v. l5	Purpose: To *gain* by trading.	v. 15 According to *several* ability
v. 14	His citizens (Jews) hated him.	Not mentioned.
v. 15	He returned having received the Millennial kingdom.	Not mentioned.
v. 16	Reward: Authority to the servants over 10 cities.	v. 21 Reward: Ruler over many things.
v. 22	Judged from his own mouth.	v. 26 Denounced as wicked.
v. 27	His enemies (Jews) slain.	v. 30 Cast him into the outer darkness. (The lake of fire)
Conclusion	The matter of equal opportunity – one pound each – appears to accent the Christian *life* and *service* and as we would therefore anticipate, it is open to *all*. There is no casting into the outer darkness – but just the loss to one servant of "that which he had" (v. 14).	**Conclusion** This is the 7th of the parables associated with the tribulation passage Matt. 24:32 to 25:30. As the punishment of the wicked servant (Matt. 24:51) is "weeping and wailing and gnashing teeth." the wicked servants would therefore be Jews, at the time when He gathers out of His Kingdom, all things that offend. (Matt. 13:41).This parable cannot be taken as applicable to the church.

The Difference between "From before The Foundation of the World" and "From the Foundation of the World"

This paper could help the reader to discover gems of truth from the Word of God, by a careful observation of the additions and omissions of even some of the most insignificant words. This is not an exhaustive study, but just aims to provoke a *careful* study of the Word of God. What we are looking at here is the usage of just *one* word, added or omitted to the phrase: "the foundation of the world", i.e. the word "before". The Scripture references are:

"From the foundation of the world"		"From before the foundation of the world"	
Matthew	13:35	John	17:24
Matthew	25:34	Ephesians	1:4
Luke	11:50	I Peter	1:20
Hebrews	4:3		
Hebrews	9:26		
Revelation	13:8		
Revelation	17:8		

1. "From Before the Foundation of the World"

"According as he hath chosen us in Him *before* the foundation of the world." (Eph. 1:4)

Being written to believers at Ephesus, it has a general application to all the believers, and therefore, to the *church* which is His body. Having "chosen us in Him, *before* the foundation of the world" takes us into an eternity past unbounded by time and lifts us to a spiritual sphere. The other two verses give us the same thought concerning our Lord:

"Thou lovest Me before the foundation of the world." (John 17:24)

"The lamb foreordained before the foundation of the world." (I Pet. 1:20)

As He was Himself loved and foreordained from before the foundation of the world, so are we chosen in *Him from before* the foundation of the world!

2. "From the Foundation of the World"

"I will open my mouth in parables; I will utter things which have been kept secret from the foundation of the world." (Matt. 13:35)

(There are six other occurrences of this phrase in the NT. Perhaps such a distinction may not be so clearly brought out in the various languages in which the Bible has been translated.)

When we examine the quotation taken from Psalm 78:2, it reads:

"I will open my mouth in a parable; I will utter dark sayings of old."

By comparison these two verses bear little resemblance in the actual words, although the underlying intent is the same, and our Lord has added to it saying *"from* the foundation of the world".

We may well note, that the Lord was speaking to Israel in parables (Matt. 13:10, 11, 34) and that this is a record of their unbelief (Matt. 13:13-15). Thus this phrase has a general application to Israel only. This particular distinction should therefore, be a help in isolating the instance, "Come ye blessed of my Father, inherit the kingdom prepared for you, *from* the foundation of the world." (Matt. 25:34). Here the King is addressing the sheep, those Gentiles who treated the Jews (my brethren) well. This verse relates to the *millennial kingdom,* and therefore also to Israel, is clear from the actual words of the verse itself.

As regards the verses in Revelation 13:8 and 17:8, (the authorised Greek Textus Receptus. from which the English AV was translated), *both* these verses speak about the *writing,* that is "names not *written* in the book of life, from the foundation of the world." Thus they clearly indicate that it was the *writing* and NOT the *slaying,* which was from the foundation of the world. It may be noted that only in verse 13:8, the reference is given about the lamb – Jesus Christ – slain, which emphasises NOT the 'act of slaying', but only the 'act of *writing'* the name in that book. The accurate translation of J. N. Darby will clear any misleading: "Whose name had not been written from (the) founding of (the) world, in the book of life of the slain lamb."

That these two verses refer to the events associated with ISRAEL, becomes apparent, when we see; that the church is in heaven from Revelation 4:1 onwards, and thus they apply to the people left behind during the great tribulation, and who are to enter into the kingdom.

Conclusion

The phrase *"from before"*, is connected with the *Church*, which is His body, that is every believer from Pentecost to the rapture.

The word *"from"* (i.e. by itself, without adding the word 'before') is connected with *Israel* and the kingdom on the earth that is the earthly Millennial Kingdom. "Thy kingdom come, Thy will be done in earth" (Matt. 6:10).

This may not, initially, appear to be a great or a vital discovery, but a careful study of the Word of; God will profit us. By distinguishing truths applicable to the *Church* from those that actually relate to *Israel* and the millennial kingdom, the true understanding of the teaching of the passages in which this word or phrase occurs, will be explicit.

The Seven Set Feasts of Jehovah and Their Prophetic Significance

(Leviticus 23)

Some of Israel's seven annual festive gatherings, given through Moses, are of a commemorative nature of the great events in their past history. They also have a prophetic purpose and were intended to foreshadow greater events of world history. They furnish us with a broad and clear outline of the entire history of the nation of Israel. In them, the great Architect of the Ages has drawn us a plan, the basic blue-print of His purposes for Israel and through them for the world.

FULFILLED	YET TO BE FULFILLED
1. THE FEAST OF THE PASSOVER (v. 5) 14th day of the first month (Num 28:16) Fulfilled as shown in "Christ our passover is sacrificed for us" (I Cor. 5:7)	5. THE MEMORIAL OF TRUMPETS (v. 24) To be fulfilled after the appearance on earth of the *Son of Man,* (a name associated with Jews; Dan. 7:13), in power and great glory (Matt. 24:30), when the angels are sent with a great sound of a trumpet to gather the scattered elect of the Jews (Deut. 30:1-11; Isa. 45:4; 65:9; Zech. 13:8, 9). The dispersed Jews, who survive the great Tribulation, are gathered, from the four corners of heaven (a phrase for everywhere and anywhere) for their review. (Num. 10:1-10; Deut. 4:30-32)
2. THE FEAST OF THE UNLEAVENED BREAD (v.6) *15th day of the first month. (Num. 28:17) To be observed for 7 days.* Fulfilled in the believers in Christ, as in "with unleavened bread of sincerity and truth". (I Cor. 5:8)	

FULFILLED	YET TO BE FULFILLED
3. THE FEAST OF FIRST FRUITS (vv. 10, 11) OR SHEAF OF THE WAVE-OFFERING (v. 15) *17ᵗʰ day of the first month. (During the feast of unleavened bread)* "On the morrow after the Sabbath" (v. 11), i.e. the first day of the week. Fulfilled in the resurrection of Christ, "Christ the first fruits". (I Cor. 15:23)	6. THE DAY OF ATONEMENT (v. 27) Apart from mourning (Zech. 12:10) because they then realised that they crucified their Messiah, they will be judged by Him, a day of reckoning (Matt. 25:19).
4. THE 50th DAY - PENTECOST (v. 15, 16) 50th day from the day of the wave-sheaf, falling in the third month. "Two wave-loaves baken with leaven" (v. 17), possibly with reference to Jews and Gentiles (Eph. 3:6) with sin no longer in dominion – leaven when baked, is no longer active – in that they are now a new creation.	7. THE FEAST OF TABERNACLES (v. 34) Now that Israel is reconciled, converted, rewarded and ready for Government (Matt. 24:47; 25:21-23) the Lord sets up His Throne (25:31) to judge the living nations (Gentiles) on the basis of how they treated His brethren, the Jews, during the great Tribulation, well or ill, (Matt. 25:40 & 45), and reward them accordingly. Sheep to go into the Millennial Kingdom, which is the Feast of Tabernacles (Zech. 14:16) – the harvest having been gathered (Matt. 13:39). This harvest is at the end of the age, i.e. after the church is raptured and there after the Tribulation period.

Israelites are commanded of the Lord to gather together in the chosen place, three times in a year (Deut. 16:16), firstly to observe the Passover and the feast of unleavened bread (a 7 day-feast), then the feast of weeks and four months later the feast of tabernacles – booths. The seven feasts are thus grouped into four and three. Every feast is a Holy convocation (Lev. 23:2).

The first four feasts took place in the first three months of the Jewish year (Lev. 23:5-15). There was a time-gap of four months (John 4:35), before the barley harvest, (for repentance) and one month later the wheat and grape harvest (for rejoicing). This long interval would remind us of the period of grace for the salvation and *gathering-out* of the Gentiles (Acts 15:14), the Church which is the bride. This *gathering-out* first from Israel and then from the Gentiles, appears to be the harvest for the poor and strangers (Lev. 23:22), the elect of Heaven.

There are two distinct companies of the seed of Abraham (Rom. 4:16). Described as 'elect':

1. *The Elect of Heaven:* The children of Abraham by faith – the Church – united with Christ in Heaven by His

Spirit (Rom. 8:33; Col 3:12; Titus 1:1; and 1 Peter 1:2).

2. *The Elect of Earth:* The children of Abraham by Promise united with Christ on earth by His Spirit, in His kingdom (Isa. 45:4; 65:9, 22; Matt. 24:22, 31; and Rom. 11:28.)

No other of the redeemed are called as *'ELECT.*

The Feast of the Unleavened Bread

The fifteenth day is specifically called "the Feast of Unleavened Bread" in Lev. 23:6. This was celebrated for a seven day period starting from the 14th day (Ex. 12:8; Num. 28:17); that is from the day of Passover till the 21st day. (Deut. 16:3). On the first and the last day (i.e. 14th and 21st days) shall be a holy convocation (Num. 28:17-18), and no servile work shall be done on these two days. These days are to be observed as a Sabbath by Israelites (Lev. 23:7, 8).

The Feast of First Fruits

This third feast falls on the 17th day of the first month of the Jewish calendar. The Passover was initially instituted on the seventh month, which month was later reckoned as the first month (Ex 12:1, 13:3, 4), for the Israelites. This month was known as 'Abib', meaning "ears of corn".

This 17th day is the day on which our Lord rose again from the dead.

It is of interest to know that the day on which Noah's ark rested on Mount Ararat was also this very day the 17th day of the seventh month (Gen. 8:4). This was before the Jewish calendar was established. This implies a new beginning and a resurrected life, after all that was on the face of the earth had been destroyed.

In the annual time-scale, there is a five month gap between this feast and that of trumpets.

The Feast of Trumpets

Israel will be re-gathered back to their own promised land (Deut. 30:1-11; Isa. 11:11, 12; Jer. 16:14, 15; 30:3, 10, 11; Ezek 37:21; Amos 9:14, 15). Matthew 24:29-31 reveals that they are to be summoned by angelic trumpeters and it will be to observe the feast of trumpets at Jerusalem.

(Please refer to "The Seven Parables relating to Israel's Future. Paper No: 04-04)

The Day of Atonement

1. On the day of atonement (6th feast), Christ shall reveal Himself to Israel as Joseph did to his brethren. "I am Joseph" to "My brethren" in type, (Gen. 45:3). Just as Joseph was made known to his brethren a *second time,* (Acts 7:13) and as Solomon was crowned king a *second time* (I Chron. 29:22), so the Lord Jesus Christ shall appear a *second time* for Israel's salvation (Heb. 9:28) and will be crowned as King. He has already appeared the first time to deal with their sin.

2. On the day of atonement, the Jews will be judged by Christ and rewarded on the basis of their prior behaviour, particularly during the great Tribulation – the time of Jacob's trouble (Jer. 30:7). They will be judged and rewarded on the basis of their service, testimony and stewardship as follows:

Service

1. *Faithful Service:* As in Matthew 24:45-47, and rewarded "Ruler over all my goods", in the Millennial Kingdom.

2. *Wicked Service:* Will cut him asunder and appoint him his portion with the hypocrites and cast him into outer darkness, where

there shall be weeping and gnashing of teeth. (Matt. 24:48-51; 25:30)

Testimony

1.   Five virgins with oil – had the light of testimony – but asleep, awakened and rewarded to go into the wedding.

2.   The other five without oil – meaning no testimony – are shut out of the Kingdom (Matt. 25:1-13).

Stewardship

1.   Rewarded according to several ability (Matt. 25:21) "I will make thee ruler over many things" in the Millennial Kingdom.

2.   The talent hid: Punished by being cast into outer darkness (Matt. 25:29, 30).

(Please note that all these parables mentioned in chapters Matthew 24 and 25 do not apply to the church.)

3.   Historically a fountain was opened for Israel for their sin and uncleanness (Zec. 13:1) at Calvary; but was rejected by them (Acts 2:23). And it will be renewed for their cleansing at the Second Advent after they are re-gathered, they will look upon Him "Whom they pierced" (Zec. 12:10), and the believing remnants accept the atonement, confessing Christ as:

"Lo this is *our God; w*e have waited for Him, and He Will save us: This is *the Lord:* We have waited for Him, we will be glad and rejoice in His salvation." (Isa. 25:9).

The appearing of our risen Lord to His disciples, including Thomas, prior to Pentecost, is a prophetic picture of Israel accepting Jesus Christ, as did Thomas confessing the Lord as "My *Lord* and my *God"* (John 20:26-29), when they would see Him and believe (see Ps. 118:28). Faith believes without seeing.

The accompanying CHART, we trust, will give a clear and graphic picture of the Scriptural truths brought out above

THE SEVEN SET FEASTS OF JEHOVAH AND THEIR PROPHETICAL FULFILMENT

	Commemorative Festivals of Israel's Past Historical Events					Festivals Shadowing Israel's Future Restoration			
	Sprinkling of the Blood (Ex. 12:1-14) 14th day	Eating the Unleavened (Ex. 12:15-20, Josh. 5:11) 14th to 21st day	The Sheaf of First Fruit (Josh. 5:12)		The Two Wave Loaves	Israel Scattered Among the Nations	Blowing of Trumpets	The day of Reconciliation	Dwelling in Booths Sabbath to Sabbath
Israel Past & Future	FIRST MONTH	FIRST MONTH	FIRST MONTH		THIRD MONTH		SEVENTH MONTH	SEVENTH MONTH	SEVENTH MONTH
	1	2	3		4		5	6	7
Old Testament Type	The Passover Lev. 23:4,5 (Deut. 16:1-8)	The Feast of Unleavened Bread Lev. 23:6-8 (7 Days)	The Feast of First Fruits Lev. 23:9-14 (Deut 16:9)	The Seven Week Interval	The Feast of Weeks Lev. 23:15-21 (Deut. 16:9-12)	The Harvest Interval Lev. 23:22 (Lev. 19:9,10; Deut 24:19-22)	The Feast of Trumpets Lev. 23:23-25 (Num. 10:7-10; 29:1-6; Ps. 81:3)	The Day of the Atonement Lev. 23:26-32 (Num. 29:7-11)	The Feast of Tabernacles Lev. 23:33-43 (Num. 29:12-40; Deut 16:13-15)
	14th day Thursday	15th day A Sabbath Day Friday	17th day Morrow After the Sabbath Sunday	Week of Sabbath Seven Sabbaths	50th day Morrow After the Sabbath Sunday		1st day Sabbath day (New moon day)	10th day	15th to 22nd day Sabbath to Sabbath
New Testament Reality	Christ our Passover (1 Cor. 5:7)	Believers holy walk in Christ (1 Cor. 5:7-9)	Resurrection of Christ (1 Cor. 15:20; Col. 1:15-18)	"Tarry ye" "Wait" (Luke 24:49; Acts 1:4)	Descent of the Holy Spirit (1 Cor. 12:12,13; Act. 2:1; James 1:18)	The Lord seated at the right-hand of God The Great High Priest (1 Pet. 3:22; Heb. 4:14-16) Israel Dispersed and blinded (Luke 21:24; Rom. 11:25) Church gathered (Acts 15:14) — Christ's Bema Seat → Dead in Christ raised (1 Thess. 4:14-17) and living saints caught up	Israel Regathered Mat. 24:31	Israel Restored (Zech. 12:10) (Dan. 9:24)	Israel Reinstated Ezek Ch 36 & 37 Zech. 14:9-21 Millennium
	Redemption	Sanctification	Justification		Pentecost		Awakening	Reclaiming	Restoration
	PAST	PAST	PAST	PAST	PAST	PRESENT	FUTURE	FUTURE	FUTURE

THE TIMES OF THE GENTILES

Nebuchadnezzar's dream of the great Image, "whose brightness was excellent" (Dan. ch. 2), Daniel's vision of four great Beasts "diverse one from another" (Dan. ch. 7), and God's prophetic revelation, concerning the nation of Israel (Dan. ch. 9), are all *concurrent happenings*, revealed to Daniel the 'greatly beloved'. They are given from the view-point of the "times of the Gentiles"-- its outward appearance (the metallic image) and its inward ferocity (the four diverse beasts) – and as related to the nation of Israel (70 week prophecy). These details are placed side-by-side in this Chart, for a clearer view and for a better understanding. For the historical dates and events and other details, please refer to "God's Prophetic Will and the Gentile Nations". Study Paper: 04 - 03

Chart No: 04 - 02

ISRAEL'S PAST HISTORICAL EVENTS AND HER FUTURE RESTORATION.	DANIEL'S PROPHCY (Dan. ch. 9) "Seventy Weeks are determined upon thy people and upon thy city" (Dan. 9:24)	NEBUCHADNEZZAR'S DREAM AND DANIEL'S INTERPRETATION (Daniel Chapter 2) A Great Image (Dan. 2:31-33) Decreasing in Value (from gold to clay)	DANIEL'S VISION (Dan ch. 7) Four Great Beasts Gentile Rule of Increasing Ferocity	THE CHURCH PERIOD AND HER FUTURE HOPE
Babylonian captivity Because of the non-observance of the sabbath - year (Lev. 25:1-22; 2 Chron 36:17-21; Jer. 25:11; 35:11; 39:1-10)	70 Years of Captivity	Head of Gold Babylon	**Beast Like A Lion**	
Re-building of Jerusalem (Dan. 9:25; Neh. 2:1-7)	7 Weeks	Breast & Arms of Silver Medo - Persia	**Beast Like A Bear**	
	62 Weeks	Belly & Things of Brass Greece	**Beast Like A Leopard**	
Messiah **Cut off** (Dan. 9:26) Israel Blinded and Dispersed (Lk. 21:24; Rom. 11:25)	Prophetic Gap	Legs of Iron Fourth - Empire	**Beast Dreadful & Terrible**	**Death of CHRIST** ✝ **The Church Age** **Church Gathered** (Acts 15:14)
Sacrifice & Oblation to cease (Dan. 9:27) **Time of Jacob's Trouble** (Jer. 30:7) Christ Coming on the Mount of Olives (Zech 14:4) **Jerusalem, The City of the Great King Jehovah Shammah (Ezk 48:35)**	70th Week	Feet Part of Iron and of Clay	Stone, Cutout without hands Christ **Tribulation Period**	**The Rapture of the Church** (1 Thess 4:16,17) Saints return with Christ (Zech 14:5; Jude 14) **Millennial Rule** (Rev. 5:10; 20:6)

A Great Mountain Filling the Whole Earth Christ's Millennial Kingdom "A Kingdom, which shall never be destroyed" (Dan. 2:44)

"The Times of the Gentiles"

The word 'times' appearing in Luke 21:24 (Strong - 2540) refers to God's divinely designed and pre-determined intervention into the history of mankind, particularly the Gentiles. The Lord spoke these words and at the same time said, "For these be the days of vengeance, THAT ALL THINGS WHICH ARE WRITTEN MAY BE FULFILLED" (Luke 21:22). Thus to correctly view the *times of the Gentiles,* we must examine the prophecies of the O.T., the things that were written to be fulfilled.

Here, it will be helpful for the reader to have a look into history. According to the chronology preserved in the Masoretic Text, the Pharoah of the oppression of Israel, who knew not Joseph (Ex. 1:8), was Thutmos III (BC 1482-1450), whilst his son Amenhotep II (BC 1450-1425) was apparently the Pharoah of the actual exodus of the children of Israel. The next Pharoah Thutmos IV was not his son, since Amenhotep's son, the heir in the god-line of Pharoah, the firstborn, was slain with the rest of the firstborn in the land of Egypt (Ex. 12:29). After about 500 years, from 9th to 7th century BC, the mighty Assyr-

ian empire dominated the ancient Gentile world, followed by the Neo-Babylonian Empire. The city of Babylon did not reach the height of its glory, until the reign of Nebuchadnezzar (BC 605 - 562).

When did the Gentiles become God's channel for world rule? When the Jewish nation continued in their disobedience to God, He allowed them to be taken captive for 70 years by Nebuchadnezzar (BC 606), who was made the world ruler of that time. From then on there were specific divine interventions sent to ensure that the Gentiles did according to the "THINGS THAT ARE WRITTEN". The whole of the period of Gentile rule is shown in the great image which appeared in the dream of Nebuchadnezzar as recorded and interpreted in Daniel, Chapter 2. We therefore will record the various PARTS OF THE IMAGE, and correspondingly on the right hand side of this tabulation, are given, details of the fulfilment of Divine intervention:

"THE TIMES OF THE GENTILES"	"YET TO BE FULFILLED"
1. FINE GOLD–HEAD "For the God of heaven hath given thee (Nebuchadnezzar) a kingdom ... and hath made thee ruler over them all. Thou art this head of gold." (Dan. 2:37, 38). The noticeable *progressive lowering* in value and weight, from gold at the top, to iron and clay at the bottom, indicates the diminishing power and effectiveness of Gentile rule.	God intervened in the fiery furnace, "the fourth is like the Son of God." (Dan. 3:25). "The kingdom is departed from thee... until thou know that the most High ruleth in the kingdom of men" (Dan. 4:31, 32). The last intervention was in the writing on the wall, "Thy kingdom is divided, and given to the Medes and Persians." (Dan. 5:27, 28).
2. SILVER–BREAST AND ARMS "After thee shall arise another kingdom inferior to thee" (Dan. 2:39) Described as a ram, in chapter 8, it is having two horns, which appear to refer to the two nations thus joined together 'breast and arms of silver' (Dan. 8:3).	History shows this, to be that of the Medes and Persians. This kingdom of the Medes and Persians involved itself, under God in the settlement of Israel back in their land, and in the rebuilding of the temple and Jerusalem (Ezra. 6:14, 15).
3. BRASS–BELLY AND THIGHS "Another third kingdom which shall bear rule over the whole earth" (Dan. 2:39). The metal here used – Brass – generally speaks of government's cold, matter of fact, political status. In Dan. 8:21, "And the rough goat is the King of Grecia; and the great horn that is between his eyes is the first king", i.e., Alexander the Great, who was succeeded by four others. (Dan. 11:3, 4)	Appreciating all that Daniel saw in revelation was later fulfilled, it is not surprising that Alexander the Great arose to conquer the Medes and Persians (obviously a divine intervention). He died of malaria at the age of 34, succeeded by his four governors of the Greek empire, namely Cassander, Lysimachus, Ptolemy and Seleucus (Dan. 8:22).

"THE TIMES OF THE GENTILES"	"YET TO BE FULFILLED"
4. IRON-LEGS Not just iron, but "as strong as iron, forasmuch as iron breaketh all these (the previous three governing systems, as each inherited its predecessor), SHALL IT BREAK IN PIECES AND BRUISE" (Dan. 2:40). The thought is that of a *threshing* instrument. Henceforth, it is this that is going to characterise the subjugating power of Gentile rule – war machines would be developed, leaving hand to hand fighting as quite secondary. The legs of iron (Dan. 2:33) may refer to the manner in which this Roman kingdom developed, with an *east* and a *west* flank, evolving further, not only militarily but religiously. This fourth kingdom is described as a beast in Dan. 8:23 that will tread down the whole earth having devoured it, and afterwards break it in pieces. This did not take place under the old Roman empire, and therefore leads us on to the consideration of the feet of "Iron and Clay".	Caesar was a title, similar to that of Pharoah, meaning *lord* – "Caesar is lord" was the test to the believer's loyalty to his lord, involving martyrdom. The other title the Caesars took to themselves was that of "Pontifex Maximus", meaning "Chief Priest". This principle was behind the "leaven of Herod" (Mark 8:15) which is the combination of religion and politics. From this it will be seen that the basis of the eventual worship of the Beast has already been laid. This divine intervention of Rome was essential, following the universal use of Greek arising from the BRASS kingdom: the Roman roads, along which the gospel would travel, had to be laid. Also the category of one known as "a Roman citizen" as also the "protective Roman legions", must evolve so that Paul may evangelise the nations – to the obedience . . . for HIS name" (Rom. 1:5).
5. PART IRON AND PART CLAY – FEET This is a development of the fourth kingdom, very expressive of weakness. While iron speaks of military might, clay refers to humanity. "Whereas thou sawest iron mixed with miry clay (i.e., sticky clay), they shall MINGLE THEM SELVES WITH THE SEED OF MEN" (Dan. 2:41-43). It is not the seed of the woman, which is Christ (Gen. 3:15) but of the 'tares', "the children of the wicked one" (Matt. 13:38). Democracy is the objective solution for human government and one world. Democracy is essentially a weak majority rule, so often seen to be essentially backed up by the stiffening presence of an army – the iron.	During this time when iron and clay are in power, (being the weakest form of all types of previous world rule) – that catastrophe, the distress of nations and the great tribulation will take over. This "times of the Gentiles" will be brought to an abrupt end by the stone cut out without hands, obviously Christ. Each kingdom as it has absorbed the previous one with its wealth, ways, wisdom and wickedness, will be broken in pieces together (clay being in the midst. See Dan. 2:45).

"And then shall they see the Son of man coming in the clouds of heaven with power and great glory" (Matt. 24:30) – the exhortation that follows must, therefore, apply to Israel –"And when these things begin to come to pass then look up, and lift up your heads; for your redemption draweth nigh", (Luke 21:28). This is referring, we are persuaded, to the signs in the sun, moon and stars of v. 25, as their Messiah will come from heaven as "the stone cut out without hands" to finish the rule of the gentiles, thus the times of the gentiles, come to an end.

Remarks

1. Attention has been drawn to the following:

The use of metal in describing these kingdoms, both as to its *inferiority* – going down from gold to iron and clay, but also as to its *cold*, matter of fact, political status, it speaks of the times of the gentiles, as seen from MAN'S VIEW POINT. It is the *outward greatness* of the image of a *MAN*.

The descriptive use of beasts in Daniel Chapter 7, adds the necessary *living characteristic* to the oppressive dictatorial rule. This speaks of *the inward character* of these world rulers in all their moral iniquity and brutality, as VIEWED BY GOD, and reveals the beastly nature of these kingdoms; hence the figures of *wild beasts*.

The action-packed struggle and oppression of the two beasts described in Daniel Chapter 8, indicates the METHOD as to how one rule will *take over* the other, as well as the details of how the government will pass *on* from one to another.

2. Daniel chapter two contains four great things, and they are:

1. **The Great Image, (v. 31)**	**Presenting "Man's Day" (vv. 1-33)**
2. The Great Mountain (v. 35)	Presenting the Kingdom of the Lord Jesus, (vv. 34-43)
3. The Great God (v. 45)	Presenting the Omnipotence of God. (vv. 44-45)
4. The Great Man and the Great Gifts (v. 48)	Presenting the earthly honours given to Daniel, who represents Israel, (vv. 46-49)

Daniel's promotion and that of his three friends, is a type of the coming exaltation of the faithful remnant, who will fill places of honour and authority in the literal earthly kingdom of our blessed Lord, during the millennial rule.

3. The whole of Daniel Chapter 8 *was future* and unfulfilled when given to Daniel the prophet. However, the first twenty two verses have since been accurately fulfilled and have been carried-out precisely. Placed beside their historical fulfilment, the correlation is conclusive that the Holy Spirit is the Divine Author of this book. We can conclude that, if the first part of this chapter (which was future when given) has no less than eight prophecies already fulfilled to the very letter, then, by the same token, the last great prophecy in the closing part (which is still future) will also be fulfilled with exactitude.

These historically fulfilled events in Chapter 8 may be detailed as follows:

1. The Assumption of the Medo-Persian Empire. (vv. 3, 20)

2. The Ascendancy of Persia over Media (vv. 3, 20)

3. The Aggression of the Persians and Medes. (v.4)

4. The Achievements of the Grecian Armies, (vv. 5, 8)

5. The Activities and Death of Alexander the Conqueror, (vv. 8-21)

6. The Appropriation of Alexander's Empire by his four Generals, (vv. 8, 22)

7. The Abhorrent Actions of Antiochus Epiphanes. (vv. 9-12)

8. The Angelic Conversation, (vv. 13, 14)

9. The Assyrian Enemy and the Desolator of Israel, (vv. 23-25)

Major events prophesied by Daniel and yet to be fulfilled:

1. The vision of the last kingdom, the kingdom of the Stone, and the interpretation of this part of the vision. (2:33-35, 41-45)

2. Future kingdom of the fourth beast, followed by the eternal kingdom of the Son of Man (7:8-14, 18, 20-27).

3. Dream-type of the anti-Christ yet to come (8:9-12).

4. Interpretation referring to the future of the king of the north (8:23-25).

5. The last 70th week and the subsequent blessing. (9:24, 26 end & 27)

6. The great tribulation and resurrection (12:1-4).

7. Certainty that the great tribulation will come to its end. (12:7-13).

The "times of the Gentiles" (Luke 21:24) referred to by the Lord in His Olivet discourse which has now been running for over 2,500 years, and no doubt coming very near to its end, may be summarised under the following five heads:

Commencement

It was not God's intention that the Gentiles should rule the earth. He placed His earthly people, the nation of. Israel, at the hub of the system of nations, and ruled from the throne of David as "the God of all the earth" (Josh. 3:13). But because of Israel's defection, their disobedience and idolatry, God disowned the throne of David and withdrew from it and ruled the world as "the God of heaven", i.e. no longer directly from an earthly throne, but from His throne in heaven, providentially.

It is reckoned that this long period, began in BC 606 when King Nebuchadnezzar of Babylon invaded Israel and Judah, besieged Jerusalem, and carried into captivity its inhabitants, including Daniel. This period would terminate with the coming in power and majesty of the Warrior King with His armies out of heaven (Rev. 19:11-16).

Continuity

Nebuchadnezzar's dream-image – the metallic man – represents Gentile imperialism, in all its pomp and power, as a whole. The first of the world emperors alone received his power directly from God, and the others who succeeded him, theirs providentially, (Dan. 2:37, 38). It is noteworthy that, twelve months prior to Nebuchadnezzar's receiving his dream, God had told Jeremiah that "these nations shall serve the king of Babylon seventy years" (compare Daniel 2:1 with Jer. 25:1, 11).

As pictorially presented in the dream-image, the times of the Gentiles would consist of four world powers, filing across the stage in succession. The divine revelation is that there would be four – no more and no less, thus apart from these four nominated, no other power would achieve world supremacy.

The order and value and specific gravity of the metals comprising the image, from the top to the bottom, tell out the historical and prophetical facts, of gradual internal disintegration, and then at last of sudden and total external demolition. The entire top-heavy colossus, struck at its most vulnerable part – the feet of iron and clay, by the Stone, cut out of the mountain without hands, is completely destroyed and smashed to smithereens to disappear for ever.

Character

The moral character of these Gentile empires is portrayed in the corresponding vision in Daniel 7, given to Daniel some 62 years after Nebuchadnezzar's dream. To Daniel they are depicted not as metals, but as monsters – visionary wild beasts emerging from the windswept turbulent waters of the Great Sea – the Mediterranean Sea. The bestial and predatory character of the Gentile world powers is thus stressed in the vision Daniel received of the four wild beasts arising out of the storm-tossed sea.

Control

God still exercises an overall control in all the affairs of men, through His chosen four Gentile world empires. He is not, at present ruling directly with His throne set up on earth, as He did in relation to Israel. God is indeed working out His sovereign will amidst all the strife and confusion men have brought into this evil world. "The most High ruleth in (over) the kingdom of men, and giveth it to whomsoever He will" (Dan. 4:32).

Conclusion

The times of the Gentiles will come to a catastrophic end, by the impact of the Stone – the Kingdom of God as ushered in by Christ in power and great glory at His appearing.

The whole image is demolished at one devastating blow, that is to say, that man's rule of all these four kingdoms will be swept away by the same impact. This would indicate that the principles of these four kingdoms will be in existence at the time of the end, when Christ comes in power and majesty as the great Warrior King (Dan. 2:44).

The final world empire will then fill the earth – the stone-kingdom, the everlasting kingdom of the Saviour who died at Calvary, then manifested as earth's universal Monarch. Righteousness shall be the principle upon which the kingdom will be established and peace will spread throughout the millennial earth. All those who survive the great tribulation will hail the King of kings and the Lord of lords and the earth will then be filled with His glory as the waters cover the sea. (Isa. 11:9; Hab. 2:14)

The blessed consummation beyond the times of the Gentiles, should give encouragement to believers today, as they view the growing darkness of the nations, knowing God's great purpose for the future.

The accompanying chart, we hope, will serve as a picturesque explanation to the Scriptural truths, brought out in this paper.

God's Prophetic Will and the Gentile Nations

Some Important Historical Dates

"The knowledge of His will" (Col. 1:9), as it involves the Gentiles, comprises *seven* Gentile Empires. They are spoken of as "seven heads", or "mountains" or 'kings' on which the great whore sits, as revealed to the apostle John in Revelation 17:9 & 10. Here it describes the totality of the *Gentile Nations,* who were under the dominion of that *whore* (Rev. 17:1 cf). In Revelation 17:18, this whore is stated to be the 'great city', the Babylon, which is vividly described in Chapter 18. Its fall and desolation is mentioned in Rev. 18: 16-19. With this the gentile kingdoms came to an end.

The Seven Gentile Kingdoms

Out of these seven Kingdoms, two, namely Egypt and Assyria existed before Nebuchadnezzar, and the other four nations, Babylon, Medo-Persia, Greece and Rome are represented in the metallic-image shown in the vision to king Nebuchadnezzar and as interpreted by Daniel (Dan 2). The seventh is not yet come, which will be a revived Rome, during the end of the Tribulation period, with feet of iron and clay. (*See Chart Appendix No.5*).

God has thus determined the *times* of all the nations, as well as their *boundaries.* We read "God... hath made of one blood all nations of men for to dwell on all the face of the earth, and hath determined the times before appointed, and the bounds of their habitation" (Acts 17:26).

Three facts of importance apply to all these nations. God appointed their *duration* (Jer. 46:17), their *boundaries* (Acts 17:26), and their *governments.* (Pro. 8:15) "The most high ruleth in the kingdoms of men, and giveth it to whomsoever He will". We see this as revealed to the Gentile king Nebuchadnezzar of Babylon, and as interpreted by Daniel (Dan. 4:17, 25).

The Times of the Gentiles

There is yet another prolonged period starting from the time of king Nebuchadnezzar, stretching through the present days and reaching forward to a point of time, when our Lord will return to establish His Kingdom on earth. (Matt. 24:30) The Word of God gives it a special name and our Lord called it, "The Times of the Gentiles" (Luke 21:24). (*See Box in the Chart – Appendix No. 5*). This period will run its course, until "the fullness of the gentiles be come in" (Rom 11:25). Thereafter a converted Israel will again assume importance – as the *head,* no longer the *tail* (Deut. 28:13, 44).

The Date-Chart

The important historical dates detailed below cover the early period of this "times of the gentiles", that is the period from Israel's 70 years captivity, as foretold by prophet Jeremiah, to that of the destruction of the Jerusalem Temple in 70 AD (Matt. 24:2). This Date-Chart is designed to highlight the important prophecies such as the 70 years of Israel's captivity, the first 69 weeks of Daniel's 70 weeks prophecy, and help to correctly picture and time-frame the major O.T. prophetical books.

In spite of vast research and desire for complete agreement among scholars, all may not agree with some of these dates. It is for this very reason, the dates have not been furnished in the Chart attached to the paper "The Times of the Gentiles" (*Paper No: 04-02*), wherein only the exposition of the prophecy is given. However, in this paper, which has a different view and purpose, the dates and the background details are furnished. It may assist to sharpen one's understanding of the historical settings of the OT events, and to appreciate to a greater measure the accuracy of the Word of God.

These dates are mostly authenticated with Scripture references. A casual reader of the Word of God may wonder at the dates and historic facts such as, "In the year that King Uzziah died, I saw also the Lord ..." (Isa. 6:1), and "In the third year of the reign of Jehoiakim, king of Judah, came Nebuchadnezzar ..." (Dan. 1:1), or the accurate cross-details given in Luke 3:1. Is it not that God thereby reveals His mind in the matter? The context, in which they are set, with the accuracy of their dates, as associated with certain kings and historical facts, takes us to a spiritual climax and reveals the importance of God's purpose of His unique revelation. They also confirm the accuracy of the Word of God to a doubting mind, and in a day of apostasy, encourage and strengthen our faith, enabling us to honour and obey His word.

NOTE: In using this date-table, it is essential to bear in mind the following:

The year given in the first column, wherever it is in relation to the Jewish history, is the Jewish year beginning with the 1st Nisan (March–April). For example, 604 BC is the year beginning with the 1st April 604; and 589 BC is the year beginning the 15th March.

According to Judahite system, the computation of the reign of kings and of the festivals is on the 1st of a new year (i.e. from the 1st of Nisan). The reign of Jewish kings, whatever the date of accession might be, was always reckoned from the preceding Nisan, so that, if for instance, a Jewish king began to reign in Adar (the last month in the Jewish calendar), the following month (Nisan) would be considered as the commencement of the second year of his reign. This rule was observed in all legal contracts, in which the reign of kings was always mentioned.

Prophets in exile, like Daniel and Ezekiel, while giving the details of various events, always reckoned the dates and viewed the situation from the exile point of view. (Examples: Dan. 2:1; 8:1, Jehoiachin's captivity Ezek. 1:2; 25th year of captivity, and the 14th year from the destruction of Jerusalem Ezek. 40:1 etc.). While prophets like Jeremiah, who spoke for God, from Jerusalem, always reckoned the events from the date of the reign of their kings (Jer. 36:1; Zeph. 1:1 etc.). Haggai and Zechariah, who were God's mouthpiece, after their return from exile, to rebuild the Temple and Jerusalem, always reckoned the events from the reign of the Gentile Kings, who granted the Edict in their favour (Hagg. 1:1; Zech. 1:1).

If this is kept in view, the chronology of the table will be found to harmonise the various details and periods contained in the Books of Kings, Chronicles, Jeremiah, Ezekiel and Daniel etc.

DATE	DESCRIPTION
B.C. 640	Josiah's 31 year reign begins. (2 Kings 22:1)
B.C. 627	Jeremiah began to prophecy on the 13th year of King Josiah (Jer. 1:2).
B.C. 626	Nabopolassar (626–605 BC), becomes king of Babylon on the death of Ashurbanipal, king of Assyria, (668 - 626 BC).
B.C. 622	Josiah's Passover, on the 18th year of his reign. (2 Kings 22:3; 23:23; 2 Chron. 35:18, 19). (*Note: This is a historical event in Israel's national life*).
B.C. 612	Fall of Nineveh, the capital of Assyria before the combined forces of Cyaxeres the Mede, Nabopolassar of Babylon, and the Scythians. Nahum prophesied this event about 100 years before it took place. (Nahum 1:1 cp).
B.C. 608	Josiah, king of Judah, slain at Megiddo (2 Kings 23:29) and Jehoahaz succeeds and reigns for just three months. Pharaoh Necho installs Jehoiakim on the throne of Judah, in the place of Jehoahaz. (2 Kings 23:33, 34; 2 Chron. 36:3-5). God's message to Jehoiakim given through Jeremiah is found in Jer. 22:3-19, and alluded to in Ezekiel's lamentations (Ezek. 19:2-4). Habakkuk prophesied during the early period of Jehoiakim's reign, who led the nation down the path of destruction (2 Kings 24:1-5). The incidents that happened during his reign are recorded in Jeremiah Chs. 35 & 36.
B.C. 606	Nebuchadnezzar (His name means "O Nabu – a Babylonian god – protect my boundary") takes Judah and Jerusalem. **The first deportation to Babylon.** Including Daniel a total of 3023 (Jer. 52:28; Lam. 1:18) taken as captives. **The 70 year Captivity – servitude – begins.** This was foretold in Isa. 39:5-7; 2 Kings 20:16-18; Jer. 25:8-11, and took place immediately after the completion of 490 years of the establishment of the kingdom under Saul. (See Appendix No. 4) Jehoiakim bound in fetters, but seems to have been released after swearing allegiance. (Dan. 1:2; 2 Kings 24:1; 2 Chron. 36:6,7; Jer. 24:1). God's message to His people during his reign is recorded in Jer. Chs. 25, 26 & 27. *Note: Leviticus 25:4, 5 states that the land was to rest one year out of every seven. Since this was not carried out during the 490 years of kingly rule, Judah was taken into captivity to Babylon, fulfilling what was told in Leviticus 26:34. The time of this captivity was to be 70 years, to fulfil the Sabbaths of the Land that had been broken (2 Chron. 36:21; Jer. 25:12; 29:10).*

DATE	DESCRIPTION
B.C. 605	Nebuchadnezzar defeats Pharaoh Necho of Egypt, (2 Kings 24:7; Jer. 46:2), and conquers all Syria and Palestine.
B.C. 604	Nebuchadnezzar hears of the death of his father and returns to Babylon to claim the throne of Babylon. Jehoiakim cuts up Jeremiah's Scroll (Jer. 36:1, 9, 27).
B.C. 602	Daniel interprets Nebuchadnezzar's dream (Dan 2:1). *Note: The events of Dan. 1:1 occurred when Nebuchadnezzar was co-regent with his father Nebopolassar. The date in Dan. 2:1 refers to his second year as sole king of Babylon.*
B.C. 598	Jehoiakim dies (2 Kings 23:36; 24:6, 7; Jer. 22:18; 19). His son Jehoiachin reigned in his stead for 3 months. Nebuchadnezzar carries on war with the Arabs of Kedar, as prophesied in Jer. 49:28-33.
B.C. 597	**Nebuchadnezzar's second attack on Jerusalem,** (2 Chron. 36: 10-21). This was on the eighth year of his reign (2 Kings 24:12). God's message to Jehoiachin is found in Jer. 22:20-30. Jehoiachin taken to Babylon along with 10,000 captives (2 Kings 24:12-16) including Ezekiel (Ezek. 1:1-3), Mordecai and Esther (Esther 2:6, 7; Jeconiah is an altered form of the Jehoiachin. Refer Jer. 24:1; 27:20 & 29:2). Mattaniah installed as king of Judah; his name is changed to Zedekiah by Nebuchadnezzar (2 Kings 24:17; Jer. 37:1). God's message to Zedekiah is found in Jer. 21:1-14.
B.C. 594	Army revolt in Babylon crushed by Nebuchadnezzar. The western provinces, including Judah, under Zedekiah, revolt (Jer. 34:21; Ezek. 17:12-20). The incidents recorded in Jeremiah Chs. 37 & 38, occurred during this year.
B.C. 593	The incidents that occurred in the fourth year of Zedekiah are recorded in Jeremiah Ch. 28.

DATE	DESCRIPTION
B.C. 592	Ezekiel begins to prophesy, in the 30th year from Josiah's Passover (2 Kings 23:22; 2 Chron. 35:18), which is the fifth year of Jehoiachin's captivity (Ezek. 1:1-3).
	Note: God's word against Babylon, given through His prophet Jeremiah, is found in Chapters 50 & 51. God used Babylon as His battle-axe and weapons of war (Jer. 51:20-26), to break in pieces the nations. God used the Gentile nations, to afflict in His wrath Israel and Judah. After using Babylon for a while in this way, God made them to "remember the Lord {Jehovah) and to bring to their heart Jerusalem" (Jer. 51:50-52). These prophecies against Babylon were written in a book which was sent to Babylon during king Zedekiah's fourth year, and there it was read and demonstrated to be a sign, "thus shall Babylon sink" (Jer. 51:59-64). It is noteworthy that these were foretold during the zenith of Babylon's glory, over 50 years before its actual fall in 539 BC.
B.C. 591	Ezekiel's vision, given in the sixth year of Jehoiachin's captivity, of the Wheels, Cherubim and the Glory of the Lord, are recorded in chapters 8 to 11 (Ezek. 8:1).
B.C. 589	The final siege of Jerusalem begins on the tenth day of the tenth month, that being the 9th year of Zedekiah (2 Kings 25:1; 2 Chron. 36: 12-20; Jer. 39:1; 52:4, 5).
	Note: This being a judgement of God over the nation of Israel, this date was specially-marked and recorded four times in God's Word, including Ezk. 24:1. While Jeremiah gave God's message to the king and His people in their home land, (2 Chron. 36: 12-17), Ezekiel was speaking the Word of God to His people in exile (Ezk. Ch 25). For the house of Israel, Jerusalem was their proud stronghold, the delight of their eyes, and the object of their affections (v 21). That city was suddenly smitten, but they would not mourn nor weep, for which Ezekiel also was made as a SIGN by God, (v 24). The prophet's wife, "the desire of his eyes" was smitten of God suddenly (v 16), and he was instructed NOT to mourn nor weep, but to put on his turban and shoes; and not even to eat the bread of sorrow. It is remarkable that a servant of God was so used to suffer such a tragedy in his family for an example to the exiled children of Judah. Would an elder or a servant of God yield himself totally to God, in these days, in a like manner?
B.C. 588	The golden image set up in Babylon (Dan. ch.3). Nebuchadnezzar's **third attack** on Jerusalem in his 18th year (Jer. 52:29). The various incidents that took place in the tenth year of Zedekiah's reign are recorded in Jer. chs 32 & 33.

DATE	DESCRIPTION
B.C. 587	**The fall of Jerusalem, "The city is smitten" and the walls of Jerusalem broken.** This was in the 11th year of Zedekiah and the 19th year of Nebuchadnezzar's first attack in 606 BC (2 Kings 25:2; Jer. 39:2). Ezekiel states this as the "twelfth year of captivity" i.e. from the year 597 BC, in which year he and others were taken captive (Ezek. 33:21), as it is part concurrent. This is a literal fulfilment of what was announced prophetically to King Hezekiah over 100 years before (2 Kings 20:12-19; Isa. 39:3-8) through Isaiah. Zedekiah's sons killed before his eyes. He sees Nebuchadnezzar, but is blinded and deported to Babylon (Jer. 39:2-7; 2 Kings 25:2-7). Jeremiah's letter to Jews taken captive to Babylon and other incidents connected thereto are recorded in Jeremiah ch. 29. Note: At first, there seems to be a discrepancy between Jer. 34:3; 2 Kings 25:7 and Ezek. 12:13. Zedekiah saw the king of Babylon but not the city itself, having lost his eye sight before being taken there.
B.C. 585	Nebuchadnezzar begins a 13 year siege of Tyre (585-573 BC), during which time, he is used to execute God's judgement, as stated in Jeremiah ch. 27, on the Moabites, Ammonites, and Idumeans. Astyrges becomes king of Media. His daughter Mandane, marries Cambyses I, a vassal Persian king and their son was Cyrus the Great.
B.C. 573	Fall of Tyre. This is the literal fulfilment of Isaiah 23:15-17. The twenty fifth year of Captivity (597 BC), and the fourteenth year from the destruction of Jerusalem (587 BC) (Ezek. 40:1), in which year Ezekiel had the vision as found in Chs. 40-48.
B.C. 570-563	It is probably during these years that Nebuchadnezzar had the vision of the Tree cut down, and he became like a beast, for a period of seven years. (Dan. ch. 4). This instance has not been recorded by the historians, is his deputies carried on the administration in the normal course, on his behalf.
B.C. 562	Death of Nebuchadnezzar and his son Evil-Merodach (562-560 BC) became king of Babylon. *Note: His name means "Fool of Merodac", i.e. a man or servant of the god Merodach.*
B.C. 561	Evil-Merodach frees Jehoiachin from prison. (2 Kings 25:27-30: Jer. 52:31-34).
B.C. 560	Neriglissar (560-556 BC), son-in-law of Nebuchadnezzar, murders Evil-Merodach and seizes the throne of. Babylon.
B.C. 559	Cyrus the Great (559-530 BC) succeeds his father as king of the small Persian Kingdom Anshan.

DATE	DESCRIPTION
B.C. 556	Labashi-Marduk, young son of Neriglissar, becomes king of Babylon, and reigns two months. He is murdered by conspirator Nabonidus (556-539 BC), who seizes the throne.
B.C. 553	Nabonidus leaves the administration of Babylon to his profligate son Belshazzar. Daniel's vision of the four Beasts (Dan 7:1), was given before the events mentioned in Daniel chapter 5.
B.C. 551	Daniel's vision of the Ram (Medo-Persia) and the He-Goat (Greece) (Dan. 8:1), which was given before the events mentioned in Chapter 5.
B.C. 547	Cyrus called 'King of Persia' for the first time.
B.C. 539	Cyrus of Persia overthrows Babylon, and enters Babylon as liberator (Dan. 1:21). Belshazzar slain. (Dan. 5:30). This is the fulfilment of Isaiah 45:1-4. The administration of Babylonia, Syria and Palestine was entrusted to Darius the Mede, a Governor appointed by Cyrus. He is the one mentioned in Dan. 5:31 & 6:1. Daniel's prophecy of 70 weeks was given during this year (Dan. 9:1, 2). **The first Gentile Kingdom (Babylon - Head of fine Gold) ends.**
B.C. 538	Cyrus of Persia reverses the cruel deportation policy of the Assyrians and Babylonians, and proclaims liberty for the Jews to return and build the House of the Lord God of Israel (2 Chron. 36:22, 23; Ezra. 1:1-4; 2:1-60). (*See Appendix No. 1*)
B.C. 537	Jews set up altar at Jerusalem (Ezra. 3:1-5) led by Zerubbabel
B.C. 536.	**The end of the seventy-year captivity.** Foundation of the Temple laid (Ezra 3:7-10). Daniel's vision of the 10th chapter, apparently the last vision, given during the third year of Cyrus (Dan. 10:1).
B.C. 535	Opposition from pagan neighbours forces Jews to stop work on the Temple (Ezra 4:1-5).
B.C. 530	Cyrus dies. Cambyses, son of Cyrus (530-522 BC) becomes Persian emperor (Ezra 4:6).
B.C. 521	Darius I Hystaspes (521-486 BC) mentioned in Dan 9:1, becomes emperor of Medo-Persia (Ezra 4:24; Hagg. 1:1; Zech. 1:1).
B.C. 520	Haggai urges resumption of work on the Temple (Hagg. 1:1 Ezra 4:24). Ezra chapters 4 - 6 give the background to the Book of Haggai. The prophet Zechariah begins his ministry (Zech. 1:1). The historical setting of Zechariah chapters 1-8 (520-518 BC) is identical to that of Haggai (*See Appendix No. 1*).

DATE	DESCRIPTION
B.C. 519	Tattenai (Tatnai) a Persian governor, writes to Darius I to challenge the rebuilding of the Temple. Darius I writes a second decree to Tattenai, commanding him to help the Jews (Ezra. 6:6, 7; Hagg. 1:14, 15). The letter to Cyrus is now kept in the library at Ecbatana.
B.C. 515	**Rebuilding of the Temple completed by Zerubbabel** (Ezra. 6:14, 15) Temple completed in the sixth year of Darius I, and was dedicated at the Passover in Nisan (Ezra 6:16-22) exactly **490 years** after the dedication of Solomon's Temple (1005 BC), and **70 years** before the date of the edict to build the city of Jerusalem in 445 BC (*See Appendix No. 4*).
B.C. 485	Xerxes (485-464 BC) son of Darius I, becomes Persian emperor. Ahasuerus (Esth. 1:1) is the Hebrew form of the Greek Xerxes.
B.C. 483	Vashti deposed (Esth. 2:16, 17) by Xerxes (Ahasuerus).
B.C. 478	Esther becomes Queen (Esth 2: 16, 17) on the seventh year of Ahasuerus' reign.
B.C. 473	The incidents recorded in Esther Chs. 3-9 all happened during this year, the 12th year of Ahasuerus, refer Esth. 3:7. Feast of Purim established (Esth. 8:12; 9:1). This is NOT a Feast of Jehovah as in Leviticus 23. The chronological span of the Book of Esther is ten years (483-473 BC) (Esth. 10:1-3).
B.C. 468	Socrates born (468-399 BC).
B.C. 464	Artaxerxes I of Persia (464 - 423 BC) becomes emperor. He is referred to in Ezra 4:7.
B.C. 458	Ezra receives a commission from Artaxerxes in the seventh year of his reign, to go to Jerusalem and enact reforms (Ezra 1:1; 7:1, 8, 9).
B.C. 445	Nehemiah commissioned by Artaxerxes, in his twentieth year, to go to Jerusalem and rebuild its walls (Neh. 2:1; 5:14). This was on the **first day of Nisan.** **The year on which Daniel's 70 weeks prophecy begins.** (See Appendix Nos. 2 & 3). Note: The first month of the Jewish calendar, was 'Abib' , meaning "*ears of corn*" (Ex. 13:3,4), which was renamed as 'Nisan' meaning '*beginning*' or '*opening*' for the first time during their captivity (Neh. 2:1; Esth. 3:7).
B.C. 444	Nehemiah arrives in Jerusalem (thirteen years after Ezra's return) and rebuilds the walls of Jerusalem in the face of great opposition (Neh. 2:11; 5:14). Nehemiah stayed on as governor of Jerusalem for twelve years (Neh. 5:14).

DATE	DESCRIPTION
B.C. 433	Nehemiah returns to Persia (Neh. 5:14; 13:6).
B.C. 429	Plato born (429-347 BC)
B.C. 424	Darius II Nothus (424-404 BC), "Darius the Persian" succeeds Artaxerxes I (Neh. 12:22).
B.C. 420	Nehemiah returns to Jerusalem (Neh. 13:6, 7).
B.C. 397	Malachi, a contemporary of Ezra and Nehemiah, prophesies. **Old Testament Canon completed.** **The end of the first seven weeks (49 years) of Daniel's 70 weeks prophecy.**
B.C. 359	Philip II becomes king of Macedonia, and Artaxerxes III Ochus (359-338 BC) becomes Persian emperor.
B.C. 338	Arses (338-336 BC) becomes Persian emperor.
B.C. 336	Darius III Codomannus (336-330 BC) becomes Persian emperor. Philip of Macedonia assassinated. Alexander the Great (336-323 BC) becomes king of Macedonia (Dan. 11:3).
B.C. 330	Alexander sacks Persepolis, and becomes prominent (Dan. 8:21). Darius found murdered. Bessus assumes the title "the Great King" in Bactria. **The second Gentile kingdom (Medo-Persia, breast and arms of Silver) ends.**
B.C. 323	Alexander falls ill and dies, an untimely death, (Dan. 8:22). His world-empire is divided by his four leading Generals (Dan. 8:8; 11:4). Which soon become merged into two kingdoms – Egypt and Syria, with Palestine as the centre "the King of the North" is Syria and "the King of the South" is Egypt.
B.C. 261	Antiochus II Theos becomes "king of the north" - Syria (Dan. 11:6)
B.C. 252	Antiochus II marries Berenice, "the kings daughter", daughter of Ptolemy II, (Dan. 11:6, 7), who is later murdered.
B.C. 245	Ptolemy III ("a branch of her roots") invades Syria, the "king of the north" to avenge the murder of his sister Berenice, and carries off 40,000 talents of silver etc. (Dan. 11:6-8).
B.C. 240	Seleucus II attacks Egypt (Dan. 11:9).
B.C. 223	Antiochus III the Great (223-187 BC) becomes king of Syria.
B.C. 219	Antiochus III referred to as 'his sons' in Dan. 11:10, invades Egypt.
B.C. 217	Ptolemy IV, "king of the south" invades Syia and defeats Antiochus III, the "king of the north", at the battle of Raphia (Dan. 11:11, 12).

DATE	DESCRIPTION
B.C. 198	Battle of Panion. Antiochus III supported by apostate Jews, "the robbers of thy people" (Dan. 11:14) in Palestine. He invades and conquers Egypt. He takes control of Palestine and desolates the land (Dan. 11:13-16).
B.C. 193	Ptolemy II Epiphanes marries Cleopatra, daughter of Antiochus 111. Antiochas hopes his daughter will subvert her husband but she supports him against her father (Dan. 11:17).
B.C. 190	Battle of Magnesia. Romans defeat Antiochus III, (Dan. 11:18). Antiochus tried to plunder the Temple of Baal, to raise tribute money, "a raiser of taxes", but furious local inhabitants killed him (Dan. 11:19, 20).
B.C. 187	Seleucus IV Philometer (187-175 BC), son of Antiochus III, becomes king of Egypt, mentioned as "in his estate (successor)" (Dan. 11:21).
B.C. 178	Seleucus IV poisoned by the Tax collector Heliodorus "A vile person", who seizes the throne, (Dan. 11:21). Antiochus Epiphanes seizes the throne of Syria (Dan. 11:20, 23). He is the one mentioned as the "little horn" in Dan. 8: 9.
B.C. 175	Antiochus Epiphanes (175-164 BC) begins a series of campaigns against Egypt, lasting until 168 BC (Dan. 11:22-28).
B.C. 170	Ptolemy VII Physcon (Euergetes) becomes co-regent of Egypt (Dan. 11:26-27). B.C. 169. Antiochus Epiphanes captures Jerusalem (Dan. 11:28).
B.C. 168	Antiochus Epiphanes defiles the Temple and suspends the daily sacrifice (Dan. 8:9-12; 11:28-31). *Note: This is not to be confused with Dan. 9:27, or Dan. 12:11, hence the warning of our Lord Jesus Christ in Matthew 24:15, "Whoso readeth, let him understand". This is yet to happen in the future, during the Tribulation period, when a man sets himself up as God (2 Thess. 2:4).*
B.C. 166	Revolt against Antiochus Epiphanes under the leadership of Mattathias the Jew, "the people that do know their God, shall be strong and do exploits" (Dan. 11:32).
B.C. 165	Judas Maccabeus recaptures Jerusalem. Re-consecration of the Temple in Jerusalem as prophesied in Daniel 8:13, 14. *Note: This is the origin of the feast of Hanukkah mentioned in John 10:22, still being celebrated by the Jews.*
B.C. 164	Death of Antiochus Epiphanes. Antiochus IV becomes king of Syria (Dan. 8:23-25).
B.C.63	The Romans under Pompey capture Jerusalem, and annex Syria and Judea. **The Third Gentile Kingdom (Greece - Belly and Thighs of Brass) ends.** (Dan. 2:39).

DATE	DESCRIPTION
B.C. 59	Julius Caesar becomes consul and adds "Pontifex Maximus", a Babylonian religious office meaning "Chief Priest" to his title 'Caesar', which in turn means 'Emperor'. *Note: Consider how the Roman Pope has adopted this very heathen title of "Pontifex Maximus".*
B.C. 44	Julius Caesar assassinated.
B.C. 31	The battle of Actium, during which Octavian (Augustus 31 BC-14 AD) defeated Antony.
B.C. 27	Octavian (Octavius) assumes the title "Augustus". (Augustus means 'Exalted'. This was a title voted to him by the Roman Senate).
B.C. 6	Cyrenius was made Governor of Syria for the first time, from 6-4 BC, after Archelaus was banished, and again a second time after about 9 years from 6 - 9 AD. During both of his terms, a census was taken, the first mentioned in Luke 2:2 and the second referred to in Acts 5:37.
B.C. 4	**The birth of Christ.** (Luke 2:1-2). See Appendix No. 3. *Note: The counting of A.D. ("Anno Domini" in Latin, meaning "In the year of our Lord") begins about 4 years after the actual birth of Christ; that is the actual A.D. 1 is effectively B.C 4. This is because of the mistake of Dionysius Exigues in arranging the Calendar of the Christian Era in 532 AD.*
B.C 3	Death of Herod the Great (37 - 4 BC). He is the one mentioned in Matt. 2:1, 19 and Luke 1:5, but not the Herod of Luke 3:1. *Note: His four sons divided his kingdom fulfilling the prophecy of Isaiah 7:16. All the four were murderers:* *1. Herod Archelaus (3 BC - 6 AD) Governor of Judaea, Idumea and Samaria. He is mentioned in Matthew 2:19-23.* *2. Herod Antipas (3 BC - 39 AD) ruled over Galilee and Perea. In Matt. 14:1 and Luke 3:19; 9:7 he is referred to as "Herod the Tetrarch". And in Matt. 14:9; Mark 6:14; & Acts 12:1, he is mentioned as 'King', because that was his popular title among the Galileans and at Rome. He killed John the Baptist (Matt. 14:10) and James (Acts 12:1), but "the Lord smote Him" (Acts 12:23).* *3. Herod Philip II (3 BC - 34 AD), Tetrarch of Iturea and Traconitis (Luke 3:1).* *4. Herod Aristobulus – Not mentioned in the Bible.*
A.D. 14	Caesar Augustus dies and Tiberius (14 - 37 AD) succeeds.

DATE	DESCRIPTION
A.D. 28	**The beginning of the ministry of the Lord Jesus Christ.** Fifteenth year of Tiberius' reign (Luke 3:1).
A.D. 32	The 18th year of Emperor Tiberius. **The crucifixion of Christ. "Messiah cut off"** (Dan. 9:26) at the fourth Passover of the Lord's ministry. (*See Appendix No.3*) **The end of the first 69 weeks of Daniel's 70 weeks prophecy.**
A.D. 70	Destruction of Jerusalem and the Temple by Titus. "Destroy the city and the sanctuary" (Dan. 9:26; Matt. 22:7). What our Lord foretold in Mathew 24:2, "Not one stone left upon another" and what He said in Luke 19:41-44, were thus fulfilled, word for word.

Remarks

Daniel chapter 11 is a consecutive prediction of events, within the period of the seventy weeks of Daniel's prophecy, and it contains over one hundred specific prophecies of historical events that literally came true. Only a few of the major events are mentioned in the above date chart.

It is generally considered that the Roman Empire ceased to exist at 467 AD. Eventually it is to be revived in the form of a confederacy of ten nations. Revelation 17:2 traces out, the ancient Roman Empire which has never ceased to exist, with its political and religious influences, as it was also influenced by its absorption of the principles of the live earlier world empires it succeeded. The spirit of this empire, its methods of justice, its administration, its name and other features remain in the broken portions of its vast dominion and its continuing history, as interpreted by Daniel, in Daniel 2:42, 43.

Each of these Gentile Kingdoms absorbed the authoritarian rule and military system of its predecessor, hence when the Stone (Christ) hits the image (Dan. 2:35), "It shall break in pieces and consume *all the kingdoms,* and it shall stand for ever" (Dan. 2:44).

Please refer to the Chart (Appendix No. 5), which pictures some of the more important events detailed above.

Appendix No I

The Rebuilding of the Temple and the Connected Events

The 70 years mentioned in Zechariah 1:12-16, should not be confused with the 70 years of the captivity of Israel, which commenced in 606 BC; but it relates to the period starting from 587 BC, when the Temple was destroyed. The burden of the message given to Zechariah is related to God's great jealousy for Jerusalem and Zion, and the Temple: "My house shall be built". With a great jealousy did God order the rebuilding of His Temple.

This rebuilding was undertaken by Zerubbabel the governor of Judea and Jeshua the High Priest under the proclamation by Cyrus the king of Persia, during the first year of his reign (538 BC). (The names Jeshua and Joshua – both are identical – meaning "Salvation of Jehovah" Ezra 3: 2, 8; 5:2). Thus the word of the Lord spoken by the mouth of Jeremiah was fulfilled, as the Lord stirred up the spirit of Cyrus the king, to grant this edict in favour of the Jews, (2 Chron. 36: 22-23, Ezra 1:1-2).

They first established the altar in the seventh month of 537 BC and resumed the daily burnt offerings to the Lord (Ezra 3:1-3). The foundation of the Temple was laid in the second month of the second year of their return, 536 BC (Ezra 3:7-10).

God not only foretold the 70 year captivity of His people through His prophet Jeremiah but He also revealed the rebuilding of the Temple (Jer. 25:12-14; 29:10-14). There is yet another prophecy spoken by prophet Isaiah in chapters 44 & 45. Though these prophetical revelations were given over a century earlier, Isaiah walking in step with Jeremiah, in a remarkable statement which even gave the name of the pagan king as Cyrus who would be anointed, "He is my Shepherd" (Isa. 44:28), to perform all the pleasure of God, setting His people free (see Isa. 44:24 to 45:7) from their captivity. This prophecy was given over 150 years before the events of Ezra chapter 1.

However, the rebuilding work of the Temple was discontinued in 534 BC, until the second year of king Darius (Ezra 4:24) 520 BC. (Darius the Mede was appointed by King Cyrus as his governor, 539 BC) over Babylonia, Syria and Palestine. However, he

becomes king in 521 BC (See Ezra 4:5 and Hag 1:1-2, 14). Ezra describes how the Samaritans hindered the building and wrote letters to the Persian king (Ezra. 4:4-10). This opposition added to the growing discouragement of the Jewish remnant, dampened the initial optimism with which they had returned to their home land. They were discouraged by the desolation of the land, crop failure, hard work, hostility and other hardships (Hagg. 1:6; 10-11). Their pessimism led to spiritual lethargy (Hagg. 1:9) and they became preoccupied with their own building projects (Hagg. 1:4). They sheltered under political opposition and the supposed idea that the Temple was to be rebuilt, perhaps only after rebuilding Jerusalem. They were saying that 'the time is not come' thus neglecting the House of the Lord (Hagg. 1:2).

It is in this context and against this background that God called His prophets Haggai and Zechariah to the same task of urging His people to complete the temple (Ezra. 5:1). Haggai was direct and practical, and he preached "consider *your ways*" (Hagg. 1:5, 7) "consider from this day" (Hagg. 2:15, 18) and "consider it" (Hagg. 2:18), while Zechariah was devotional and spiritual, his theme being "consider *Him*" (Zech. 2:10-13; 6:12, 13; 14:9, 20, 21). However, they worked harmoniously fulfilling God's purposes bringing Him glory. It is interesting to note the precise dates given by the Holy Spirit through these prophets.

84

Hagg. 1:1	520 BC	First day of the sixth month	The first rebuke.
Hagg. 1:15	520 BC	24th day of the sixth month, the spirit of His people and they worked on the House of the Lord.	The Lord stirring up
Hagg. 2:1	520 BC	The feast day, the 21st day of the seventh month, *(See Note # #)*	The first encouragement.
Zech. 1:1	520 BC	Eighth month	Call to repentance.
Hagg. 2:10	520 BC	24th day of the ninth month	The second rebuke.
Hagg. 2:20	520 BC	24th day of the ninth month	The second encouragement.
Zech. 1:7	519 BC	24th day of the eleventh month	God's word to His people through the eight visions of the prophet.
Zech. 7:1	518 BC	Fourth day of the ninth month	Rebuke for hypocrisy and call to repentance.
Ezra. 6:14, 15	515 BC	Third day of the twelfth month, Adar	Rebuilding of the Temple completed.

 # # NOTE: This is the seventh day of the Feast of Tabernacles, as they dwelt in booths, (Lev. 23:33-43). This feast was not apparently celebrated after they came to the Promised Land, which was revived only now, after the 70 year captivity. This was the result of the reading of the law, (Neh. 8:14-18).

Haggai and Zechariah (Zech. Ch 1-8) were ministering to the remnant on their return after exile during the reconstruction of the Temple, and Malachi joined Zechariah (Zech. Ch 9-14) after the Temple was completed, while Daniel (Dan. 1:6) and Ezekiel (Ezk. 1:1) ministered to His exiled people in Babylon.

Thus, after 14 years of neglect, the work on the temple was resumed in 520 BC and was completed in 515 BC (Ezra. 6:15). It began under the reign of King Cyrus (539-530 BC) and was completed under Darius I (521-486 BC).

There were *three waves* of deportation of His people to Babylon by king Nebuchadnezzar first in 606 BC (Dan. 1:2; 2 Kings 24:1; 2 Chron. 36:6,7) then in 597 BC (2 Kings 24:12,16; 2 Chron. 36:10-21) and the third in 587 BC (Jer. 52:29). Similarly there were *three stages* in their return to Jerusalem, first in 537 BC under the leadership of Zerubbabel (Ezra. 3:2) during the reign of King Cyrus. The second, after about eighty years, in 458 BC under Ezra (Ezra. 1:1, 7:1, 8&9), and the third in 444 BC under Nehemiah (Neh. 2:11; 5:14), both under the commission granted by king Artaxerxes (464-423 BC). Neither time nor world powers will hinder God fulfilling His purposes, for there is no power but of God (Rom. 13:1). By Him "Kings reign and rulers decree justice" (Pro. 8:15), God says: "the king's heart is in the hand of the Lord, as the rivers of water: He turneth it whithersoever He will" (Pro. 21:1).

Appendix No 2

The Seventy Weeks of Daniel

Daniel 9:24-27

Some Bible teachers regard the letter of Artaxerxes I given to Ezra in 458 BC (Ezra 7:11-26) as the beginning point of Daniel's 70 weeks prophecy (Dan. 9:24-27). Yet others regard the commission of Nehemiah (Neh 2:1; 5:14) by the same king, given in 445 BC as its starting point. By using either a Solar calendar with the former date (458 BC) or Lunar calendar with the latter date (445 BC), one can arrive remarkably close to the date of our Lord's public entry into Jerusalem, as, king. (Matt 21:7-11).

However, as God spoke to Daniel concerning Judah, as *"Thy* people" and Jerusalem as *"Thy* Holy City" (Dan. 9:24) and because of the mention of "the streets and wall" (Dan. 9:25), it confirms that the edict referred to, is that issued to rebuild the city Jerusalem. Further as Israel had a "Lunar" calendar, we can safely use the dates, relating to their history, from the Jewish Lunar calendar only. The number of days such as 1290, 1335 (Dan. 12:11; 12) given to Daniel relating to the "end of the days" in relation to Jews, make sense only if taken according to the Lunar calendar. Hence, we conclude that the commission of Nehemiah, in 445 BC, determines the date of commencement of the 70 weeks prophecy.

If this be so, the first lap, or stage of this 70 weeks, that is the first 7 weeks (49 years), specifically segregated out of the **total** period will end in BC 397, marking the completion of the rebuilding of the city of Jerusalem and also that of the completion of OT Canon, with the last prophet Malachi.

The late Sir Robert Anderson, an honoured head of Britain's Police investigation centre, known as Scotland Yard, a man "long accustomed to deal with evidence in difficult and intricate inquiries", provides us with the most convincing countdown from the edict of King Artaxerxes I in his book "Daniel in the Critics' Den", as follows:

He puts the edict of king Artaxerxes I for the rebuilding of the city of Jerusalem (Neh. 2:1; 5:14), as on the first day of Nisan, 445 BC. From that date to Messiah the Prince, was to be 69 x 7 = 483 years. The Hebrews used a 360 day Lunar calendar. Thus 483 years x 360 days = 173,880 days. Sir Robert's calculations show that from the first day of Nisan 445 BC to the 10th of Nisan in the 18th year of Tiberius Caesar. This was the day the Lord made His public, triumphant entry into Jerusalem, when He presented Himself to the nation (Matt. 21:1-10) as "Messiah the Prince". This title is used by Gabriel (Dan. 9:26) as a proper name or title of Christ. Thus the Lord showed Himself to Israel as their Messiah and on the fourth day, He was "cut off" by crucifixion.

Appendix No 3

The Date of Nativity and Crucifixion

Historians have assigned the death of Herod the Great, thirty seven years after he had been declared king by the Romans. He was declared king in 714 AUC (Anno Urbis Conditoe: i.e. the year in which the City – Rome – was founded), which is parallel to 39 BC. Thus adding 36 complete years, Herod's death is placed on 750 AUC or 3 BC, which is in all probability during the month of Adar (Feb/March) of 3 BC, just before the Passover of that year.

This detail will help us to have a clear understanding about the circumstances and the date of the birth of Jesus our Lord, with the background picture portrayed in Matthew chapter 2. "For they are dead, which sought the young child's life" (v.20).

It has also now been well established that Cyrenius was *twice* governor of Syria and that his first term of office was from the latter part of BC 4, when the first taxing was ordered by Caesar Augustus (Luke 2:1,2). This confirms the birth of our Lord Jesus to the autumn (Sep/Nov) of 4 BC.

The date of Tiberius Caesar's reign is known with absolute accuracy as the 19th August 14 AD, and that his 15th year would begin in the autumn 28 AD. This date in fact would have been well *before* the completion of our Lord's 31st year, "And Jesus Himself began (His public ministry) to be *about thirty years of age*" (Luke 3:23). In this connection, we have to carefully note that in reckoning the years from BC to AD, *one year* must always be omitted; for it is obvious that from 1 BC to 1 AD, *was not two years* but one year only, as 1 BC ought to be

described as BC 0, and it is so reckoned by astronomers. *(See Note #)* Thus autumn 4 BC, to autumn 28 AD makes a little over 30 years, confirming the statement of the Evangelist, "about thirty years".

The Lord's ministry on earth lasted for a period of *above three years,* and the crucifixion took place at the fourth Passover. The first Passover is thus fixed by the Gospel narrative itself. He stayed at Capernaum "not many days" after the wedding-miracle at Cana, when the "Jew's Passover was at hand" (John 2:11-16), i.e. in Nisan 29 AD. The other two are mentioned in John 5:1 and 6:4 and the last in John 11:55; 13:1-2, i.e. in Nisan 32 AD.

He went up to Jerusalem on the 8th Nisan (John 11:55; 12:1), which that year was Friday. He spent the Sabbath at Bethany, and then entered the city of Jerusalem the following Sunday morning (Zech 9:9; Matt 21:4, 5). This was the tenth day of the first month, as Jehovah commanded Israel in Exodus 12:3. Our Lord Jesus Christ, as the *true substance* of that shadow, the Passover Lamb, was kept up until the fourteenth day (Ex 12:6), and died "between the evenings", (Num. 9:3 JND & Newberry Margin) of 32 AD, as the fourteenth day began.

(See "The 10th to the 14th day of Christ as the Passover Lamb". Paper No: 08-09)

Oh! with what marvellous accuracy this fits in with Daniel's 70 weeks prophecy, as found in Daniel 9:24-27! !

Note:

For Example the number of years from the 1st January 2 BC to 1st January 2 AD is not 4 but 3 years:

1ˢᵗ Jan. 2 BC to 1 BC = 1 year
1ˢᵗ Jan. 2 BC to 1 AD = 2 years
1ˢᵗ Jan. 2 BC to 2 AD = 3 years

In the light of the foregoing as we read Daniel 9:24 - 27, we observe:

"**Seventy weeks** (of years, in contrast to weeks of days, Dan. 10:2) **are determined** (Literally cut out or divided) **upon thy people,** (Daniel's people, Israel) **and upon thy holy city** (Jerusalem, Matt. 27:53; Rev. 11:2) **... Know therefore and understand, that from the going forth of the commandment to restore and to build Jerusalem** (Neh. 2:1, BC 445), **unto Messiah the Prince** (unto His coming as prince of Peace to establish His kingdom; in all a seventy weeks period thus divided) **shall be seven weeks:** (7 x 7 = 49 years, during this period) **the street shall be built again, and the wall, even in troublous times** (see Nehemiah) **and threescore and two weeks; And after the three score and two weeks** (these with the seven weeks mentioned before makes sixty-nine weeks or 483 years) **shall Messiah be cut off,** (the crucifixion of Jesus Christ the Messiah, the King of the Jews, was on the 14th of Nisan 32 AD) **but not for Himself:** (Isaiah 53). (From the crucifixion till Antichrist, time is not reckoned because during this period Israel is not regarded as God's people, nor Jerusalem as the holy city; thus the seventieth week is cut off or segregated from the previous sixty-nine weeks of years. Therefore, the present Church-Age falls as a parenthesis or as an interlude) **and the people** (the Roman people) **of the prince that shall come** (Antichrist) **shall destroy the city and the sanctuary;** (under Titus, 70 AD) **and unto the end of the war desolations are determined.**"

Appendix No 4

Table of Chronological Parallelisms and God's Programme of 490 Years

The point of contact between sacred and profane chronology, and therefore the first certain date in Biblical history, is the accession of Nebuchadnezzar to the throne of Babylon (Dan. 1:1; Jer. 25:1). From this date i.e. 604 BC we reckon on to Christ and back to Adam. The agreement of the chronologist guarantees that David began to reign in BC 1056 - 55 and therefore, that all dates subsequent to that event can be definitely fixed. But before this epoch, certainty vanishes.

Furnished below are the most striking features that appear in the chronology of the sacred history. The call of Abraham is the *central point* between the creation and the crucifixion.

From Adam to the covenant with Abraham (4141 BC to 2055 BC) is	2086 years
From Abraham to the crucifixion of Christ (2055 BC to 32 AD) is	2086 years
From Adam to the Flood (4141 BC to 2485 BC) is	1656 years
From Flood to the Covenant with Abraham (Gen 15:18) (2485BC to 2055BC) is	430 years
From the Covenant to the Exodus (2055 BC to 1625 BC) is	430 years
From the Exodus to the Crucifixion (1625 BC to 32 AD) is	1656 years

With awesome wonder, we view these chronological details of world history (pictured in the diagram below) as BUT part of God's plan of "Times and Seasons" (Acts 1:7):

4141 BC	ADAM	The Creation			1656 years	2086 years
2485 BC	NOAH	The Flood	430 years			
2055 BC	ABRAHAM	The Covenant (Gal. 3:17)		430 years (Ex. 12.40)		
1625 BC	MOSES	The Law			1656 years	2086 years
32 AD	CHRIST	The Crucifixion				

God's Programme based on a sequence of 490 (70 x 7) years relating to Israel's history:

1.	The entrance into Canaan (1586 BC) unto the establishment of the kingdom under Saul (1096 BC) was	490 years.
2.	The establishment of the kingdom under Saul (BC 1096) unto the beginning of the captivity (servitude) in Babylon (606 BC) was	490 years.
3.	The dedication of Solomon's Temple (BC 1005) unto the dedication of the second Temple (515 BC) in the reign of Darius was	490 years.
4.	The decree to rebuild Jerusalem in Nehemiah 2, (445 BC) unto Messiah cut off in Daniel 9 (69 weeks of years = 483 years) and adding the 70th week (7 years of Tribulation) – leaving the whole of the present church-age in parenthesis – unto the coming of Christ in Millennial glory makes a total of	490 years.

"How unsearchable are His judgements, and His ways past finding out" (Rom. 11:33).

Note: Please refer the Chart given under Appendix No. 5

The Date of the Flood from the Creation

According to the details given in Genesis Chapter 5 and 7:6; 9:28, 29, we are able to determine as to when exactly the Flood came upon the earth. The workings are furnished below:

Year from Creation	Name	Begat when	Further lived up to	Total Age	Death after creation
1	Adam	130	800	930	930
130	Seth	105	807	912	1042
235	Enos	90	815	905	1140
325	Cainan	70	840	910	1235
395	Mahalaleel	65	830	895	1290
460	Jared	162	800	962	1422
622	Enoch	65	300	365	987 *God took him*
687	Methuselah	187	782	969	1656
874	Lamech	182	595	777	1651
1056	Noah		–	–	–
1656	The Food *(Gen. 9:28, 29)*	600 Noah after the Flood	350	950	2006

It is noteworthy, that Adam died when Lamech was 56 years of age. He had known all except Noah before the Flood. And Methuselah (the meaning of his name is: "When he dies it shall be sent") died just before the Flood.

The Seven Parables Relating to Israel's Future in Fulfilment of the Feasts of Trumpets, of Atonement and of Tabernacles

(Matthew chs 24 & 25)

Of the five great discourses of our Lord, found in Matthew's Gospel, the last one is given in chapters 24 & 25, in which our Lord outlines vividly Israel's future course in seven distinct parables. These two chapters fore-tell in detail the happenings during the period portrayed by the unique and most striking events of the Lord's return in power and great glory (Matt. 24:30), *with* His saints, and the setting up of His Throne, at the end of the Tribulation period. And He will judge the living Nations (Matt. 25:31).

The Seven Parables in these two chapters involve God's earthly people the Jews, or Daniel's people ("thy people" Dan. 12:1), and have special regard to their behaviour while their Messiah was absent. At the end of His discourse, (Matt. 25:31-46) the Lord deals with the Nations, that too, in relation to Jews. These parables have as there background the period of the Great Tribulation - the time of Jacob's trouble (Jer. 30:7). Needless to observe, as the Lord returns with His saints, the bride of the Lamb, *these seven parables do not refer to or involve the church.* Elsewhere in these papers *(The Seven Set Feasts of Jehovah, Paper No: 04-01)*, we have

seen that the Feast of Trumpets for the re-gathering of the scattered Israel will be fulfilled, as our Lord fore-told in Matthew 24:31. "His elect" refers to Israel and Judah (Isa. 45:4 & 65:9), the elect of the earth. The heavenly elect of Romans 8:33; Col. 3:12 & 1 Pet. 1:2, is the Bride of the Lamb, who will return to the earth *with* the Lord.

Thereafter, the implications of the last two feasts of Leviticus 23 are described by our Lord in Matthew 24 & 25. At that time, the situation would involve a much sobered and changed Israel, having come out of the Great Tribulation. The setting and implications of the return of Israel's rejected King are vividly described and portrayed in these seven parables as detailed below:

1. The Fig tree putting forth leaves (Matt. 24:32-35):

– Israel's lack of discernment of the times.

This parable deals with the certainty of Israel's national restoration within a generation. The unbelieving Israel (typified as a fruitless fig tree), now begins to put forth leaves – that is to be a nation as happened in 1948, together with other nations, that is "all the trees" (Luke 21:29). The State of Israel has now been set up, though in unbelief, which will change, when as a result of the Great Tribulation (Deut. 30:1-10), their hearts will be circumcised (Deut. 30:6), they will truly trust, and enthrone their King, whom they have so long rejected (Zech. 13:9).

This parable reveals Israel's lack of discernment of the times.

(Please see this paper for the significance and meaning of Israel as a fig tree).

2. The suddenness of the Judgement, like that of the Flood in Noah's Days (Matt. 24:36-42).

– Israel's un-preparedness, as to the unexpected suddenness of Messiah's coming.

This parable deals with the quite unexpected return of the King and is based upon the illustration of the Flood, in the days of Noah, "and knew not until the flood came, and took them all away" (Matt. 24:39). Israel will be unprepared though incessantly warned, as in Noah's days.

This parable highlights the character of that day – un-preparedness.

3. The thief-like unexpected character of the Judgement (Matt. 24:43-44).

– Israel's lack of preparedness and watchfulness.

This parable deals with the unpreparedness of the nation, the house of Israel, "good man of the house", who was caught completely off-guard, through unbelief, "in such an hour as ye think not".

This parable stresses Israel's negligence.

The above three parables, therefore, set the stage as to Israel's *state* and *attitude,* at the time of the return of the Son of Man, their rejected King. However, a nation will be born suddenly, as foretold by His prophet in Isaiah 66:7-9:

> "Before she travailed, she brought forth; before her pain came, she was delivered of a man child, who hath *heard* such a thing? Who hath *seen* such things? Shall the earth be made to bring forth in *one day?* Or shall a nation be *born* at once? – Shall I bring to the birth, and not cause to bring forth? saith the Lord."

Compare this with Zech. 12:10-14 & Rom. 11:26, 27.

The remaining *four* parables concern Israel's 'service', 'testimony' and 'stewardship' in the absence of the king, during the period of the reign of the Beast, which includes the Great Tribulation period. At the end of this seven year period, most unexpectedly (as portrayed in the first three parables), scattered Israel will be gathered out, fulfilling the Feast of Trumpets, from the "four winds of heaven". And then approaches the Feast of Atonement, as a day of reckoning to Israel. This will be followed by the Feast of Tabernacles of Millennial joy.

4. The faithful and wise Servant (Matt. 24:45-47).

– Faithful service during the Great Tribulation and its reward in Millennium (Mat 24:47).

This parable deals with the faithful and wise Jewish servant, whom his lord (King) has made ruler over his household (Israel), and to give them meat, in due season – particularly during the Great Tribulation. He will receive from the King his reward in the Millennial Kingdom (Feast of Tabernacles) which follows, by making him a "ruler over all His goods".

5. The evil Servant (Mat 24:48-51).

– Wicked service during the Great Tribulation and its Judgement.

This wicked Jewish servant, is being reviewed, in this parable, in respect of his unfaithful service

– Israel's unfaithful service will be reviewed – and accordingly he is appointed his portion by punishing him in the lake of fire.

Note: How "in an hour that he is not aware of" (v 50) confirms the third parable, (v 44).

6. The Ten Virgins, with their lamps (Matt. 25:1-13).

– Testimony during the Great Tribulation period and its reward, for their preparedness to meet the Bridegroom.

The oil in the lamps, or no oil, speaks of witness and testimony. They that took oil in their vessels with their lamps and at midnight "trimmed their lamps" (witness) and went in (Matt. 25:10), to the marriage, (here simply described as the marriage, this being a parable only), pointing to the marriage of the Lamb (Rev. 19:9), which develops into the Feast of Tabernacles or Millennium. Whereas, the other five virgins, foolish and unwise, "took no oil with them", that is, they were without testimony. The door was shut, and so was pronounced, "I know you not", because they had no testimony to their Messiah, and not knowing the day or the hour when the Son of Man will come.

7. Five Talents – Two Talents – One Talent (Matt. 25:14-30).

– Wise stewardship during the Great Tribulation period, its Millennial rewards, and the joy of the Lord.

This parable speaks of the talents delivered unto the servants "to everyman according to

his several ability" who were made accountable. "After a *long time* the Lord of those servants cometh and reckoneth with them" (v.19). The King has now returned, and the stewards are reviewed and rewarded suitably, as to their faithfulness, as like the faithful service and faithful witness, brought out in the earlier parables. Their reward is "to rule over many things" in the Millennial Kingdom, but the unfaithful and "unprofitable" steward, was cast into outer darkness.

Note: Please refer to remarks given under the Day of Atonement, in "The Seven Set Feasts of Jehovah" Paper No: 04-01.

Israel Typified In Scripture As A Fig Tree

The NT Scripture provides, as detailed below, a vivid background picture of disobedient and unbelieving Israel, as a "Fig Tree", to which they are typified in the first of the above seven parables.

1. The fig tree planted in the vineyard (Luke. 13:6-8).

A fig tree in a vineyard is out of place. The vineyard, the house of Israel, (Isa. 5:1-7), was unfruitful, broken down and the desolate vine carried away to Babylon, was however planted back in the land as an unbelieving Fig Tree, from which no fruit matured during the Lord's "these three years" of ministry. Yet, another year was granted, "let it alone this year also", which speaks of God's extended grace, - "I shall dig about it, and dung it" - over rebellious Israel. However, it had to be finally "cut down" in 70 AD, by the destruction of the City of Jerusalem including the Temple (Matt. 24:2) as they would not hearken and repent at the preaching of the Gospel by the Apostles (Acts 3:11-26; 4:13-21; 7:1-59; 13:15-42; 22:1-21 and 28:23-29), which was in fact the digging and dunging.

2. The cursing of the Fig Tree (Matt. 21:18-20).

Israel, the unbelieving Fig Tree, is cursed by the Lord "let no fruit grow on thee hence forward forever", and it quickly withered away. "How soon is the fig tree withered away", for their unbelief in crucifying their King as foretold in Deuteronomy chs. 29 & 30. Thus for nearly 2,000 years the nation of Israel has been scattered among the Gentile nations. Israel is thus set aside once for all, "until the fulness of the Gentiles be come in" (Rom. 11:25).

3. The Fig tree putting forth leaves (Matt. 24:32-34), and the Fig Tree and all the trees (Luke 21:29-30).

While "all the trees" speaks of the Gentile nations, the fig tree is now seen putting forth its leaves, indicating a new beginning for Israel, as ultimately being a vehicle for carrying out the purposes of God in Millennium, and as promised in OT prophecies. Israel's salvation out of Great Tribulation is now literally at the doors. Her unbelief will be removed forever. The events described in Luke 21:6-28, will be accomplished within the time-span of one generation (Luke 21:32).

Whereas Israel, before being carried away into Babylon was always depicted as a *'vine'* only (Ps. 80:14,15; Isa. 5:1-7; 27:2,3; Jer. 12:10,11), after returning from Chaldea (Babylon) Judah as in Jeremiah 24:5, is likened to *'figs'* and further developed as such in the NT Scripture, as shown above. However, Romans 11:24 speaks of Israel once again being grafted in, but this time into an *'olive'* tree. The Vine, Fig and Olive are, therefore, pictures of Israel as given by the Holy Spirit, over the *three* dispensations of her history:

1. Israel as a Nation out of Egypt – Vine. (Isa. 5:1-7)

2. Israel after the Babylonian captivity – Fig. (Matt. 24:32-35; Luke 13:6-8)

3. Israel inheriting the Promised Land during Millennium – Olive. (Jer. 11:16; Rom. 9:25, 26; 11:24)

PROPHECY

The Day of the Lord
"In That Day, When I Make up My Jewels"

(Isaiah 2:11 & 17 and Malachi 3:17 expounded)

The prophetic expression, "The Day of the Lord" is a comprehensive term. In Joel 2:1, 2 it is spoken of as "a day of darkness and of gloominess", a day about which the prophet mentions five times (1:15; 2:1, 11, 31; 3:14). But this day of darkness, turns out to be a wonderful day, as we read in Joel 3:17-21, where the prophet mentions as *"in that day"*.

The readers of the OT Scriptures will wonder how comprehensive the expression "the day of the Lord" is. The comparable expression "in that day", will be found repeated quite often in the OT, as we read from Isaiah 2:11, through to Malachi 3:17, the first and the last mention of it.

The expression *"in that day"* is repeated 88 times by the OT prophets, as follows:

Isaiah	42	Obadiah	1
Jeremiah	5	Micah	3
Ezekiel	6	Zephaniah	3
Hosea	2	Zechariah	20
Joel	1	Malachi	1
Amos	4		

And therefore, this phrase would appear to embrace all the various phases and aspects of the expression "The Day of the Lord".

The repetition of this expression indicates the importance God has attached to it. "In that day" occurs 42 times (7 x 6) in the prophecy of Isaiah alone, the last mention found in 52:6. Here God directly reveals to His people thus:

"Therefore, they shall know IN THAT DAY that I am He that doth speak: "Behold it is I" and again in verse 9, *"Break forth into joy, sing together, ye waste places of Jerusalem, for the Lord hath comforted His people, He hath redeemed Jerusalem".*

This wonderful prophecy about the future fulfilment of the promises and hopes of centuries concerning Israel needs to be *believed,* and that is exactly how Isaiah 53 begins: "Who hath believed our report?" In understanding and interpreting Isaiah chapter 53, although the great Gospel truth expressed here is often used, as we find in Acts 8:32, 33, this contextual background is usually overlooked.

So we ask, what "that *report"* is? And "to whom it is *revealed!"* (Isa. 53:1). Here, we shall first consider the question "to whom is the arm of the Lord *revealed!"* The word 're-vealed' is rendered in the margin as "made bare". This is from Isa. 52:10. "The Lord hath *made bare* His holy arm in the eyes of all the nations". By what follows in this verse "and all the ends of the earth shall see the salvation of our God", we can conclusively say that it speaks of the Lord's Second Advent and not his first.

The passage "All the ends of the earth" (52:10) will help us to understand as to who are these people, who "shall see the salvation of our God". They are the Jews, who were scattered to the uttermost parts of heaven. Their God scattered them because they rejected their king. However, in grace, He promised to regather them (Deut. 30:3, 4; Ezk. 39:28; Matt. 24:31). This re-gathering "the salvation of our God", would be a revelation, (that which is revealed) and would be realised immediately after the great Tribulation, (Matt. 24:19), when the Son of Man shall appear, coming in the clouds of Heaven, with power and great glory.

Thus is the *report* and the good tidings of God, "that publisheth salvation", mentioned in Isa. 52:7, which they shall see, eye to eye, when the Lord shall bring *again* Zion. Hence, "break forth into joy, sing together" etc. Thus to benefit from the report of this wonderful good news, Israel has to believe it, after the "bare arm" of the Lord is revealed in judgement of the nations. Unless this "bare arm" of the Lord is properly understood, it will not be possible to rightly divide these prophecies and the future events, as to when exactly they will take place.

Then follows the prudence of "My servant" and His exaltation, which refers to Messiah in Millennium. "Behold, My servant shall deal prudently, He shall be exalted and extolled, and be very high" (Isa. 52:13). This would astonish many that He should be so exalted, since during His first advent, all Israel and the nations and the kings saw Him, this same Messiah, being put to grief, accursed and afflicted, hanging on the tree, His

visage so marred more than any man, and unrecognisable as found in Isaiah 52:14.

"The Day of the Lord" has its *two* aspects, (1) "The terrible day of the Lord" (Joel 2:31) and (2) the joyful reconciliation day of Millennial blessing, when Israel will be made His Jewels (Malachi 3:17). We should rightly divide the expression "in that day" found 42 times in Isaiah under these two aspects:

1. The terrible day of the Lord *(20 mentions in Isaiah):*

2:20; 3:7 & 18; 5:30; 7:18 & 23; 17:4 & 9; 19:16; 18 & 19; 20:6; 22:8,12,20 & 25; 23:15; 24:21; 27:1; and 31:7.

2. The day of comfort and redemption for Israel *(22 mentions in Isaiah):*

2:11 & 17; 4:1 & 2; 7:21; 10:20 & 27; 11:10 & 11; 12:1 & 4; 19:23 & 24; 25:9; 26:1; 27:2, 12 & 13; 28:5; 29:18; 30:23 and the final, 52:6.

A study of these two categories of references will widen our understanding, clarifying our perception of the future events.

We should observe the wide gap between verses 31:7 and 52:6 the final references of the above two categories. In the first, *the fear of the ensign* is expressed: "His princes shall be afraid of the ensign, saith the Lord, whose fire is in Zion, and His furnace in Jerusalem" (31:9) and in the second, *He Himself is the ensign, with His arm made bare* "Behold it is I... the Lord hath made bare His holy arm". The significance of making "bare His holy arm" (Messiah's holy arm), is to give Him full freedom in wielding His sword of justice against the foes of Israel on "The Day of Vengeance of our God" (61:2; 63:4). And their blood shall be 'sprinkled' upon My garments and I will stain all my raiment (63:3). This brings salvation to His people, to enable them to leap for joy, and to exalt their Messiah, Who has come to reign, "Surely they are my people ... so He was their saviour" (63:8). "My own arm – the holy arm that was made bare – brought salvation unto Me" (63:5).

But *"who hath believed our report?"* and in that day *"to whom will the arm of the Lord be revealed?"*

The descendents of Israel, who crucified their Messiah at His first advent, will recognise that *self same One,* now exalted as the Ruler, with power and great glory. Isaiah 53 clearly depicts the picture of how Israel would react to Him, both in His first coming (vv. 2-4) and in the Second Advent (vv. 5-12), the details of which are given below:

AT HIS FIRST ADVENT	ISRAEL'S REACTION
He hath no form nor comeliness (53:2) (His agony instead of His regal glory)	There is no beauty that *we* should desire Him (53:2) (They expected a royal conqueror, but He came in the form of a Servant Phil 2:7)
He was despised and we hid as it were, our faces from Him. (53:3).	And *we* esteemed Him not; *we* hid (Marg: hiding) our faces from Him (53:3).
Surely He hath borne our griefs, and carried our sorrows (53:4) as quoted in Matt. 8:17.	Yet *we* did esteem Him stricken, smitten of God and afflicted (53:4). **Israel's belief and confession at His second advent, when "the arm of the Lord" is revealed.**
He was wounded,	For *our* transgressions
He was bruised,	For *our* iniquities,
The chastisement was upon Him,	For *our* peace,
With His stripes (53:5).	*We* are healed (53:5).
Every one has turned to his own way (53:6).	The Lord hath laid on Him the iniquity of *us* all (53:6).
He was stricken (53:8).	For the transgression of My people (53:8).
He made His grave with the wicked and with the rich in His death. (53:9).	Because He hath done no violence neither was any deceit in His mouth (53:9).
He made His soul an offering for sin (53:10).	Yet, it pleased the Lord to bruise Him (for *our* sake) (53:10).
He shall bear their iniquities (53:11).	By his knowledge shall My righteous Servant justify many (53:11).
He was numbered with the transgressors (53:12).	He bare the sin of many (53:12).

Note: The words 'we', 'our' and 'my' indicate a repentant Israel identifying herself with her confession.

Israel's change of heart, evident in the confessions above mentioned, is the confir-mation that she has returned to Jehovah, with all her heart (Deut. 30:1-3). They have indeed *believed the report* brought by the beautiful feet, and that the Lord hath made bare His holy arm of judgement against all the nations and thus Israel has seen *"the salvation of our God"* (Isa. 52:10; 63:2, 6).

Regarding the remaining references of *"in that day"*, attention has already been drawn to the last one found in Malachi 3:17 of the day in which the Lord Jehovah will "make up His jewels". He will spare Israel out of the great tribulation (Matt. 24:21, 22) as one who will spare his own son that serves him. (Malachi 3:17).

Grace knows no bounds!! The children of those Jews who stand condemned by the blood of the Lord Jesus (Matt. 27:25), are now made up as "My jewels", by the same blood – "the blood of the everlasting covenant" which has been mediated to them (Heb. 8:6; 13:20; Jer. 31:31-34). Such is the certainty and clarity of these prophetical features! Thus we can easily rest with certainty upon the meaning of this oft repeated expression, "in that day", as inclusive of all the aspects and events at the return of Israel's Lord, "after a long time" (Matt. 25:19). This includes the Day of Atonement, leading on to the Feast of Tabernacles – the Millennial Day!

"And the pleasure of the Lord shall prosper in His hand" (Isa. 53:10).

It is a sobering thought, when considering Matt. 7:22, 23. "Many will say to me *in that day* calling 'LORD, LORD'" (Matt. 7:21) and claiming:

1. Lord, Lord, have we not prophesied in thy name?

2. And in thy name have cast out devils (demons)?

3. And in thy name done many wonderful works?

These claims as grounds for entry into the Kingdom of heaven were bluntly rejected. Those who in our day practise prophecy, cast out demons – evil spirits – in His name, and do wonderful works are all nothing but counterfeits as is the current spate of miracles. They are but fraudulent claims, and are of the devil. The Lord disowns them saying "I never knew you: *depart* from Me, ye that *work iniquity"*, against their claim of "wonderful works" which the Lord condemns as "iniquitous works".

We live in the apostasy period of 2 Thes. 2:3, 4 when deception and delusion are dressed-up as angels of light, (compare 2 Cor. 11:14 with v.13). False apostles of Christ are gaining ground. Congregations with itching ears, draw to themselves "the teachers" and "the teaching" they desire to have. Truth and righteousness are pushed aside and no longer valued and this will continue after the rapture, culminating in the revelation of the man of sin.

The 'maranatha' shout is imminent. "Hold fast the *confidence"* and "cast not away your *confidence"* (Heb 3:6; 10:35). ('Confidence – Strong - 3954 – means outspokenness, frankness, bluntness). Let us not shun speaking out loud the truth, always rejoicing in the blessed hope of His coming.

Let us be "firm unto the end" (Heb. 3:6).

The Mount of Transfiguration – His Exodus

A comparison of three men each of whom knew the manner of their exodus.

Scripture reading: Matthew 17:1-9; Luke 9:28-36; Mark 9: 1-9; John 1:14 and 2 Peter 1: 16-20.

Points of Comparison and Contrast	MOSES Who wanted to enter the promised land but whom God buried.	ELIJAH Who wanted to die but whom God took, by a whirlwind.	THE LORD JESUS Who went to the Father through death, resurrection and ascension.
Their exodus (Luke 9:31). (For 'decease' read 'exodus'. The Greek word used here is "*Exodos*" meaning: 'a way out', hence, "a departure especially from life i.e. decease").	He wanted to enter into the promised land. An optimist.	"It is better for me to die than to live". A pessimist.	Christ voluntarily offered Himself. He need not have died. The divine Son of God, knowing all things, *chose* to die and rise again.
	His exodus – death. (Deut. 34:5; Jude 9) Divinely planned.	His exodus in a whirlwind. (2 Kings 2:11). Divinely provided.	His exodus which *HE* should accomplish. (Lk. 9:31) "When he had by *Himself* purged." (Heb 1:3).
Christ's exodus is compared here with the 'exodus' of two notable men, who represented the *law* and the *prophets*.	God buried him in the land of Moab (Deut. 34:6).	The chariot of Israel was sent that he should not die. (2 Kings 2:12)	It was not a passing cloud that received Him, but a *glory-cloud* sent from Heaven, as He will return (Acts 1:11; Matt. 24:30).

	Moses died because he called Israel, 'Ye rebels', and did not sanctify God. Moses thus misrepresented God and failed as a prophet. (Num. 20: 10-12; Deut. 32:50-52).	Elijah was taken into heaven (2 Kings 2: 11). A shadow of the Lord's exodus.	Christ died for the sins of many and His burial and resurrection was according to the Scriptures. (I Cor. 15:3.4; Luke 24:44, 51).
Each had 70 men involved with them.	Had 70 elders to help (Ex. 24:1; Num. 11:16)	Brought judgement on 70 sons of Ahab (2 Kings 10:6-7)	Commissioned 70 messengers with the gospel of the Kingdom (Luke 10:1)
Each stood before proud kings.	Pharoah: to deliver His people (Ex. 5:1)	Ahab: to deliver Israel from Baal worship (I Kings. 17: 1; 18:37)	Herod: to expose his pride and curiosity (Luke 23:8)
Each made intercession for Israel	To pardon their iniquity (Ex. 34:6-9)	"Thou art the God of Israel – I am Thy servant" (I Kings. 18:36)	To forgive their sin of having numbered Him with the transgressors (Luke 23:34; Isa. 53:12b)
Each had angels minister to them.	Ex. 23:23	I Kings 19:5	Mark 1:13; Matt. 4:11; Luke 22:43.
Each experienced testing for 40 days.	In Sinai (Ex. 24: 18)	In Horeb, which includes Sinai (I Kings 19:8)	Tempted of the Devil in the wilderness (was this also in Horeb?) Luke 4:1
Each were men of mountain experience.	Sinai: A mountain smoking with fire and earthquake (Ex. 19:18)	Carmel: Fire from heaven (I Kings 18:38) "The Lord, he is the God" (I Kings 18:39)	Transfiguration: His raiment white and glistering, 'Jesus only' (Luke 9:29)
Each were prophets and therefore were stewards of the word of God.	Given direct revelation. Not by vision or dream (Num 12:8)	"The Lord before whom I stand" (I Kings 17:1)	But in Heb 1:2, 'Spoken in His Son', and we have the command "Hear ye Him". (Matt 17:5).
Each controlled the mighty waters.	Moses needed a *rod* (Ex 14:16)	Elijah needed a *robe* (2 Kings 2:8)	The Lord with simply a *word*: "Peace, be still" (Mark 4:39)

100

Each accounted for his responsibility.	Said: "It is too heavy for me" (Num 11:14)	Cried: 'It is enough' (I Kings 19:4)	Prayed "I have *finished* the work which Thou gavest me to do" (John 17:4) i.e. He completed the revelation of the true God and cried 'It is finished' (John 19:30) The redemption.
Their successors.	Joshua: His name means: "Jehovah-Saviour"	Elisha: His name means "My God is Jehovah".	*No* successor: Our Lord lives in the power of an endless life and has an un-transferable priest-hood (Heb 7:24), and HE *IS* JEHOVAH
Each directed men in obeying God.	His service enabled Israel to promise "We will do" (Ex 19:8), but ended in failure.	His ministry made Israel to confess, "He is God" (I Kings 18:39), but ended in failure.	The Lord writes His laws in our hearts (Heb 8: 10), and the new man (I John 5:18) sinneth not.
Each knew the day of his exodus.	(Deut 32:50) To die, which was accomplished for him.	(2 Kings 2: 1-10) To be translated, which was accomplished for him.	(John 17:1; Acts 1:9). He died and rose again. To be received by the Father– "Which *He* should accomplish at Jerusalem" (Luke 9:31)
Each experienced exclusivism.	Numbers 11:28,29	2 Kings 2:23 (In Elisha's double portion)	Luke 9:49, 50

NOTES

1. The *contrasts* in the Gospels:

Matthew 17	Accentuates	His	Face	--	Of the King (Pro 20:8)
Mark 9	Accentuates	His	Clothes	--	Of the Servant
Luke 9	Accentuates	His	Attitude	--	Of the dependent Son of man (Praying)

God *singled out* the Lord Jesus as, "MY beloved Son, in whom I am well pleased" (Matt. 3:17; 17:5).

2. The conditions mentioned of *elevation* High Mountain" and *separation* 'apart' must be satisfied before the Lord's glory is to be seen. In every way, the Lord is *greater* than either Moses or

Elijah, who represents the LAW and PROPHETS, but is only fulfilled by our Lord. We must, now, "Hear HIM" only.

3. Peter was rebuked because he equated the Lord with Moses and Elijah, and thought that he was in the feast of tabernacles; but eventually learned the lesson as an eye witness of this incident, in his account in 2 Peter 1:16-20. "No prophecy of the scripture is of any private interpretation". Shall we learn this lesson?

Conclusion

The above devotional study, concerning the Person and Work of our Lord Jesus Christ, would result in the better understanding and appreciation of "The Lord of Glory" (I Cor. 2:8), and to exalt Him in our daily life.

"We beheld His glory, the glory as of the only begotten of the Father". (John 1:14)

"We see Jesus crowned with glory" (Heb. 2:9)

His Moral glory:

The beauty and perfection of His character, shone forth in all His words, works and ways, as He passed through this world among all conditions of men. Is Christ the great *attraction* of our hearts?

His Official glory:

His excellence and superiority of His office as Apostle, Prophet, High Priest, Redeemer, Shepherd and Head, calls us to *'consider'* Him (Heb. 3:1), and to own Him. His claims as the One sent of God, His words and actions of prophetic fulfilment, His service on our behalf as High Priest, His claims upon us as Redeemer, His care for us as Shepherd, and His glorious position as our Head, the source of all our authority, life and blessing – we surely need them all. We are called to avail ourselves of His Office.

His Eternal glory:

"His glory that He had with the Father before the world was", that essential, incommunicable glory, is His alone. Neither angel nor man can share this glory.

We shall 'behold' (John 17:24) it and adoringly acknowledge (Rev 5:11). However, the glory given to Him by the Father, we shall partake of (John 17:22; I Pet. 5:1). The church 'arrayed in glory' (Eph. 5:27), not her own but His, will be presented faultless in the day of His coming. And when He returns in manifested power and glory to the world (Col. 3:4), His saints will 'appear with Him', in that glory as followers in His train (Rev. 19:14). That glory His saints shall bear, and through endless ages display (2 Thess. 1:10; Rev. 21:11) before all worlds.

102

The Difference between a Believer's State and Standing

(In Relation To Eternal Security)

The parable of the sower (Mark 4:1-20) clarifies fruit - bearing (30, 60 and 100 fold) as the evidence of eternal life generated by the power of the Holy Spirit through the Word of God. Hence, "by their fruits ye shall know them" (Matt. 7:20).

Our *standing* in Christ *cannot* change, but our *state* certainly does. Note the use of the word *'in'* from Ephesians 1:1, 4,7,11,12 & 13 etc The current erroneous teaching of being lost after having been saved is shown in this paper as false by the simple statements of truth from God's Word.

"This is the Father's will, which hath sent me, that of all which he hath given me I should lose nothing" (John 6:39). If Christ could lose one of His own, He is not omnipotent or omniscient.

1. "Being Born Again"

Being born again, is the work of God, and has nothing to do with any work from our side. "Being born again, not of corruptible seed, but of incorruptible, by the Word of God, which liveth and abideth for ever". (I Pet 1:23). We simply believe God and are credited with His righteousness.

Note, therefore, the difference between "believing God" and "believing in God". All should "believe in God", but all believers "believe God" (James 2:19).

The verse I Peter 1:23, itself invalidates the use of the modern phrase: "making a commitment", in order to obtain the "Christian" status. Salvation is regeneration by the living Seed, the Word of God and is not obtained by any human commitment. "Be born again" of water even (Gr. Kai=even, also. This word has a cumulative force) of the Spirit (John 3:6)

2. "Backsliding"

'Backsliding', is an Old Testament word, and is not found in the New Testament.

There are three temperatures mentioned in Revelation 3:16; 'Hot', 'Cold' and 'Lukewarm', and the Lord is seen standing *outside* the assembly. If ever backsliding should have appeared in the NT, Revelation chapter 3 would have been the place. Even if backsliding were in the NT, and applicable to the Church (and not to Israel, as it is in the OT), it would not have a different meaning to its OT counterpart.

103

A backsliding heifer, ('Heifer' means "a young cow that has not calved") as we find Israel compared to in Hosea 4:16, describes lack of willingness to be fruitful – to produce a calf – and so become a fruitful cow and no longer a heifer.

"For Israel *slideth back* like a backsliding heifer".

The picture presented here in this verse is that Israel slideth back, like an unwilling or stubborn heifer causing the bull to slide off her back, thus making fruitfulness (conception) impossible.

Note: The Hebrew word for 'backsliding' is "*sah-rar*" and it is derived from the primary root "to back away", meaning, morally "to be refractory, backsliding, rebellious, stubborn and withdrawing". This word is translated in AV as 'withdrew' in Neh. 9:29; 'pulled away' in Zec. 7:11; 'rebellious' in Ps. 66:7, Isa. 1:23 'revolters' in Jer. 6:28; Hos. 9:15; and 'stubborn' in Ps. 78:8; Pro. 7:11

The above usages of this Hebrew word are given in detail to help readers, as well as translators, to understand this Scripture text better. As the various language Bible translations give just the meaning of 'rebellious' or 'stubborn', and thus do not imply the idea of the cow sliding away from the bull, and will not allow him to mount her for the purpose of fruitfulness in conception. Unless we understand the picture presented in this verse, by the Holy Spirit, comparing Israel to that of a stubborn heifer, this text will have no meaning. We trust the translators will present this illustration clearly.

The NT fruitfulness comes from abiding in the true vine yielding 'fruit', "more fruit", and "much fruit", "so shall ye be my disci-

ples". (John 15:2, 5, 8). And again we find, "by their fruits ye shall know them" (Matt. 7:20).

Thus we find that both in OT and in NT, fruitfulness results from *abiding*.

3. VINE Branches : *"Taketh Away" and "Burned"*

The vine tree is for fruit bearing, and if not, *it is not meet for any work, except for fuel.* "It is cast into the fire for fuel" (Ezek. 15:2-4). This observation given by the Holy Spirit should help us to understand correctly John 15:2 & 6 and the words "taketh away" and "burned":

Taketh Away

Taketh away from what? The branches of the vine plant, if allowed to fall and touch the ground, will begin to take root and draw sustenance there from, instead of from the vine and so become fruitless. How to make it fruitful? It is simple. Just "lift up" (upwards) the branch, or "take away" such branches, to avoid earth – rooting so that they may yield fruit. So the meaning of "take away" is not *removing* or *cutting off* but is lifting up. Grapes will not appear on a branch, one end of which is attached to the vine and the other end rooting itself in the earth (the world) some believers try this, (even suggesting a television is not harmful) but they bear no fruit for God.

Burned

We find that the word *'as'* is used twice and is used by way of illustration:

"As the branch cannot bear fruit	Positive aspect.
.. except it abide in the vine" (v.4)	Useful because fruitful.
"If a man abide not in me, he is cast	Negative aspect.
forth as a branch, and is withered" (v.6)	Useless, but still a branch.

The meaning of this illustration is obvious. Except the branch abide in the vine and draw its sustenance there from, it cannot bear fruit. This confirms verse 2.

Verse 6 poses a question. The word 'as' in this verse, proposes a similitude. What use is a fruitless branch, except for burning? Consider Ezekiel 15:2-4, burning as fuel would normally be the case. Here the burning is not hell fire but because of its barrenness or fruitlessness, *it is fit only for fuel.* It is useless and worthless, nevertheless indicating it remains as a branch unhappily, and this is the point - withered without fruit.

We interpret this passage as above, because the word 'as' is used twice as an illustration for a fruitless believer "in Christ".

4. "Nor Any Other Creature Shall Be Able To Separate Us."

Let us have a look at Romans 8:39. Because of the word 'other', used in this verse, the saved-and-lost theorist implies that a person is able to separate himself from Christ. This interpretation is not correct, because the Greek word used here is not 'allos' (ie. another of the same kind), but 'heteros' (ie. another of a different kind). This verse means, "Any other creature" of a different kind will not be able to separate us from Christ.

However, if we take it to mean, that one of the same kind (Allos) will be able to separate him from Christ. Then it would contradict the assurance, "he cannot sin, because he is born of God" (1 John 3:9) and also the truths expressed in the first chapter of Ephesians, as a believer being *"in* Christ" (v.1); "blessed *in* Christ" (v.3); "chosen *in* Christ" (v.4) etc. This is the result of divine choice, quite unalterable, and made by God before the foundation of the world. As our salvation is of grace with no part whatsoever from our side, (Eph. 2:8), this position (condition or state) cannot be altered or nullified from our side.

With the correct and clear understanding of just the few passages, as seen above, we conclude that our standing in Christ is eternally unchangeable. A believer's standing in Christ indicates he possesses eternal security.

The Eight Baptisms

Few appreciate that there are some EIGHT different baptisms mentioned in the Word of God. Each involves *four* things:

1. A *place* where the baptism is enacted.
2. A *baptiser*.
3. A *medium* in which to baptise.
4. A *subject* to be baptised.

Further, the improper use of prepositions such as 'by', 'of', 'in' and 'with' etc., has brought confusion over this subject of baptism.

The following tabulation proves that the four above mentioned points are essentially relevant to each of the eight baptisms found in the NT. And it will *not* be right to use phrases like:

"They have been *by the Spirit's power* baptised into one body" as one sect puts it.

nor "Baptised *by* the Holy Spirit"

nor "Baptised *of* the Holy Spirit"

to describe the "baptism *in the Spirit*".

Neither is it correct to use the expression *"Spirit's* Baptism" or "Baptism *in* the Holy Spirit" to describe the truth of being "filled with the Spirit" (Eph. 5:18).

The risen Lord Jesus Christ (the baptiser) baptised the whole body of Christ, (the sub-ject) (all those to be saved, from the day of Pentecost until the rapture, that is, the church which is His body) *in* the Spirit (the medium), in heaven (the place), when all the above four essentials were present at one and the same time. "For by one Spirit are we all baptised into one body, whether we be Jews or Gentiles, whether we be bond or free; and have been all made to drink into one Spirit." (1 Cor. 12:13).

The Lord stated; "Ye shall be *baptised with* (Gr. 'en' which is correctly interpreted as 'in' (see Newberry Margin) the Holy Spirit not many days hence" (Acts 1:5). This baptism of His body, could not take place before the Lord Jesus ascended to His Father, forty days after His resurrection, according to John 16:7. It *had* to take place after the Lord ascended, but before the Holy Spirit descended on the day of Pentecost (Acts 2:33), to fulfil, "... but ye shall receive power after that the Holy Spirit is come upon you" (Acts 1:8), which is the *filling* (and not the baptism) of the Holy Spirit. See Acts 2:4.

Note: It is observed that in many of the Indian language Bibles, the prepositions such as 'by', 'of', 'in', 'with' etc. have not been accurately translated as found in the original Greek text. We request our readers, particularly the translators to note this vital point and render correctly as found in Greek, and point out any inconsistency found in their language Bibles.

Sl. No	NAME	SCRIPTURE References	LOCATION 1	BAPTISER 2	MEDIUM 3	SUBJECT 4
1.	The Flood α	I Pet. 3:20, 21	On the earth	God	Flood	Noah's Family
2.	John's Baptism	John 1:26 Acts 13:24; 19:3, 4	Bethabara beyond Jordan – Aenon-Salim (John 3:23)	John the Baptist	Water	Jews
3.	Lord's Baptism	John 3:26	-do-	Lord and His disciples	Water	Jews
4.	Lord's own Baptism	Luke 12:50	Calvary	God	Judgement over sin of the world for which He died.	Jesus
5.	Baptism in the Spirit	Matt. 3: 11, I Cor. l2:13, Acts 1:5; 11:16	Heaven	The Lord Jesus	The Holy Spirit	The whole Body of Christ δ
6.	Jewish Baptism β (before salvation)	Acts 2:38	Anywhere with deep enough water	Apostles and Disciples	Water. This was a "washing away" (Acts 22: 16) and not simply- a burial.	Only Jews γ
7.	Gentile Baptism (upon salvation)	Acts 10:47, 48	-do-	Peter and Disciples	Water – The believers who are dead to sin are symbolically buried in water and	Any saved Gentile

					raised again. (Rom 6:3-5)	
8.	Armageddon	Matt. 3:11, 12; Rev. 16:14-16; Ezek 39:4, 10, 14; Zech 14:12	Armageddon at Megiddo;* and Jerusalem .(Zec. 12:11)	The Lord Jesus	Fire	The Living Gentile – nations

* Megiddo, from the root *'gowdad'*, means to gather or assemble by troops (Rev. 16:16)

Explanation:

1. α The flood (item No. I above) being an illustration of baptism, declares: "A good conscience before God", and would be applicable to the points relating to Jewish Baptism, before salvation and Gentile Baptism upon salvation (items 6 & 7 above)

2. β Jewish Baptism, before their salvation (item No 6 above) is to deal with the sin of crucifying Christ, which proved the genuineness of the one baptised. Hence the instruction: "He that believeth and is baptised shall be saved" (Mark 16:16). After baptism the Holy Spirit came upon them (Acts 2:38).

3. γ We may conclude that this Jewish Baptism (item No 6 above) ceased with the dispersion of the Jewish Nation and thereafter the Jews who are saved are baptised in the same manner as Gentiles, without any difference (Gal. 3:28; Col. 3:11).

4. δ The total of all members of the body of Christ, (item No 5 above), was baptised into that *one body* in one Spirit (I Cor. 12:13). When the Lord ascended on high, He received gifts for men, that is for the complete body of Christ, that "the Lord God might dwell amongst them" (Ps. 68:18; Acts 2:33). And subsequently gave gifts to men as we read in Eph. 4:8, 11. Thus we conclude that this baptism into one body took place in the presence of God in heaven.

That the complete Body of Christ already existed, is in keeping with "God which calleth those things which be not as though they were" (Rom. 4:17). Other illustrations of the same principle are:

1. All died in Adam – "As in Adam all die" (I Cor. 15:22)

2. All died in Christ – "If we be dead (died) with Christ." (Rom. 6:8).

3. All buried with Christ – "We were buried with Him", by baptism (Rom. 6:4).

4. The nations as in Gen 10:32 were divided with Israel in view, although Israel did not exist. (Deut. 32:8).

5. "Blood which *is* shed" (Luke 22:20) – when Calvary was still a future event.

6. Redemption from Egypt (Ex. 12:27) – Before it actually took place.

The Eternal Security of the Believer in the Lord Jesus Christ

The present day believers are confused with the constant repeated warnings found in the Epistle to the Hebrews, and wonder whether they fall foul of any of them. Many teach errors, particularly from Hebrews chapter 6, and mislead sincere Christians. This paper will help clarify such misgivings and misunderstandings.

The reader would, please take account of Mark 4:13, "Know ye not this parable? (The parable of the sower) and how then will ye know all parables?" So using this *divine key* to revelation and understanding, (so much of the Word of God, old and new testaments, is parabolic), we have drawn up the following table, assuming that the reader does understand the parable of the sower. We chose Mark's account of the parable of the sower, because of features not mentioned in Matthew and Luke. *(Please see "The Seven Parables of the Kingdom" Paper No: 08-04).*

The wayside, the stony and the thorny grounds, "yielded no fruit". The basic understanding of this parable is this: No fruit-bearing as a result of hearing the Word of God, is no hearing at all. We find words such as "and hearing they may hear, and not understand" (Mark 4:12), "have heard" (Mark 4:15, 16), and "such as hear the word" (Mark 4:18, 20), all of which draw attention to the result of hearing or even hearing with faith. Consider "Not being mixed with faith, in them that heard it". (Heb. 4:2).

The Word is divinely generated and "did *yield fruit* that sprang up and increased" (Mark 4:8), God gives to the seed of His Word a body, which has been divinely quickened in the believer. But how are we to be sure? The proof is, it yields fruit. This alone is the outward evidence: "By their fruits ye shall know them". Such would depart from iniquity, and "the Lord knoweth them that are His". (2 Tim. 2:19).

The parable of the sower and the *seven warnings* in Hebrews, are compared and contrasted in the following tabulation, in order to highlight the eternal security of the believer in the Lord:

The Seven Warnings in Hebrews.	The Parable of the Sower	Remarks
1. If we neglect to *hear*, (2:1-4) lest let slip. "How shall we escape?"	When they have *heard*, Satan cometh immediately and taketh away the word (Mark 4:15)	Comparison in the hearing.
2. An *evil heart* of unbelief (3:12-19)	Which in an honest and *good heart*, having heard the word, keep it and bring forth fruit with patience (Luke 8:15)	CONTRAST in a man's heart.
3. Lest *any fall in unbelief.* (4:1-11).	And have *no root* in themselves and endure for a time; when affliction or persecution ariseth, for the word's sake, immediately they are offended (Mark 4:17)	Comparison in depth and reality.
4. Impossible to renew them again. But that which beareth thorns and briers is *rejected* and is nigh unto cursing. (6:4-8)	Sown among thorns – such as hear the word – things entering in, *choke* the word and it becometh unfruitful. (Mark 4:18, 19)	Comparison of thorns / briers, "things entering in".
5 Of how much *sorer punishment* – for if we sin wilfully after we have received the knowledge of the truth ... fiery indignation which shall devour the adversaries. (10:26-31)	It was *scorched* (Mark 4:6)	Comparison of Eternal fiery Judgement.
6. Lest any man *fail* (12:15-17).	And it becometh *unfruitful* (Mark 4:19).	Comparison of the final result.
7. If we *turn away*, we shall not escape, (12:25) answering to No. 1 above "How shall we escape?"	For the word's sake ... are *offended* (Mark 4:17)	Comparison of the reason for the final result.

A clear understanding of Hebrews 6:1-8, will save us from worry and concern, regarding the erroneous teaching by many, as these verses are used by them unsparingly as an argument that the saved can lose their salvation. The persons described in Hebrews chapter 6, were never saved in the first place, which we will discover, as we examine the words used to describe their *actions*.

Hebrews Chapter 6 verse 4 and 5 reads of those who:

1. were once *enlightened*.	'enlighten' (Strong - 5461) means "to shed rays of light", or "brighten – up".
2. have *tasted* the heavenly gift.	'tasted' (Strong - 1089) figuratively "to experience".
3. having been made *partakers* of the Holy Spirit.	'partakers' (Strong - 3353), means "a sharer" "an associate".
4. *tasted* the good (spoken) word of God, and	'tasted' as in 2 above
5. *tasted* the powers of the world to come.	'tasted' as in 2 above

The above three words were chosen by the Holy Spirit, to describe those who are charged with crucifying "to themselves the Son of God afresh", and so it is impossible to "renew them again to repentance", (v 6). Thus it becomes obvious that such were never saved, never born of God, never the sons of God.

The teaching of Hebrews Chapter 6 depends on the right understanding of these three words used in the verses 4 and 5.

Enlightened:

This is light shining *upon* a person instead of *in* a person. The same word is used in John 1:9, "This was the true light, which shineth upon every man, coming into the world"; that is "the light is come into the world" for the purpose of turning the people to God, and for revealing the response in them, on whom it shined. For example, it shined on Nicodemus and Peter for good, but upon Pilate and Simon the sorcerer (Acts 8:20-24) to their detriment. This is not what happens when a believer comes into salvation, as we find in 2 Corinthians 4:6. "For God, who commanded the light to shine (Strong - No. 2989, "to beam", or "radiate brilliancy") out of darkness, hath shined (same Strong - 2989) *in* (not *on* as with John 1:9) our hearts to give the light (Strong - 5462, 'photismos', ('illumination') of the knowledge of the

"glory of God in the face of Jesus Christ". The persons referred to in Hebrews 6:4 are those *upon* whom the light has shined, but not shined *in* them, to result in their new-birth.

Tasted:

Believers comprising the body of Christ are made to DRINK into one Spirit (I Cor. 12:13). Of course, there is a world of difference between 'tasting' and 'drinking'. Satisfaction is found only in drinking. The Lord Jesus Christ said, "Whoso drinketh of the water that I shall give him shall never thirst" (in no wise thirst for ever, John 4:14). The persons addressed in Hebrews 6:4 had only *tasted,* but never *drunk* – not taken a deep satisfying drink. In other words, they were not born-again. Let us therefore take a closer look at those who only tasted – in whom no deep work of God took place, under the three headings given in Hebrews:

1. *Tasted the heavenly gift (6:4).* The Lord Himself is that gift. "This is life eternal that they might know Thee the only true God and Jesus Christ, whom Thou hast sent." (John 17:3). The mighty works, which have been done in Capernaum, is a taste of that heavenly gift, the Lord Himself. However, "they repented not". Had such mighty works been done in Sodom, it would have remained until this day. (Matt. 11:20, 23).

111

2. *Tasted the good word of God (6:5).* "All bare Him witness and wondered at the gracious words which proceeded out of His mouth" (Luke 4:22). They certainly tasted and agreed the taste was good, but immediately following they "rose up, and thrust him out of the city, and led him unto the brow of the hill whereon their city was built, that they might cast him down headlong" (Luke 4:29). This is nothing but "crucified afresh" as our text in Hebrews, says.

3. *Tasted the powers of the world to come (6:5)* Matthew 8:29 speaks of the judgement in the world to come (John 16:11), already known to the demons. The demons manifested a power of another world, (under world) which was met by the Lord Jesus Christ the very "powers of the world to come". "Even the wind and the waves obey Him".

Partakers:

Partakers of the Holy Spirit (Partaker = "a sharer" or "an associate"). This word is *never* used in relation to a believer in this context. "He (Christ) shall be *in* you" (John 14:17). A believer is *indwelt* by the Holy Spirit (I Cor. 6:19). This was Simon the Sorcerer's problem, who did sorceries or magic (Acts 8:9-24). He partook (associated) in the incident when the Holy Spirit came upon the Samaritans (v.17), but as Peter clearly differentiates between a true believer, and one like Simon, with the words "thou hast neither part nor lot in this matter; for thy heart is not right in the sight of God" (v.21). Remember, Simon was 'baptised' as a Jew (v 13), but did not receive the Holy Spirit (Acts 2:38).

Conclusion

Careful consideration of the above matters should conclusively show that these persons in Hebrews Chapter 6, who "crucify to them-selves afresh the Son of God", were never true believers. This takes the whole ground away for using this against 'backsliders', and those who go back from their profession of faith of the true believers. Hebrews 6:9 continues: "But, beloved, we are persuaded better things of you, and things that accompany salvation, though we thus speak", i.e. about those in verses 4-6, who were not truly the Lord's, but only tasters and not drinkers.

Currently the Pentecostal and Charismatic movements are causing delusions by 'wresting' of these verses 6:4-6, and by wrongly assuming that such a person as described in verse 4 is a true believer. To safeguard against such error, the passage Hebrews 6:7-8 includes a parable (ever heard the word 'parable' before? Mark 4:13), which clearly repeats the principle of fruit bearing.

> *Heb. 6:7* Herbs are the fruits brought forth by the earth with the blessing of God.
>
> *Heb. 6:8* Thorns and briers (where seed fell), were brought forth by the earth and are rejected. They are only fit for burning. It is impossible to renew them again to repentance – for a change of mind (v 6).

A spiritually minded believer will find it easy to apply the true meaning of Hebrews 6:4-8, and to all the other six warning-passages in rightly dividing the Word of God. "Know ye not this parable of the sower? And how then will ye know *all* parables?"

In conclusion, we may comment that anything otherwise would demonstrate a misunderstanding of the correct interpretation of the parable of the sower and so of the Epistle to the Hebrews.

Note: This paper should be considered along side that entitled, "The Difference Between a Believers State and Standing", Paper No: 06-01.

112

The Devil Tempting the Lord

On an enquiry as to the conviction of Dr Billy Graham and his associates with regard to whether Christ was *not able to sin* or *able not to sin* the following reply was received from the London Office of the Billy Graham Evangelistic Association:

"With regard to the question that you asked, Dr Graham believes that as a man Jesus could have sinned – but he did not. If he had been unable, to sin like the rest of us, he could not fully be identified with us. The temptations would have meant nothing at all if he could not have succumbed to them anyway."

This means that the Lord Jesus Christ was like Adam before his fall, and therefore He was able to sin, but did not; while Adam fell, Christ did not.

This paper will help us to understand the plain Scriptural truth, concerning our Lord Jesus Christ, God incarnate who was "made flesh and dwelt among us" (John 1:14), and seeks to answer whether Christ was able to sin like the rest of us. If God incarnate could sin, then our salvation and security are at stake. Some even reason that His divine nature would not allow His human nature to sin! The reply cited above, is a damnable heresy; damnable since it concerns the person of the

blessed Lord Jesus Christ the Son of God, and heresy because it is against God's Word.

The issue here is, whether the Lord Jesus "is *able not to sin*" or "*not able to sin*".

The Scripture says that the Lord Jesus was "led up of the Spirit into the wilderness, to be tempted of the devil". The word 'tempt' leads to misunderstanding. One of the meanings for this word is, "inciting or enticing to evil or to seduce". This always presupposes evil present in some form, the possibility that the person tested, can be enticed and incited to do evil; that in his person there is something which responds or may respond to the evil placed before him. This could never be the case with the Lord. There was no sin, no evil in Him. He is absolutely holy. Therefore the word 'tempt' with the above meaning, can *never* apply to Jesus Christ.

The Greek word *'peirazo'* translated as 'tempt' actually means "to test or try". This word is made use of in John 6:6, where the Lord questioned Philip as to how they would feed the 5000, and "this He said to *prove* him". Again, another such use is in "By faith Abraham, when he was *tried*, offered up Isaac" (Heb. 11:17). All these were *tests of faith* and not temptations to sin. Thus the word 'tempt' means, "put to test", to bring to trial and examination and to compare with a standard. It is in this sense only, that it refers

113

to our Lord. When we say He was tempted, it means, *He was tested to verify as to His PERSON, that He was indeed God.* Satan had met One, whom he could not harm, and the *temptations* proved, and declared that our Lord was the only One who was able to do the work He came to do. The testing was to bring out and establish that He is the pure gold, the Holy one, the Spotless One, the One who alone can do the specific work for which He came, "to put away sin by the sacrifice of Himself" (Heb. 9:26).

Philippians chapter 2 says that Christ Jesus was made in the likeness of men, and became obedient unto death, Whom God has highly exalted. When He took the form of man, He was not tainted by man's fallen nature. He took human nature in wondrous grace, but it was *not fallen nature*, or even flawed nature. His humanity was more than innocent. He was "holy, harmless, undefiled, separate from sinners" and perfect (Heb. 7:26). There was nothing in Him to respond to the evil suggestions of the master-tempter. "Satan cometh and hath nothing in me" (John 14:30).

The Lord's temptation was genuine. It covered all the aspects of His total dependence upon His Father. It was not designed to bring out whether there was any weakness or failure in this perfect Man; but was only to prove and to manifest His *flawless perfection.*

Temptation is not sin; but yielding is. Suffering through temptation will result in victory, not defeat. "He Himself hath suffered being tempted" (Heb. 2:18). Christ suffered being tempted, because Satan who tempted Him was:

1. One of His creatures,

2. A creature who had been the pre-eminent shining cherub,

3. One who had fallen into sin through pride, "I will be like the Most High" (Isa. 14:14),

4. One who tested "The most high" even Christ,

5. One to whom, in a measure, the Lord submitted Himself for testing, and so suffered in that very act.

Satan's suggestions were so contrary to His holy nature, and this added to His sufferings.

In His temptations, Jesus, even as God incarnate never went beyond the limitations of His humanity, proving He was the perfect man by depending upon God's Word, "It is written . . ."

The Lord Jesus employed the Word of God as a weapon, as the sword of the Spirit, evidencing complete trust and dependence on God His Father.

He kept the Father's commandments	This is dependence (John 15:10)
He would not allow Satan to tempt God	This is eschewing doubt. So He quoted Deut. 6:16
Nevertheless He proved to be the dependent Son	This is trust, "I will put my trust in Him" (Heb 2.13)

Satan's suggestions involved self-will, which was foreign to the will of Christ. – "Lo, I come to do *thy* will, O God" (Heb 10:9), thus identifying Himself with God and also as God.

So the last Adam, driven (which means "led by irresistible force") by the Spirit, into the wilderness, faced the assaults of the tempter by the sword of the Spirit, the Word of God, in simple dependence and in subjection to God, gained the victory. The first man Adam, in perfectly ideal circumstances, "crowned with glory and honour" (Ps. 8:5) failed. The last Adam, the second man, is the Lord from heaven (I Cor. 15:45, 47), was in a place of disadvantage, but withstood Satan. Angels ministered to the Lord Jesus, but cherubims and a flaming sword obstructed the way of the first man (Gen. 3:24).

Let us now consider and compare the two Gospel narratives, as recorded in Matthew and Luke.

As to the order given, Matthew narrates the challenge to jump from the top of the Temple as the *second* temptation, and as the last, the offer of all the kingdoms of the world and all their glory as bait, for surrender. Luke records the latter as the second temptation, and the challenge to jump from the Temple pinnacle, as the last.

Matthew's order is the *chronological order,* that is, the order in which they actually took place, climaxing in the offer of the kingdoms of the world, keeping with his portrayal of the King. Consider these verses:

"*Then* the devil taketh Him up into the holy city."

"*Again the* devil taketh Him up into an exceeding high mountain" (Matt. 4:5 & 8).

The words 'then' and 'again', in these verses fix the *time order.* This is also confirmed in that, the Devil did not stay with the Lord further, after he was ordered to flee, "Get thee hence … , then the devil leaveth Him" (Matt. 4:10, 11). This was after the temptation about the world's kingdoms and its glory offered as a reward for worshipping him.

On the other hand, Luke arranges them according to the *thematic order* touching the needs of the body, the soul, and the spirit.

The absolute impeccability of this sinless Man full of compassion is the subject of Luke, setting Satan's request for a spectacular display before men, as the final temptation. Luke has the *moral order* of I John 2:16, thus:

1. "The lust of the flesh" As to BODY

2. "The lust of the eyes" As to SOUL

3. "The pride of life" As to SPIRIT

Stones made bread.

Showed unto Him all the kingdoms.

Cast thyself down . . . He shall give His angels charge, lest thou dash thy foot.

These are highlighted below:

MATTHEW'S GOSPEL (4:1-11) THE CHRONOLOGICAL ORDER	LUKE'S GOSPEL (4:1-13) THE THEMATIC ORDER
If thou be the Son of God, command that these stones be made bread (4:3)	If thou be the Son of God, command this stone that it be made bread (4:3) (Refers to the Physical realm)
Setteth Him on a pinnacle of the temple... if thou be the Son of God, cast thyself down (4:6)	All the power will I give Thee, and the glory of them (4:6). (Relates to the soul, satisfying the ego.)
All these things will I give Thee, *if* thou wilt fall down and worship me (4:9).	If thou be the Son of God, cast Thyself down from hence. (4:9). (Refers to the spirit, implying spiritual subtlety)

On a study of these two Gospels, we are able to arrive at the following:

1. Matthew's Gospel closes with a climax, as the Jewish leaders, mockingly said to Him while He was hanging on the cross: "If thou be the Son of God", and "For He said, I am the Son of God" (Matt. 27:40, 43) touching the claims of His Sonship. While Luke's narration closes with "Art thou the Christ?" (Luke 22:67), as Luke is dealing with the compassionate Son of Man.

2. Matthews Gospel commences Christ's service with a challenge to the Devil over his use of "it is written", wherein the Devil deletes from, and adds to the Word of God. The Lord does so by adding the word *"again"* in His reply, "It is *written again,* thou shall not tempt the Lord thy God" (Matt. 4:7), as given by Matthew. Whereas, Luke omitting 'again', records as "it is said, thou shalt not tempt the Lord thy God" (Luke 4:12). The Lord's 'again' in Matthew is vital in understanding the Lord's rebuke of the Devil, for misquoting and corrupting God's Word.

3. After his third repetition of 'if' the Devil is dismissed with "get thee hence Satan" (Matt 4:10). The basis of the word *'if'* used here for the third time is as a *condition* and not as a *doubt.* "I will give Thee *if thou wilt* fall down and worship me" (Matt. 4:9). In Matthew 16:23 Peter is dismissed for a like ulterior reason, that is, of attempting to dissuade the Lord from going to the cross.

The three temptations are addressed to the Lord in the *three* aspects of His character, as that of *man,* of *Messiah* and of *Son of Man.* These may be viewed in the following tabulation.

Tempted	1.	2.	3.
as	Man	Messiah	The Son of Man
Through	the lust of the flesh (as to body)	the lust of the eyes (as to soul)	the pride of life (as to spirit)
By	stones made bread	showing "unto Him all the kingdoms"	"cast Thyself down" etc,
With	the *evil motive* being	*evil motive* being, "All	the *Devilish motive* of the

to persuade Him to satisfy His own physical need, which He never would (Luke 9:58)	this power and glory . . is delivered unto me". The Devil offers back the usurped power and glory, to the One whose it is and to Whom it will eventually be given.	Deceiver seeking to introduce 'chance' (which is his attractive gambling weapon) "at any time", (into the Divine pathway and His time table). The Devil added these three words "at any time", as if they were actually in the text of the law, giving an impression of divine inspiration, unnoticeable to the general reader.

Christ showed exemplary patience and wonderful use of the written Word of God by answering, "it is *written* ... " being personally responsible to God in making use of the Book of Deuteronomy, which demands obedience and details the privileges that belong to His people, Israel. Three times He quoted from this book, given in the wilderness at the end of the forty years of wanderings, (8:3; 6:13; & 16). At the end of 40 years, Israel needed reminding of God's Word; at the end of the 40 days, Satan needed rebuke from God's word. The Lord quoted from just one book of the law out of five, as David slang one stone from his bag of five (I Sam. 17:40).

The way the Lord answered Satan is nothing but what we find in John 12:49, 50 "The Father which sent me, He gave me commandment what I should say and what I should speak ... as the Father said unto me, so I speak".

What then was the reason that the word 'again' was added to "it is written"? (Matt. 4:7).

The first reason is that, indeed, "it is written again", that is, it *is* written *twice,* the first in Exodus 17:7 and the second in Deuteronomy 6:16. However, even in Exodus 17:7, the stress to be put upon 'again' becomes apparent, when we notice Israelites tempting God at Massah saying, "Is the Lord among us or not"? Thus we realise the significance of Satan's "If thou be the Son of God". Israel was tempting "the Lord thy God", and undeniably the gushing waters from the rock at Horeb (Ex. 17:6), proved "that rock was Christ" (I Cor. 10:4). So did Satan test that Rock, even Christ, who's refreshing Divine Words were like waters to a thirsty soul.

The second reason was, because the Devil had evidently altered the very Word of God, by omission of "in all thy ways", and addition of "at any time", which is clearly, prohibited in Deuteronomy 4:2, being another Scripture from the same book.

This demand to cast Himself down from the Temple pinnacle, involving a spectacular display of His power, was meant discarding the entire revealed prophetic OT programme. Knowing the subject of Psalm 91, Satan deliberately misquoted it. In that Messianic Psalm, the Lord's position is as dwelling in the secret place of the Most High (v 1); Jehovah being his refuge and fortress (v 2), without any fear on earth, when Jehovah is His habitation (vv 5, 9). Consequently there was the promise of complete deliverance (vv 3, 6, 10-12), where the last deliverance refers not to the physical falling from the Temple pinnacle, but to the deliverance from hurt, lest "thou dash thy foot against a stone". "Therefore will I deliver Him: I will set Him on high" (v 14), indicating Christ's resurrection and ascension. Hence the angelic ministration, "angels charge over thee" (v 11), which is certainly spiritual. Here the Lord by adding to God's words, 'again', exposes the misapplication of the text referred to by Satan with the words: "Thou shall not tempt the Lord thy God", challenging Satan in his, altering of the Word of God, for the Lord is verily among us (Ex. 17:7), even Christ the Son of God. This viewed in the context of Deuteronomy 6:24 & 25 would mean that the Lord God's preservation is certain since His commandments will be obeyed by Christ. Thus the Lord rebukes Satan, the god of this world, for dissuading Him (thy God) from obedience to His own Word, reminding him that he was standing before 'thy God' Himself. Here, the Lord's answer to Satan's inducement is two-told:

1. that he must not tempt "thy God" to unrighteously fulfill Psalm 91, and

2. that he must not tempt the Son of God, "the Lord thy God" from obedience to His own word, deceptively trying to prove the truth of Psalm 91:12.

The quotation, "The Lord thy God", is no other than the Lord Jesus Himself, **who was not able to sin**, proving Who He was. Rejection and denial of such a glorious truth, concerning our Lord Jesus is rejection of the "Lord thy God".

It is not without significance to consider the actual words in Psalm 91:11, *omitted* by the Devil, *"to keep thee in all thy ways"*. Why did he omit these words? It is because the ways in which He, the Messiah, will be kept are all the ways of God. "Thy ways", are indeed His very ways, which declare "the determinate counsel and fore-knowledge of

God" as irreversible. This temptation or testing would be nothing but testing and proving Jesus ("Thy God") – to be verily God Himself.

Again, compare the words he *added* to the Psalm 91:12, "at any time". This consideration, "at any time", could never enter into the times and the pathway of the Lord. To "dash thy foot", found in the verse employed by Satan, surely in this context has some reflection upon God's declaration, "It shall bruise thy head, and thou shall *bruise His heel"*, (Gen. 3:15), but not just *dashing the foot* against a stone.

Satan constantly plays the game of chance, bringing uncertainty into the written Word, by omitting or adding a word or phrase from and to the inspired text. When he came to Eve, he said, "hath God said ..." and to Christ "if Thou be the Son of God". Both cast doubt and unbelief. Following this suggestion, Satan misquotes the Word of God, taking it out of context and denying it by misapplication. To Eve he said, "Lest ye die", when God had actually said, "Thou shall surely die" (Gen 2:17 with 3:3). To the Lord the Devil first denies the truth by omission of words and then contradicts by adding more of His own words. This principle of omission and addition is evident in all the modern translations of the Bible.

(Please write to us for the booklet 'Why Not NIV?' and the leaflet "The NIV and GNB - Shocking Expose".)

When verses are pulled out of context, which is a typical ploy of the cultists, one must always be cautious and careful to examine the context. Had the Devil ever seen the verse that follows the one which he referred to? Had he not ever read?

"Thou shalt tread upon the *lion* and the *adder,* (Marg: asp) the young *lion*

118

and the *dragon* shall thou tread under foot." (Psalm 91:13)

The Conqueror of this temptation, would Himself soon tread on this very tempter, Satan, who is the adder and the dragon (Rev. 12:9). He is also a roaring lion (I Pet. 5:8).

How manifestly was our Lord "kept in all His ways"? There was not a single mistake in any of His words or His deeds. The Lord *was* among us of a truth, declaring Himself to be the "the Sent-One" from the Father, as THE Son of God (not *"a son of the gods"* as NIV has in Daniel 3:25), and as the ONE without origin (not "whose *origins are from of old"* as NIV puts Micah 5:2).

Thus we find that God allowed Satan to test the Lord Jesus Christ, and So He was "led by the Spirit into the wilderness", in order to demonstrate to Satan the perfection of the Son of God, the One who is *not able to sin.* And "when the Devil had ended all the temptation" (Luke 4:13), having tempted the Lord, he had demonstrated in all respects, of body, soul and spirit, his impotence to seduce "the second Man", the Lord from heaven (1 Cor. 15:47).

Conclusion

We can now clearly discern that although Christ was tempted "in all points like as we are, *yet without sin"* (Heb. 4:15). *He was tested for testing sake*, to prove His divine character and quality, as one Who was NOT ABLE TO SIN.

The false-accuser the Devil is continuing his age old tactics down the centuries, which he employed on Eve and on our Lord. How easily has he succeeded in duplicating this deception today? The mighty mustard tree with the political birds in its branches (Matt. 13:32), controls the many waters of religion, through the scarlet woman (Rev. 17:2). World-conquest, influence and power are its

objectives. Let us not bow our knees to this system by using 'Bibles' into which have been introduced deletions and additions to God's Word. Our rebuke to all such is, "It is written".

Satan's methods employed in Eden and in the wilderness have spawned numerous false teachings and doctrinal errors, now passing on almost unnoticed as God's Word, resulting in confusion and creating ineffectiveness in the witness of His people.

His method of *adding* and *removing* words, phrases, and verses from the written Word of God, still continues. It is sad to see that the very inspired and eternally established Word of God has been shamefully mutilated again and again by the translators, and committees of modern translation. Over hundred of these publications are being *copy-righted* with a view to financial gain. It is part of Babylon's business, conducted by the present day scholars in earning a living. Ecumenical scholarship is bulldozing ahead with *"dynamic equivalence"* in their modern translations. This is a method of translation, which by its very nature denies both inerrancy and the need for inerrancy. It attempts "thought for thought", not "word for word", as with the actual equivalence of verbal translation. Thus these so called scholars bring out as to what *they thought* God would have meant in the original language. However, God's Word says, "Who hath known the mind of the Lord or who hath been His counsellor", which thought is repeated four times in the Scripture (Job 11:7-9; Ps 36:6; Isa 40:13 & Rom 11:34). Beware of these modern versions and shun them; nay, let us reject them!!

(Please also see "The Divine Accuracy of the Words used in the Holy Scripture". Paper No: 07 - 03.)

"Times"

The word 'Times' occurring in the Scripture, can have at least two meanings, which unless clarified may obscure understanding of God's Word.

In Acts chapter 17 we find this word 'Times' occurring twice. The different meanings of this word are: "A specific *point of time*", as in Acts 17:26, and "A *specific period of time*", as in Acts 17:30.

I "TIMES" (Gr. *'Kairos'* Strong - 2540) "*A Divinely Designed Intervention*"

This word primarily means due measure or due proportion, when used of time, signifies a fixed or definite period or special occasion.

God "hath determined *times* before appointed" (Acts 17:26). Some of the times before appointed, the times of Divine intervention, are as follows:

1. The *universal flood* in Noah's day and the institution of the rainbow which limited another such divine intervention. (Gen. ch. 9).

2. The *confusion of tongues,* from a position of one language to many, in order to stop the furtherance of Cain's religion in the worship of the sun and the principle of "united we stand, divided we fall" – early trade unionism. The people had become un-restrainable (Gen. 11:6), would not spread abroad (Gen. 9:1), but built and dwelt in cities (Gen. 10:10-12) therefore God intervened.

3. The *division of the nations* that resulted from this divine intervention (Gentiles, Gen 10:5 Ham and Shem, 10:20, 31) and by these were the nations divided in the earth after the flood (Gen. 10:32).

4. The *earth itself was divided* into continents during the days of Peleg (Gen. 10:25) as a means of separating the people into nations. In mixing the nations, against God's will, man is currently reaping untold difficulties.

5. The divine *judgement of Sodom and Gomorrah* for the sins of Rom. 1:27. Had this not taken place civilisation would have destroyed itself – (with AIDS or such other thing) – and keeping in mind the royal seed of Gen. 3:15, the sin of Sodom and the violence of Noah's day, may have been one of Satan's ways of defeating God's plan concerning him – the bruising of his own head at Calvary.

6. The *seven years of famine* (Gen. 41:30, 31), was a divine judgement to overthrow the Egyptian king, the heathen god-line, in the death of Pharaoh's firstborn, thus to deliver Israel out of Egypt, and also in their final de-

liverance across the Red Sea (I Cor. 10:1). These were, fore-ordained of God to be an example and for the admonition for the saints of NT period as found in I Cor. 10:11.

7. The *destruction of Jericho* (Joshua ch.6) and the saving of Rahab, the great-great-grandmother of David and thus establishing the Royal line (Mat 1:5).

8. The *appointed day* of judgement (Acts 17:31)

9. The *times of the Gentiles* (Luke 21:24)

(This is dealt with in a separate paper No. 04-02).

In all these judgements, we see a silver line of grace, which brought great blessing. Divine intervention by a God of love, even in judgement, is essential; "Because they have no changes, therefore they fear not God" (Psalm 55:19).

II. "TIMES" (Gr '*Chronos*' Strong - 5550) "*A Continual Chronological Sequence*". This word means, a space of time or interval.

Secondly we have the same word again used: "And the *times* of this ignorance God winked at" (Acts 17:30).

1. "The '*times*' of this ignorance God winked at (Margin 'overlooked')" (Acts 17:30). The meaning of this is very different to the one considered above, and refers to the constant repetition of idol worship ignorantly practised, as the idolaters were not aware that the true God was not made of gold etc., or that they were His offspring.

2. There was nothing epoch making about times that continually recurred as in the above. However, to understand the argument that Paul was using, the two words for 'times' must be well *differentiated*. *The* argument is this:

i. The philosophers of Mars Hill did not acknowledge such a thing as resurrection (Acts 17:18) which is a divine intervention. It implies accountability and that to God, which the philosophers were not willing to acknowledge.

ii. Paul assures them that they are accountable to God, because the day of judgement has already been appointed (Acts 17:31), which would be one of those times of divine intervention, epoch times, this was provable and assurance of the proof was on the grounds that the judge has already been appointed, being already raised from the dead. This reasoning not only gave proof of the resurrection, but proved that divine intervention was still the way in which God dealt with men over accountability. There will be a final day of reckoning and judgement. The basis of this argument is irrefutable. One philosopher acknowledged this to be so, and turned to Christ (Acts 17:34).

The Difference Between OT Verses And Those Quoted In The NT Scripture

Difficulties present themselves, in that many OT quotations appearing in the NT do not agree. We may ask should this be so?

This problem has a relevance, particularly to the quotations taken from the book of Isaiah, in that a complete copy of the Scroll of Isaiah in Hebrew Massoretic Text was recovered in the 1950s, from a cave in Qumran in Palestine, commonly known as "The Dead Sea Scrolls". These Scrolls are dated by experts about 200 to 150 BC and are considered to be the oldest and most accurate manuscript of OT Scrolls available.

Difficulties arise in understanding the particular passages our Lord Jesus read from Isaiah chapter 61 in the Synagogue, as recorded in Luke 4:17, and also the Ethiopian Eunuch, read from the book of Isaiah chapter 53 as in Acts 8:32.

The variations appearing in these NT readings, from that of the OT passages are generally accounted to be been taken directly from the Greek translation of the OT Scriptures, known as 'Septuagint'. This is a well accepted common explanation. (This Greek version of the OT is the translation by the 70 Scribe Scholars – 'septa' meaning 70, and hence 'Septuagint'. The need for this transla-

tion arose because most of the Jews no longer spoke Hebrew, after their Babylonian captivity).

We are not able to confirm or deny this claim. According to one American scholar in Greek and Hebrew, there are internal evidences to show that the Septuagint version was not in existence, until after the NT Scriptures were written. The Greek Faculty of the Edinburgh University are currently examining this claim.

Thus we do not have a direct and relevant answer to this problem. However, what is presented in this Paper, may be of help to our readers, as we trust, this will exalt our Lord Jesus Christ. "The well is deep" (John 4:11) indeed!

Alexander the great, had imposed Greek as the official language throughout his vast empire, the then known world. He had also commanded that *each* Greek word should have *only one meaning*. This is vital to the understanding of the particular slant in the interpretation of Greek words. An example may be cited:

"To see with the *eyes*" *in* not the same as, "The see with the *mind*" (that is to understand).

Thus *two different* Greek words are used in John 20:5 and 8, but are translated in *one* English word, 'saw'. This one word 'saw' obscures the nicety, aptness and the beauty of the Greek text. Could a language with such accuracy, obscure the exactness of the Hebrew OT text? We would infer that it could not be so.

Isaiah 53:7, 8

The following comparisons given of the OT quotations in the NT, it is hoped, will be helpful and enlarge our appreciation of our exalted Lord and His fulfilment of the Scriptures to the very letter:

OT Quotation	NT reiteration word difference *italicised*	Comments and Observations
Isaiah 53:7, 8: "He is brought as a lamb to the slaughter and as a sheep before her shearers is dumb, so He openeth not His mouth."	Acts 8:32: "He was led as a *sheep* to the slaughter; and like a *lamb* dumb before *His shearer,* so opened He not His mouth".	When our Lord fulfilled Isa. 53:7, 8, what actually happened is described in Acts 8:32. Ewe sheep as a type of our Lord, so valuable, so caring for their young, as Luke so graphically states, "Why, what evil hath He done?" (Luke 23:22) was asked of Him for the *third* time. Why demand crucifixion for such a wonderfully caring full-grown sheep?
The above statement is quite normal: Lambs are slaughtered, and ewe sheep are shorn, never making any bleeting, their mouths closed.	The above statement shows what actually happened in the case of our Lord.	Then notice "before *His shearer*", whereas OT is "before *her shearers*", which is simply the Holy Spirit applying the Scripture to the changed circumstances; 'Her' to '*His*', and plural to singular as applicable to our Lord. Then there is also the fact of a lamb shorn, (instead of "ewe-sheep" mentioned by Isaiah) *lambs* generally are not shorn, but as we view the ferocious treatment shown to our Lord at Calvary, it was as if it were shearing a defenceless *lamb.*
Isaiah 53:8: "He was taken from prison and from judgment".	Acts 8:33 "In His *humiliation* His judgment was taken away".	This NT translation, is helpful in regard to the above, the judgment given was, "No fault in this man", which was a true and righteous judgment, given by Pilate – who in desperation as in Matthew 27:24. When he saw that he could prevail nothing, but that rather a tumult was made, he took water and washed his hands before the multitude saying "I am innocent of the blood of this *just* person, *see ye to it*". Indeed *His judgment was taken away,* and He was humiliated beyond measure.

123

Apart from considerations involving the Septuagint, other problems, present themselves. Had Isaiah 53:7, 8 appeared twice in the NT, a comparison would have been very interesting.

Actually there are other OT quotations which appear more than once in the NT, and the careful reader will notice that words have been changed in *each* NT quotation of that one OT verse. One of such most notable spiritual passages concerning Israel's blindness

is mentioned *four times* in the NT, and none of them agree. Normally "God speaketh once, yea twice, yet man perceiveth it not" (Job 33:14). So important is this passage that God has spoken it four times in the NT.

Isaiah 6:9, 10

The passage Isaiah 6:9 & 10 is quoted four times in the NT, as shown below and each time the words differ:

Reference	Verse Quotation	Comments
Matt. 13:15	"For this people's heart is waxed gross, and their ears are dull of hearing, and their eyes they have closed; lest at any time they should see with their eyes, and hear with their ears ... and should be converted and I should heal them."	What *the Jews did.*
John 12:40	"He hath blinded their eyes, and hardened their heart; that they should not see with their eyes, nor understand with their heart, and be converted, and I should heal them."	What *Satan did* to the Jews.
Acts 28:27	"For the heart of this people is waxed gross, and their ears are dull of hearing, and their eyes have they closed; lest they should see with their eyes, and hear with their ears, and understand with their heart and should be converted, and I should heal them."	What had *now happened* to the Jews.
Romans 11:8	"God hath given them the spirit of slumber, eyes that they should not see, and ears that they should not hear; unto this day".	What *God did* to the Jews.

It appears that the Holy Spirit, the Divine Author and Writer, wrote through the Apostles amending the OT quotation suiting to the context of the times of the NT days. Taking the above four NT references serially, the import appears to be the difference in *the action*. None of these four variations seem to rest on the changes of the Septuagint translation, (which should be identical in all the four places) but on the Holy Spirit's intention.

124

Psalms 40:6

So also with Hebrews 10:5: "But a body hast Thou prepared me", which was a quotation from Psalm 40:6 reading: "Mine ears hast Thou opened (or digged)". As there is no apparent similarity between these two statements in either Greek or Hebrew (the OT was written in Hebrew and the NT was written in the Greek), what then, is the explanation?

In seeking to understand this, such an explanation must exalt and not denigrate the Lord and His Word. What are the hall-marks in this particular *change of words?*

1. Hebrews 10:5 are words *spoken by the Lord Himself,* "when He cometh into the world", while Psalm 40:6 is a statement *written before the Lord came* into the world.

2. To have the ear opened or digged may relate to the servant (Ex. 21:5,6; Deut. 15:17), whilst gaining his freedom through serving for six years may show his attachment to his master, by having his ear bored through with an 'aul' and thereafter never leaving his 'master'.

3. Although quoting the OT, a much *larger* consideration was before this Servant, the Lord Jesus Christ. This Servant, in knowing the demands of the will of God, "I come to do Thy will" (Heb. 10:7), knew that His whole body, not just an ear, was demanded of Him, in which to accomplish God's will, "He gave Himself" (Gal. 1:4).

4. Although most of this Psalm 40 was clearly prophetical of the Lord Jesus, that which fell short of Him, is enlarged in Hebrews.

5. Who but the Lord, could stand in such a position, as to enlarge and add to the word of God? Do not such considerations, accord exactly with the whole

purpose of Hebrews? "Hath in these last days spoken unto us *in* Son" (Heb. 1:2).

6. In Matthew chapter five, the Lord amends the OT statements *seven* times with the words: "But I say unto you", which is only His prerogative! (vv. 20, 22, 28, 32, 34, 39, & 44).

Isaiah 11:1

Contextually Isaiah 11:1 looks forward to a millennial day, when the Lord Jesus, as King, will rise to reign over the Gentiles. The Apostle Paul in Romans 15:12, uses it as a verse to support the gospel going out to the Gentiles to confirm the promises made unto the fathers i.e. Abraham, Isaac and Jacob. There is no doubt that in doing so, the Holy Spirit is breathing His words through Paul, and the verses are the inspired word of God. Amen.

A comparison of Isaiah 11:1 and 10 with Romans 15:12, shows that Paul by the Spirit omits the opening words of Isaiah 11:10, "in that day", which refers to the day of the Lord, as the millennium opens. This allows a general use of Isaiah 11:10 in respect of the *Gentiles* and the *Gospel* during the Church age. In other words, we find that the Holy Spirit changes words and quotations from the OT, as it suits Him to fit in with "the eternal purposes" of God (Eph. 3:11). Holy men, like Paul here, wrote as they were moved by the Holy Spirit (II Peter 1:20, 21).

Conclusion

Disagreement between NT quotations of OT verses is NOT necessarily the result of translation into the Greek. The spiritual mind must act here, as a king - since "It is the glory of God to conceal a thing: but the honour of kings is to search out a matter" (Pro. 25:2). To suggest 'discrepancies', is somehow reflecting on the reliability of the Word of God, and would be to act contrary to that of a king.

The Divine Accuracy of the Words Used in the Holy Scripture

"No prophecy of the Scripture is of any private interpretation. For the prophecy came not in old time by the will of man: but holy men of God spake as they were moved by the Holy Ghost" (2 Pet. 1:20, 21). This verse, which speaks of the inspiration of Holy Scripture, should be read along with Jeremiah 36:17, 18 & 32, to understand its real implications. "Tell us now, how didst thou write all these words at his mouth?" Then Baruch answered them, "He pronounced all these words unto me with his mouth, and I wrote them with ink in the book". After king Jehoiakim cut the roll with the pen knife (who was himself cut off from the Lord's royal genealogy, given in Matthew's Gospel) he cast it into the fire. Jeremiah as instructed by God took another roll, in which Baruch wrote all the words, "from the mouth of Jeremiah", as given by the Holy Spirit, that were in the first roll, and there were added besides unto them "many like words" (Jer. 36:32). Here the phrase "many like words" are words of Divine inspiration, similar to those written earlier. The holy men of God who wrote the actual words of God as they were moved by the Holy Spirit, did not understand all that they wrote, as we read, "the prophets have enquired and searched diligently" (I Pet. 1:10-12). Now, for us, it is the Holy Spirit that gives the understanding of what is thus written (I Cor. 2:12, 13) and "He (the Holy Spirit) will guide you into all truth" (John 16:13).

All Scripture is Given by the Inspiration of God

The following facts taken from the Word of God will enable even a simple believer to appreciate the meaning of 2 Peter 1:20, 21. It is not for us, therefore, to *alter, modify, remove or add* any word, to the given inspired Word of God.

The *Original* manuscripts were inspired by God:	"Holy men of God spake as they were moved by the Holy Ghost" (2 Peter 1:20, 21).
Copies of the originals were used as the inspired Holy Scripture:	"From a child thou hast known the Holy Scriptures" (2 Tim 3:15).
Each *letter* in the word is inspired:	"Till heaven and earth pass, one *jot* or one *tittle* shall in no wise pass from the law, till all be fulfilled." (Matt. 5:18).
Each *word* is inspired:	"He saith not 'and to *seeds*' (plural), as of many: but as of one.' and to thy *seed* (singular), which is Christ" (Gal. 3:16).
All words are inspired:	"For I have given unto them the *words* which Thou gavest Me." (John 17:8).
All *tenses* are inspired:	"I *am* the God of Abraham and the God of Isaac and the God of Jacob, (present tense) God is not the God of the dead, but of the living" (Matt. 22:32).
Psalms are considered as law:	"Is it not written in *your law:* I said, Ye are gods" (John 10:34 quoting Psalm 82:6), indicating even a portion of a verse in a Psalm is to be regarded as law, taking its place of authority, equal to and alongside the law of Moses.
All that was to be recorded in the Gospels is the inspirational work of the Holy Spirit:	"He shall bring all things to your remembrance, whatsoever I have said unto you" (John 14:26). So that all that the Lord *'said'* could be recorded, and thus we have four Gospels.
All that was to be penned in the Epistles and in the book of Revelation were also of the Holy Spirit:	"He will guide you into all truth; for he shall not speak of (or from) Himself; but whatsoever He shall hear, that shall He speak; and He will shew you things to come" (John 16:13). ("Things to come" are prophetical, as in the Epistles and in the book of Revelation).

The New Testament Language

It would be profitable to note that words with *double meaning* were never used in the Greek of the New Testament. This is because, each Greek word was made to denote one meaning only, by an edict of the Emperor Alexander the Great. He was about to lose a battle, as his Greek commands, using words with double meanings were misunderstood by his army men, such as:

EIMI : means "to go" and or "to be",

ARCHOMAI: means "to begin" and or "to come",

EGEIRO : means "to awaken" and or "to resurrect".

Since then each NT Greek word has only one meaning, thus God prepared in advance, a language to convey His divine message, clearly and distinctively, without misleading of thoughts or intents.

Modern Translations

The following quotes taken from the Forward and Preface to the 1994 Revised Edition of the Good News Bible, expose the translator's/reviser's presumption, whereby they claim to give the meaning that God wanted the readers to understand:

"The Good News Bible is a new translation which seeks to state clearly and accurately the *meaning* of the original texts ... It attempts to present the biblical *content* and *message*. The aim of this Bible is to give today's readers maximum understanding of the *content* of the original texts."

"The primary concern of the translators was to provide a *faithful translation of the meaning* of the Hebrew, Aramaic, and Greek texts. Their first task was to under-

stand correctly *the meaning of the original.* . . . After ascertaining as *accurately as possible the meaning of the original,* the translators' next task was to express that meaning in a manner and form easily understood by the readers. . . . Consequently there has been no attempt to reproduce in English the parts of speech, sentence structure, word order and grammatical devices of the original languages." (Italics our)

The Preface also states that the revisers were concerned where passages in which the English style was unnecessarily *masculine – oriented.* "In practical terms it means that, where references in particular passages are to both men and women, the revision aims at language that is not exclusively male – oriented. At the same time, however, great care was taken not to distort the historical situation of the male-dominated culture of Bible times".

In the light of what we have seen in 2 Peter 1:20, 21, we leave the readers to consider how the translators/revisers view their own scholastic abilities. Are they not arrogantly displacing the prerogative of the blessed Holy Spirit, Who wrote them?

Was it a Matter of Semantics?

When comparing translations, we often hear people say, "Well, it's only a matter of *semantics!*" What do they mean by this? Possibly, the hearer has never heard before the word 'semantics'. This word means, "Relating to the meanings in languages or relating to connotations of words." Had the Lord Jesus not laid such stress on the importance of a single *jot* or a *title* of the Word of God, (Matt. 5:18; Luke 16:17), it would NOT be possible to fully appreciate the meaning of the prohibition expressed in Revelation 22:18, 19 and the hollowness of "it is only a matter of semantics". A translation must be found faithful to every single word, tense, number,

128

gender etc. of the inspired text. Our understanding of the Godhead is entirely dependent upon *His revelation* of Himself, which in turn is subject to God's *chosen Words.* "For I have given unto them the *words* which Thou gavest Me and they have received them, and have known surely that I came out from Thee and they have believed that Thou didst send Me" (John 17:8).

We need, therefore, to "hold fast the *form* of sound words, in faith and love which is in Christ Jesus" (2 Tim. 1:13). Here the word 'form' means the actual letters that make up these words. The stated intention of the modern Bible translators is to give what they conclude as the general meaning of Hebrew and Greek texts as they understood them, which they term as the *"dynamic equivalent".* This means, they would bring out their own ideas/judgements and translate, "thought for thought" and *not* "word for word", ignoring the accuracy of the *words* chosen by God the Holy Spirit, and thus denying inerrancy. Thus all we have as a result, is the understanding of the translators and their opinion on the text they translate. They adopt a posi-

tion wherein they claim to know and to be able to project what God meant in the original languages. Let God's Word speak to us on this matter: "Who hath known the mind of the Lord or who hath been His counsellor", which is expressed repeatedly in His word. (Psalm 36:6; Isa. 40:13, 14; Rom. 11:34 & 1 Cor. 2:16).

We are to appreciate what our Lord said in John 16:13, concerning the sending of the Holy Spirit, that is, to guide us into all truth and to glorify Him. To say that it is only a matter of semantics, that is, relating to the meaning or connotations of words used in the original languages ignores the very purpose for which the Holy Spirit is given to us, that is of guiding us into all truth even the objective of glorifying Christ. Who can deny that the very opposite has been the result of these modem translations and revisions? The following comparative table of the NIV and the revised 1994 GNB verses, with that of the Authorised King James version, will clearly reveal how much these modern translations have lowered our Lord, instead of glorifying and exalting Him.

Authorized (King James) Version	Good News Version (1994 Edition)	New International Version
Gen *3:15* And I will put enmity between thee and the woman, and between thy *seed* and her seed;	*Gen. 3:15* I will make you and the woman hate each other; her offspring and yours will always be enemies.	**Gen.** *3:15* And I will put enmity between you and the woman, and between your offspring and hers;
Prov 8-22 The Lord *possessed* me in the beginning of his *way,* before his works of old.	*Prov. 8:22* "The Lord created me first of all, the first of his works, long ago.	*Prov.* *8:22* "The Lord brought me forth at the first of his works, before his deeds of old;
Isa. 7:14 Behold, *a virgin* shall conceive, and bear a son, and shall call his name Immanuel.	*Isa. 7:14* A young woman who is pregnant will have a son and will name him 'Immanuel.' (see also Luke 1:27)	*Isa. 7:14* The virgin will be with child and will give birth to a son, and will call him Immanuel.

129

Authorized (King James) Version	Good News Version (1994 Edition)	New International Version
Dan. 3:25 the form of the fourth is like *the Son of God.*	*Dan. 3:25* the fourth one looks like an angel."	*Dan. 3:25* the fourth looks like a son of the gods."
Micah 5:2 yet out of thee shall he come forth... whose *goings forth* have been from of old, from *everlasting.*	*Micah 5:2* but out of you I will bring a ruler for Israel, whose family line goes back to ancient times."	*Micah 5:2* *out* of you will come for me one who will be ruler over Israel, whose origins are from of old, from ancient times."
Matt. 1:25 And knew her not till she had brought forth her *firstborn* son: and he called his name Jesus.	*Matt. 1:25* But he had no sexual relations with her before she gave birth to her son. And Joseph named him Jesus.	*Matt. 1:25* But he had no union with her until she gave birth to a son. And he gave him the name Jesus.
Matt. 8:2 And, behold, there came a leper and *worshipped* him saying *Lord.*	*Matt. 8:2* Then a man suffering from a dreaded skin disease came to him, knelt down before him, and said, "Sir,	*Matt. 8:2* A man with leprosy came and knelt before him and said, "Lord,
Matt. 27:24 I am innocent of the blood of this *just* person:	*Matt. 27:24* "I am not responsible for the death of this man!	*Matt. 27:24* "I am innocent of this man's blood,"
Luke 2:33 And *Joseph* and his mother marvelled	*Luke 2:33* The child's father and mother were amazed	*Luke 2:33* The child's father and mother marvelled
Luke 23:42 And he said unto Jesus, *Lord,* remember me when thou comest into thy kingdom.	*Luke 23:42* And he said to Jesus, "Remember me, Jesus, when you come as King!"	*Luke 23:42* Then he said, "Jesus, remember me when you come into your kingdom."
John 6:69 And we believe and are sure that thou art that *Christ, the Son of the living God.*	*John 6:69* And now we believe and know that you are the Holy One who has come from God."	*John 6:69* We believe and know that you are the Holy One of God."
John 9:35-36 Dost thou believe on the Son of God? He answered and said. Who is he? *Lord that* I might believe on him?	*John 9:35-36* "Do you believe in the Son of Man?" The man answered, Tell me who he is, sir, so that I can believe in him!"	*John 9:35-36* "Do you believe in the Son of Man?" "Who is he, sir?" the man asked "Tell me so that I may believe in him."

130

Authorized (King James) Version	Good News Version (1994 Edition)	New International Version
1 Cor. 15:47 The first man is of the earth, earthy; the second man is the *Lord from* heaven.	*1 Cor. 15:47* The first Adam, made of earth, came from the earth; the second Adam came from heaven.	*1 Cor. 15:47* The first man was of the dust of the earth, second man from heaven.
Col. 1:14 In whom we have redemption *through his blood,* even the forgiveness of sins:	*Col. 1:14* by whom we are set free, that is, our sins are forgiven.	*Col. 1:14* in whom we have redemption, the forgiveness of sins.
1 Tim. 3:16 And without controversy great is the mystery of godliness: *God* was manifest in the flesh,	*1 Tim. 3:16* No one can deny how great is the secret of our religion: He appeared in human form,	1 *Tim. 3:16* Beyond all question, the mystery of godliness is great: He appeared in a body,
Titus *1:2 God, that cannot lie,*	***Titus 1:2*** God, who does not lie,	***Titus 1:2*** God, who does not lie,
Heb. 1:5 Thou art my son, this day *have I begotten thee?*	**Heb. 1:5** "You are my Son; today I have become your Father."	*Heb.1:5* "You are my Son, today I have become your father"?

The G.N.B. and N.I.V. also *completely* omit: Matt. 17:21, 18:11, 23:14; Mark 7:16, 9:44, 9:46, 11:26, 15:28 ; Luke 17:36, 23:17; John 5:4; Acts 8:37, 15:34, 24:7, 28:29 and Rom. 16:24.

Semantics Employed by the Holy Spirit

With further reference to 'semantics', the modern Bible translators have taken upon themselves to change and alter the accurate and definite words used in the inspired Word of God, to accord with what they consider God meant With the deviousness of the human mind, it would be thus easy to change doctrine, as modern translations plainly reveal. On the other hand, various expressions are found in the inspired Word, wherein semantics employed by the Holy Spirit, reveal and guide us into all truth. See for instance the expressions "The Word made flesh" and "The Word of God". They are in a way semantic, and thus they should be appreciated and understood in their right perspective. We shall now try to express this aspect of truth found in the Word of God, and so be guided into Divine truth.

THE WORD OF GOD
is quick and powerful . . .
a discerner of the thoughts and intents
of the heart.
Neither is there any creature that is not
manifest in

HIS SIGHT,
but all things are naked and opened unto

THE EYES OF HIM
with Whom we have to do (Heb. 4:12-13).

This verse identifies the *Word of God* with the *Lord Himself.* As the Lord sees and discerns the hearts of men (Rom. 8:27), so does the Word of God. God reveals the thoughts and intents of our hearts, as we read His

131

Word. The eyes of the Lord look deep into the hearts of men, through His Word. This characteristic of God's Word has the *three-way* manifestation, as found in the above text:

The INCARNATE WORD
(The Lord Jesus Christ), through

The WRITTEN WORD
(The Holy Scripture), speaks out from

The PREACHED WORD,
by the Holy Spirit

The above three-fold aspect is borne out by numerous texts from the Word of God, clearly manifesting that every word is God inspired. They are God breathed. (2 Pet. 1:20, 21).

The following tables reveal some of these similarities. The first tabulation deals with THE WORD MANIFEST IN FLESH and THE WRITTEN WORD. The second deals with similarities attributed to CHRIST and also to THE HOLY SCRIPTURE. These tabulations underline, Hebrews 4:12, as above quoted, and refer *both* to the LIVING WORD and to the WRITTEN WORD. The following tabulated summary will assist us in perceiving how the Holy Spirit guides us into all truth, with His words of wisdom (1 Cor. 1:24). This He has accomplished by comparing spiritual things with spiritual in the Word of God. If a translation, in any way, disagrees with another verse of the Holy Scripture, it must, therefore, be spurious, and be rejected. A comparison given on page 4 of the NIV and the (revised!) GNB will illustrates this most crucial point and we trust, act as a warning to all. Do not let them rob you of your inheritance of an uplifted glorious LORD, expressed in words taught of the Holy Spirit.

TABLE- 1

"THE WORD MANIFEST IN FLESH"

Compared and identified with

"THE WRITTEN WORD"

THE WORD MANIFEST IN FLESH		THE WRITTEN WORD	
His name is called THE WORD OF GOD	Rev. 19:13	They pressed upon Him to hear THE WORD OF GOD.	Luke 5:1
The *Prince* of PEACE.	Isa. 9:6	The *Gospel* of PEACE.	Rom. 10:15
Jesus said "No man cometh unto the Father, but BY ME".	John 14:6	Make me to go in the PATH of thy COMMANDMENTS.	Ps. 119:35
Jesus saith unto him, I am THE WAY.	John 14:6	Teach me, O LORD, the WAY OF *Thy statutes*.	Ps. 119:33

THE WORD MANIFEST IN FLESH		THE WRITTEN WORD	
I am ... the TRUTH.	John. 14:6	*Thy Word* is TRUTH.	John. 17:17
Christ – Full of grace and TRUTH,	John. 1:14	All *Thy commandments* are TRUTH.	Ps. 119:151
These things saith *He* that is TRUE.	Rev. 3:7	The *Judgements* of the Lord are TRUE.	Ps. 19:9
Jesus Christ. This is the true God and eternal LIFE.	1 John. 5:20	Holding forth the *Word* of LIFE.	Phil. 2:16
A Bone of *Him* shall not be BROKEN.	John.19:36	*The Scripture* cannot be BROKEN.	John. 10:35
I am the Living Bread . . . if any man eat of *this Bread* he shall LIVE for ever.	John 6:51	Man shall not LIVE by bread alone, but by *every Word of God.*	Luke 4:4
With *Thee* is the FOUNTAIN OF LIFE	Ps. 36:9	The *Law* . . . is a FOUNTAIN OF LIFE.	Pro. 13:14
Jesus said, I am the LIGHT of the world.	John. 8:12	"*Thy Word* is a LIGHT unto my path".	Ps. 119:105
The *Life* was the LIGHT.	John. 1:4	The *Law* is LIGHT.	Pro. 6:23
Thou art my LAMP, O Lord.	2 Sam. 22:29	Thy *Word* is a LAMP unto my feet.	Ps. 119:105
I, saith the Lord, will be unto her a wall of FIRE.	Zech. 2:5	Is not My *word* like as a FIRE? saith the Lord.	Jer. 23:29
The *light of Israel* shall be for a FIRE.	Isa. 10:17	I will make *My Words* in thy mouth FIRE.	Jer. 5:14
Unto you which believe, *He* is PRECIOUS.	1 Pet. 2:7	Exceeding great and PRECIOUS *Promises.*	2 Pet. 1:4
My beloved is.... the chiefest among ten THOUSAND	Song 5:10	The *Law of Thy mouth* is better unto me than THOUSANDS of gold and silver.	Ps. 119:72
His Mouth is most SWEET.	Song 5:16	How SWEET are *Thy Words* unto my taste.	Ps.119:103

THE WORD MANIFEST IN FLESH		THE WRITTEN WORD	
His Name shall be called WONDERFUL	Isa. 9:6	*Thy Testimonies* are WONDERFUL.	Ps. 119:129
Christ, the POWER OF GOD.	1 Cor. 1:24	The *Gospel* of Christ is the POWER OF GOD.	Rom. 1:16
Lord, "*Thou* art GOOD and doest GOOD.	Ps. 119:68	GOOD is the *Word of the Lord.*	Isa. 39:8
Ye have known *Him* that *is* FROM THE BEGINNING.	1 John 2:13	*Thy* Word is true FROM THE BEGINNING.	Ps. 119:160
From everlasting to EVERLASTING *Thou* art God.	Ps. 90:2	The righteousness of Thy *Testimonies* is EVERLASTING.	Ps. 119:144
Thy throne O God, is FOR EVER AND EVER.	Heb. 1:8	Thy *Testimonies*. . . Thou hast founded them FOR EVER.	Ps. 119:152
The *Lord* shall ENDURE for ever.	Ps. 9:7	The *Word of the Lord* ENDURETH for ever.	1 Pet. 1:25
Christ ABIDETH for ever.	John 12:34	The *Word* of God . . . ABIDETH for ever.	1 Pet. 1:23
Worship *Him* that LIVETH for ever.	Rev. 4:10	The *Word of God* LIVETH for ever	1 Pet. 1:23
A Kingdom which. . ."shall STAND FOR EVER"	Dan. 2:44	The *Word of God* shall STAND FOR EVER.	Isa. 40:8
THE STONE, "on whomsoever it shall fall, it will grind him to powder".	Luke 20:18	Is not *my Word*. . . saith the Lord, like a HAMMER that breaketh the rock in pieces?	Jer. 23:29
Christ "A STUMBLING Stone."	Rom. 9:33	Even to them which STUMBLE at the *Word.*	1 Pet. 2:8
Lo, *I am* with you ALWAY, even unto the end of the world. Amen	Matt. 28:20	Thy *Commandments* . . . are EVER WITH ME.	Ps. 119:98
Christ may DWELL in your hearts by faith.	Eph. 3:17	Let the *Word* of Christ DWELL in you richly.	Col. 3:16
Christ said, "ABIDE in me, and I IN YOU".	John 15:4	If . . . my *Words* ABIDE IN YOU.	John 15:7
Hereby we know that *He* ABIDETH in us.	1 John 3:24	The *Word* of God ABIDETH in you.	1 John 2:14

THE WORD MANIFEST IN FLESH		THE WRITTEN WORD	
Christ was called, "FAITHFUL and True".	Rev. 19:11	Thy *Testimonies* . . . are very FAITHFUL.	Ps. 119:138
Out of *His Mouth* goeth a sharp SWORD.	Rev. 19:15	*The Word of God* . . . is sharper than any two edged SWORD.	Heb. 4:12
The *Lord* TRIETH the right-eous.	Ps. 11:5	The *Word* of the Lord TRIED HIM.	Ps. 105:19
Christ a "TRIED Stone".	Isa. 28:16	The *Word* of the Lord is TRIED.	Ps. 18:30

TABLE – 2

SIMILARITIES OF WORK ATTRIBUTED TO

CHRIST AND TO THE WORD OF GOD

WORK ATTRIBUTED TO CHRIST		WORK ATTRIBUTED TO HOLY SCRIPTURE	
"Whosoever is BORN of God"	1 John 5:18	Born . . . by the *word* of God	1 Pet. 1:23
BEGOTTEN us . . by . . *Jesus Christ.*	1 Pet. 1:3	BEGOTTEN you through *the Gospel.*	1 Cor. 4:15
The *Son* QUICKENETH whom He will.	John 5:21	*Thy Word* hath QUICKENED me.	Ps. 119:50
You hath *He* QUICKENED who were dead.	Eph. 2:1	*Thy Precepts* . . . with them thou hast QUICKENED me.	Ps. 119:93
He that *eateth* me, even he shall LIVE by me.	John 6:57	Desire the sincere milk of *The Word,* that ye may GROW thereby	1 Pet. 2:2
Christ hath made us FREE	Gal. 5:1.	The *Truth* shall make you FREE	John 8:32
The Blood of Jesus Christ . . . CLEANSETH us from all sin.	1 John 1:7	Ye are CLEAN through the *Word,* which I have spoken.	John 15:3
Christ "is able also to SAVE them to the uttermost that come unto God by Him".	Heb. 7:25	Receive . . . the engrafted *Word,* which is able to SAVE your souls.	James 1:21

WORK ATTRIBUTED TO CHRIST		WORK ATTRIBUTED TO HOLY SCRIPTURE	
SANCTIFIED in *Christ Jesus.*	1 Cor. 1:2	SANCTIFIED by the *Word of God* and prayer.	1 Tim. 4:5
SANCTIFIED through the offering of the body of *Jesus Christ* once for all.	Heb. 10:10	SANCTIFY them through THY TRUTH. Thy *Word* is truth.	John. 17:17
Christ Jesus who of God is made unto us WISDOM.	1 Cor. 1:30	The *Holy Scriptures* . . . able to make thee WISE unto salvation.	2 Tim. 3:15
"And He HEALED them'.	Matt. 4:24	He sent His *Word* and HEALED them.	Ps. 107:20
Striving according to *His Working* which WORKETH in me mightily	Col. 1:29	The *Word of God* which effectually WORKETH also in you that believe.	1 Thess. 2:13
The *Lord Jesus Christ* . . . shall JUDGE the quick and the dead.	2 Tim. 4:1	*The Word* that I have spoken . . . shall JUDGE him. .	John 12:48
I will go . . . unto *God,* my exceeding JOY.	Ps. 43:4	*Thy Word* was unto me the JOY and rejoicing of my heart.	Jer. 15:16.
"The Word of our God shall stand for ever." Isaiah 40:8.			

Genesis Finds its Compliment in Revelation

The Bible, in its object as a whole, wonderfully presents to us God's glorious revelation of His essential fullness, and the manifestation of all that He is. It brings back into that enjoyment of Him and His fullness, those who are made partakers of His nature and are made capable of comprehending and loving His counsels. How all this began and how it was wonderfully and beautifully achieved is recorded in its first and last book.

Genesis is the book of beginnings and Revelation makes a splendid finish to the Divine library, inspired of God.

Genesis has a character of its own, and as the beginning of the Book of books, presents to us all the great elementary principles which find their development in the history of the relationship of God with man. As such Genesis is the *seed-plot* of the whole Bible, and it is essential to the true understanding of its every other part. It is the foundation on which the Divine Revelation rests, and on which it is built up. It is not only the foundation of all truth, but it enters into and forms part of all subsequent inspiration.

Revelation is the *grand-finale* of His Holy Writ, and the completion of the Canon. It deals with the future events, unfolds the matters previously hidden and contains Christ's final message to the church as well as to the world of men. It is the last book of grace. There is no further revelation.

There are two books in the Bible which the great enemy of mankind hates. Satan has used all his energy to discredit and they are Genesis and Revelation. He has attempted to overthrow Genesis by attacks of scientists and other higher critics, and Revelation by persuading men that it is too mysterious and dreamy. Why this his dislike? Because they both prophesy his downfall and doom – Genesis tells us *Who* would bring this about, and Revelation details *how* it will be accomplished.

If Genesis contains the seed-plot of the Bible, then Revelation shows its harvest in a grand scale. There is a striking balance which exists between the books of Genesis and Revelation.

In Genesis there is a garden, which is the home for man, in Revelation there is a City, the home for His people. All the problems of life opened first to divine scrutiny in Genesis, are balanced at the end of Revelation with the unfolding of the new heavens and the new earth, wherein dwells righteousness. In Genesis the first man, Adam falls; in Revelation the last Adam – Jesus Christ the Lord – reigns as King of kings and Lord of lords. In Genesis there is the first grim appearance of that great enemy Satan, in Revelation there is his final doom. In Genesis there is the inauguration of sorrow and suffering, we hear the first sob and see the first tear drops; in Revelation there is no more sorrow and no more pain, and all tears are wiped away. In Genesis we hear the pronouncement of the curse, which falls because of sin, in Revelation we read, "There shall be no more curse". In Genesis we see man driven out from the garden and the tree of life, in Revelation we see him welcomed back, with the tree of life at his disposal; and the first Adam and Eve represented by the last Adam, Christ, and the church His spotless bride in paradise.

The following tabulation explains how Genesis finds its compliment in the book of Revelation:

GENESIS	APOCALYPSE
1. Genesis, the book of the beginning.	1. Apocalypse, the book of the end.
2. The Earth created (1:1)	2. The Earth passed away (21:1)
3. Satan's first rebellion.	3. Satan's final rebellion (20:3, 7-10).
4. Sun, moon and stars for Earth's government (1:14-16)	4. Sun, moon and stars, connected with Earth's judgment (6:13; 8:12; 16:8).
5. Sun to govern the day (1:16).	5. No need of the sun (21:23).
6. Darkness called night (1:5)	6. "No night there" (22:5).
7. Waters called seas (1:10)	7. "No more sea" (21:1).
8. A river for Earth's blessing (2:10-14)	8. A river for the renewed Earth (22:1, 2).
9. Man in God's image (1:26).	9. Man headed by one in Satan's image (13).
10. Entry of sin (3).	10. Development and end of sin (21, 22).
11. Curse pronounced (3:14-17).	11. "No more curse" (22:3).
12. Death entered (3:19).	12. "No more death" (21:4).
13. Cherubim, first mentioned in connection with man (3:24).	13. Cherubim finally mentioned in connection with man (4:6).
14. Man driven out from Eden (3:24).	14. Man restored (22).
15. Tree of life guarded (3:24).	15. "Right to the Tree of life" (22:14).
16. Sorrow and suffering enter (3:17).	16. No more sorrow (21:4).
17. Man's religion, art, and science, resorted to for enjoyment, apart from God (4)	17. Man's religion, luxury, art and science, in their full glory, judged and destroyed by God (18).

GENESIS	APOCALYPSE
18. Nimrod, a great rebel and king, and *hidden* anti-God, the founder of Babylon (10:8, 9).	18. The Beast, the great rebel, a king, and *manifested* anti-God, the reviver of Babylon (13-18).
19. The flood from God to destroy an evil generation (6-9).	19. A flood from Satan to destroy an elect generation (12:15, 16)
20. The Bow, the token of God's covenant with the Earth (9:13).	20. The Bow, betokening God's remembrance of His covenant with the Earth (4:3; 10:1).
21. Sodom and Egypt, the place of corruption and temptation (13, 19).	21. Sodom and Egypt again: (spiritually representing Jerusalem) (11:8).
22. A confederacy against Abraham's people overthrown (14).	22. A confederacy against Abraham's seed overthrown (12).
23. Marriage of first Adam (2:18-23).	23. Marriage of last Adam (19).
24. A bride sought for Abraham's son (Isaac) and found (24).	24. A Bride made ready and brought to Abraham's Son (Jesus Christ) (19:9). See Matt. 1:1.
25. Two Angels acting for God on behalf of His people (19).	25. Two witnesses acting for God on behalf of His People (11).
26. A promised seed (Israelites) to possess the gate of his enemies (22:17).	26. The promised seed (Jesus Christ) coming into possession (11:15-18).
27. Man's dominion ceased and Satan's begun (3:24).	27. Satan's dominion ended and man's restored (20, 22).
28. The old serpent causing sin, suffering, and death (3:1).	28. The old serpent bound for 1,000 years (20:1-3).
29. The doom of the old serpent pronounced (3:15).	29. The doom on the old serpent executed (20:10).
30. Sun, moon, and stars, associated with Israel (37:9).	30. Sun, moon, and stars associated again with Israel (12).

A Comparison of Moses as a Type of Christ in Divine Service, Involving Seven Mountains

"A Prophet like unto Me." -- Moses in Deuteronomy 18:18

THE SEVEN MOUNTAINS	MOSES – A PROPHET	CHRIST – AS PROPHET
The Mountain of Commission	The mountain of God–Horeb (Ex. 3:1, 2) Israel, the bush that burned and yet could not be consumed, was to Moses a revelation of God's intentions for His people (we believe "The Bush" to be Israel and not Christ.)	Christ required no commissioning; but commissioned others and empowered them. (Mark 3:13-19) Coming down from the mountain Christ was rejected by others. (Mark 3:22)
	"Moses whom they refused" (Acts 7:35). The Law given through Moses was broken.	"My words shall not pass away"(Mark 13:31)
The Mountain of Intercession.	Jehovah-Nissi (Ex. 17:9, 15). This revealed to Moses, his dependence on God, and of his utter inability and weakness. At this mount God revealed to Moses, Israel's total dependence on Him (Ex. 17:11)	Christ departed into the mountain (Mark 6:46; John 6:15) revealing His commission as well as His relationship with the Father (Heb. 1:5; Ps. 2:7; 2 Sam. 7:14)
	"If thy presence go not with me" (Ex. 33:15) expresses Moses' dependency and his incompetence.	"Glorify thy Son" (John 17:1) expresses the Son's equality with the Father and the certainty of His request being fulfilled.

THE SEVEN MOUNTAINS	MOSES –A PROPHET	CHRIST - AS PROPHET
The Mountain of Legislation	Given at Mount Sinai (Ex. 19:2, 3), Exodus and Leviticus contain the basic laws by which Israel was regulated. To Moses' credit, the laws of the tabernacle were faithfully copied by him (Ex. 40:19, 21, 23, 25, 27, 29 & 32).	The sermon on the mount, reveals the laws of the Kingdom, to be established when the King returns (Matt. 24:31). (Nevertheless, the principles enunciated therein are relevant in many respects to the church.)
	Moses as a servant obeyed the law and taught His people (Heb. 3:2-5).	The Son (Heb. 3:6) as the King enunciated these laws and fulfilled them all (Matt. 5:17).
The Mountain of Instruction.	Moses as a servant needed instructions (Ex. 24:12-18). The passage Ex. 40:17-32, traces back his obedience seven times "as the Lord commanded Moses" to those instructions detailed in Exodus chapters 25 to 27 & 30.	But Christ, as Son (Heb. 3:6), needed no instruction for He was the Author and Finisher (Heb. 12:2). Nevertheless, in the Mount of Olives (Matt. 24:3) and in the mountain in Galilee, (Matt. 28:16) He instructed His disciples
The Mountain of Communion and Revelation.	In Mount Sinai, Moses learned the meaning of the name of the Lord (Ex. 34:5). As "The Lord, the Lord God, merciful and gracious, long suffering and abundant in goodness and truth," (v.6). Moses received this - a revelation.	In the Mount of Transfiguration, Christ gave a revelation of Himself, (the abounding grace of God) in the presence of the Law (Moses), and the prophets (Elijah), which He came to fulfil. (Matt. 17:1-9 and Matt. 5:17).
The Mountain of Contemplation.	On Mount Nebo (Deut 34:1, 4). "This is the land which I swear unto Abraham unto Isaac and unto Jacob... but thou shalt not go over there". Moses was not permitted to enter into the Promised Land.	On a Mount in Galilee (Matt. 28:16-20). "All authority is given unto me in heaven and in earth. Go ye therefore... teach...baptize..." Thus His presence would be with them always, even unto the end of the age of Grace.

THE SEVEN MOUNTAINS	MOSES –A PROPHET	CHRIST - AS PROPHET
The Mountain of Completion.	In Mount Nebo (Deut. 34:1) Moses work was incomplete.	In the Mount of Transfiguration, Moses acknowledged Christ would complete His work by accomplishing His own exodus. He and Elijah talked with Christ (Matt. 17:3). They spoke of His decease (exodus), which he should accomplish at Jerusalem (Luke 9:30).
	He could not go into the land. He failed to accomplish and complete his mission.	Christ completed His mission. "It is finished".

NOTE:

It will be appreciated from the above that the comparison between Moses and Christ found in Deuteronomy 18:18, "A prophet like unto me", was *really as a vehicle of revelation.* However, Christ as 'Son', revealed the Father, and His purposes in and through Himself (Luke 10:22).

Moses as a prophet, taught His people, having been given revelation from God, particularly on Mount Sinai. However he was above all other prophets. Consider very carefully, Numbers 12:6-8.

Christ was the Prophet and in Him was the fountain of Truth. "Ye have heard it was said by them of old time" – "But I say unto you" (Matt. 5:20, 22, 28, 32, 34, 39 & 44), seven times He repeated this and altered what was said of old.

Christ is the Author and Finisher of our faith (Heb. 12:2), and He is the Truth (John 14:6). Moses was only a *servant* but Christ *is the Son.* See Heb. 3:5, 6.

The Aaronic Priesthood and
The Great High Priesthood of Christ

AARON	CHRIST
1. Aaron was called of God (Heb. 5:4)	Christ is forever high Priest, confirmed by God's oath, therefore Heb. 5:10 called (i.e., "Rather be saluted") of God (Heb. 7:20; Ps. 110:4)
2. Aaron: Simply *one* of the many High Priests.	Christ: is the *only* Great High Priest. (Heb. 4:14)
3. He was taken from among men – He had no background as a Priest (Heb. 5:1).	This cannot be applied to Christ. He has an *everlasting* Priesthood.
4. He was ordained for men in things pertaining to God. ('Ordained' meaning, "to designate or constitute") (Heb. 5:1).	While priests are constituted for this purpose, Christ is God Himself (John 10:30).
5. He was to offer both gifts and sacrifices. His work was *unfinished* (Heb. 5:1).	Christ offered one sacrifice for sins *forever*, and sat down. (Heb. 10:12)
6. Who can have compassion on the ignorant and on them that are out of the way, but was unable to give grace. (Heb. 5:2)	Christ is able to give grace in time of need, which Aaron could not give. (Heb. 4:16)
7. For that He himself was compassed with infirmity – He himself needed grace. (Heb. 5:2)	Does not apply to Christ, as He is sinless (Heb. 7:26).
8. And by reason thereof he ought, as for the people, so also for himself, to offer for sins. (Heb. 5:3)	Christ, who did no sin, neither was guile found in His mouth. (I Pet. 2:22; Heb. 9:14).

Note: The correct meaning of Heb 5:10 is: "Saluted of God as High Priest according to the order of Melchisedec."

The Seven Parables of the Kingdom

(Matthew 13)

Each of the four Gospels presents different aspects of the Lord Jesus Christ.

Matthew – Presents the *King* of God's chosen Nation Israel, "The King of the Jews" and sets out to prove that Jesus is son of David – that promised Messiah.

Mark – With no genealogy, or birth details, presents *Jehovah's Servant,* moving day by day, fulfilling God's will. Note the repetition of the words: 'immediately', 'forthwith' and 'straightway' etc., marking His *continuous* service.

Luke – Presents the compassionate *Son of Man,* in just five chapters (4:14 to 9:51) condensing His three years of ministry, while up to 4:13, we have the details before He entered His public ministry. Chapter 10 onwards give the details of His ministry of His last days before his crucifixion, and also after His resurrection.

John – Presents the *Son of God,* drawing His Deity to the attention of the Jews.

We would therefore rightly expect that matters relating to the King and His Kingdom would appear most explicitly in the Gospel according to Matthew.

The Gospel According to Matthew

Matthew's Gospel presents the Lord Jesus Christ to the Jewish people as their promised Messiah. The Holy Spirit, through Matthew, a tax-collector, a reject of his own nation, presents to the nation Jesus as their King, and thereafter from chapter 11 records the nation's rejection of her King.

Before the first of the five great discourses of our Lord commences in Chapter 5, God allows us to hear seven voices of confirmation, that without any doubt or rival claims, Jesus of Nazareth has the title to the Throne. He is indeed the rightful King of the Jews as follows:

1. The voice of genealogy	The right line (1:1-17)
2. The voice of the Angel	The right mother (1:18-25)
3. The voice of the star	The right City – Bethlehem (2:1-12)
4. The voice of the Prophets	The right Root – The NETZER (Hebrew word "Netzer" means "a branch" (2:13-23)
5. The voice of the Forerunner	The right words (3:1-12)
6. The voice of His Father	My Beloved Son (3:13-17)
7. The voice of the King Himself	It is written (4:1-11)

After the forerunner is put in prison, the King begins His ministry by leaving Nazareth for good, and taking up residence at Capernaum. There His opening message is: "Repent, for the Kingdom of heaven is at hand". (4:12-17).

Three out of the five of His great discourses, take place after He was rejected as detailed in Chapters 11 and 12. Words such as "When Jesus had finished these sayings" follow each of these five discourses.

1.	The Laws of the Kingdom (5:1 to 7:27)	"When Jesus had *ended* these sayings" (7:28)
2.	The Directions to the Servants of the Kingdom (10:5-42)	"When Jesus had *made an end* of commanding His twelve disciples" (11:1)
3.	The Panoramic and Prophetic outline of the Kingdom (13:1-53).	"When Jesus had *finished* these parables" (13:53)
4.	The basis of humility and that of forgiveness for the citizens of the Kingdom (18:1-35)	"When Jesus *had finished* these sayings" (19:1)
5.	The manifestation of the King and the setting up of His Kingdom (24:1 to 25:46)	"When Jesus had *finished* all these sayings" (26:1)

145

Matthew Chapter 13
Analysed

There are eight parables in Chapter 13, seven of which form a panoramic and prophetic outline of the Kingdom.

But why parables? Parables are the *effective means* of conveying spiritual truths to His people, yet *withholding those truths from those who would not believe,* "to them it is not given" (v.11), thus fulfilling the Scripture (Isaiah 6:9-10). The use of parables is foretold in Psalms 78:2.

The "parable of the Sower," which contains the *divine principles* operating over the centuries, during the *whole period* of the Kingdom of Heaven, is followed by seven parables, each commencing with the words, "the kingdom of heaven is like". They are:

1. The good seed and the tares (vv. 24-30)	These were spoken to the multitudes (v 2, 36) and have an evil aspect, and speak of the outward view and status of that Kingdom.
2. The grain of mustard seed (vv. 31-32)	
3. Leaven hidden in three measures of meal. (v.33)	
4. Treasure hid in the field (v. 44)	These were spoken to the disciples, inside the house, (v 36) having a good aspect, and speak of the true inward characteristics of that Kingdom.
5. One pearl of great price (vv. 45-46)	
6. A net cast into the sea (vv. 47-50)	
7. A householder's treasure (v. 52)	

Matthew Chapter 13
It's Setting

Mark 4:13 indicates that the "parable of the Sower" is the *key* for our understanding.

"Know ye not this parable? And how then will ye know all parables?"

Symbols and *parabolic* suggestions are intricately woven throughout the Gospels. We draw attention to just a few:

Old Bottles (Luke 5:37)	Judaism
The strong man armed (Luke 11:21)	Satan
A stronger than he (Luke 11:22)	The Lord Jesus Christ
The man out of whom the unclean spirit is gone (Luke 11:24)	The Nation Israel, established after their 70 years captivity
I (the evil spirit) will return unto my house (Luke 11:24, 25)	Evil Israel returning to their land after the Babylonian captivity.
The last state of that man (Israel) is worse than the first (Israel's earlier state of idolatry before being carried away captive to Babylon). (Luke 11:26)	Only to crucify God's Son.

The spiritual mind will recognise the symbolisms seen in this chapter. Verse 1 *& 2* indicate the day on which the King made this declaration. "The same day" that is, the day on which He was rejected (see ch. 12), He "went out of the House", that is He was rejected by the house of Israel and "went into a ship" - on the waters, symbolic of the Gentile nations (Rev. 17:15) "and sat" (Matt. 13:2), (Refer to Rom. 11:25).

Consider how helpful the Lord Jesus Christ is, in giving us the meanings in the parable of the tares (vv. 36-43). They are as follows:

The Sower of the Seed	The Son of Man "The Lord of the Harvest" (Matt. 9:38).
The Field is the World	It is both a place and a sphere of influence.
Good Seed	Children of the Kingdom (of Heaven).
Tares	Children of the Wicked one (Satan).
The Enemy Sower	The Devil (Diabolos = False accuser).
The Harvest	The end of the World (i.e. age) "until the fullness of the Gentiles be come in" (Rom. 11:25).
The Reapers	The Angels (Rev. 19:11-14).

Similar meanings were not given for the following:

The mustard seed and the man that sowed – The birds of the air or of the branches in which they lodged.

The Leaven – The three measures of meal and the woman who hid it.

The Treasure hid. – The field. (Although this is given as the world in the parable of the tares v. 38)

The Merchant man – The one pearl of great price.

The net – the good – the bad. His treasure.

However the meanings of these, we can find without searching very far, by using the key found in the parable of the sower (Mark 4:13) and also in the parable of the Tares. For instance:

The birds of the air – Fowls (v 4, 19) which refers to the wicked one, Satan and his demons.

The leaven – The leaven is a principle of evil, mentioned several times elsewhere in the Scripture (Ex 12:15; 1 Cor. 5:6-8; Matt. 16:6, 12; Mark 8:15; Luke 12:1).

For the rest, the meanings and teaching are given in the diagrammatical exposition, which follows in this paper.

Matthew Chapter 13
It's Purpose

No earthly king has ever been able to successfully prognosticate about the future of his reign, nor how his kingdom would develop, nor the very principles upon which it would operate and such other details. However, the King of the Jews, as presented in Matthew's Gospel, though being rejected by His own subjects (Ch 11 & 12) traces out accurately how His kingdom would develop *in His absence* (Ch 13). This Divine King, in His final discourse (Chs. 24 & 25), reveals and describes in vivid details the conditions that would prevail before and upon His very return and how He would set up His Kingdom on the earth – His Millennial Kingdom. – *(Please refer to Paper No. 04-04)*

Therefore, to approach and to appreciate this Divine King and His Kingdom, who even in His very birth was the "King of the Jews" (Matt. 2:2) – no other was a king at his very birth – we are given the details of these seven parables, each commencing with, "The Kingdom of Heaven is like..."

They are spoken of by our Lord as "Mysteries of the Kingdom of Heaven" (v. 11). Taken together, they describe the results of the preaching of the Word in this world, "the field" (v. 38). This time of "seed-sowing", began with John the Baptist preaching the Gospel of the Kingdom (Matt. 3:2), and continued with the preaching of the Gospel of the grace of God (Acts 20:24) during the present Church Age. This seed sowing will end with the further preaching of the Gospel of the Kingdom during the great Tribulation period (Mat 24:14), and will culminate with the harvest (13:40-43), at the return of our Lord, Who will then establish His Millennial Kingdom.

This expression "The Kingdom of Heaven" includes the development of the Kingdom on this earth, *while the King is absent.* Hence there is an *evil side,* "An enemy hath done this" (Mat 13:28) by the sowing of evil seed – tares, which is set forth in the first three parables, narrated to the multitude on the sea-shore. He as the then-rejected King, sits upon the waters, ("went into a ship and sat" v.2) brings before us the waters of people, multitudes, nations and tongues (Rev 17:15). It also has a *good side,* which was set forth only to His disciples, in the last four parables (v.36). Back, inside the house, the King develops against the background of the parable of the sower, the *spiritual principles,* as set out in vv 18-23, which were to continue in the form of the Gospel of the Kingdom and also of the Gospel of the Grace of God. This Kingdom when preached is reacted-to, either for or against, by believing or rejecting, from the time of John the Baptist and up to the return of the King of the Jews.

The expression "Kingdom of *Heaven*" which occupies Matthew Chapter 13 is not synonymous with that of "Kingdom of *God*". We have to bear in mind, that "The Kingdom of God" has a *moral aspect,* while "The Kingdom of Heaven" has a *prophetic view. (For a full treatment on this subject, please see "The Kingdom of Heaven and the Kingdom of God Differentiated" Paper No: 08-05).*

The following diagram will enable the readers to have a clearer view of these parables of the kingdom, as recorded in Matthew chapter 13.

THE PARABLE OF THE SOWER
FROM WHICH HANG THE SEVEN PARABLES

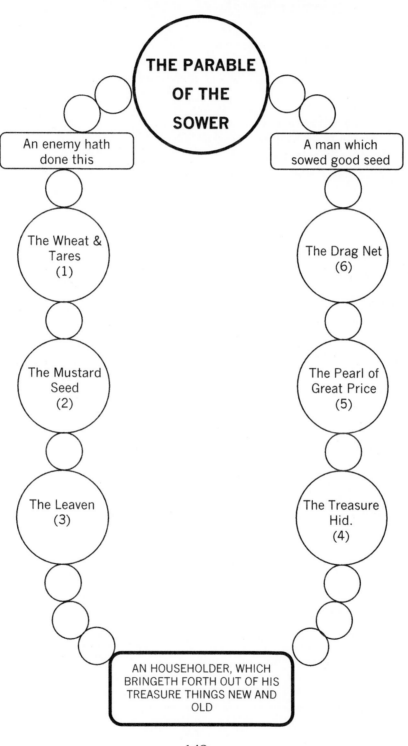

THE PARABLE OF THE SOWER

An enemy hath done this

A man which sowed good seed

The Wheat & Tares (1)

The Drag Net (6)

The Mustard Seed (2)

The Pearl of Great Price (5)

The Leaven (3)

The Treasure Hid. (4)

AN HOUSEHOLDER, WHICH BRINGETH FORTH OUT OF HIS TREASURE THINGS NEW AND OLD

THE KINGDOM PARABLES	
THE *EVIL SIDE* OF THE KINGDOM *(The result of sowing evil seed – tares)*	**THE *GOOD SIDE* OF THE KINGDOM** *(The result of sowing the good seed of the word of God)*
The prominent teachings given to the *multitudes* (vv.1-3), concern the *outward appearance* of the Kingdom.	The prominent teachings given to His *disciples* (v 10, 36) concern the *inward character* of the Kingdom, and of God's mind.
I. Wheat and Tares (vv 24-30)	**VI. The Net (vv 47-50)**
Good preserved and evil judged at the coming of the King (after the rapture of the church, and the great Tribulation).	Good preserved and evil judged at the end of the Millennium.
1. There was an enemy to the man with the good seed, who operated in the dark, sowing evil seed in this world.	1. "A net" – A drag-net for trawling the seas to catch fish. Consider this as symbolic of the final round-up of all the nations. (Rev. 20:7-10).
2. The final reckoning was the harvest.	2. "At the end of the world (age)" (The end of the Millennial-age)
3. The tares were burnt. The wheat was gathered into the barn.	3. "And sever the wicked from among the just" (v 47) and "gathered the good into vessels" (v 48).
4. All things that offend (tares) were to be removed from this kingdom – one (tare) taken for judgement and the other (righteous-good seed) left for blessing. (Matt. 24:40) to shine as the sun, in the Kingdom.	4. "When it was full, the angels sat down", for emptying of this huge drag-net at the final scene, which closes the kingdom of heaven on earth.
II. Mustard Seed (vv 31-32) ***External* appreciation and value.**	**V. The Pearl of Great Price (v 46)** ***Inward* preciousness and value.**
1. It was just one grain of seed and the least of all the seeds. But it is not, as of flesh enticing and thrilling religion, a substitute for the true seed.	1. This travelling (margin) Merchant – from heaven to earth and back again to heaven (Eph. 4:9-10).
2. "Which a man took" – Could this be 'the way of Cain' and 'the error of Balaam' (Jude 11) involving 'Works', instead of 'Grace'?	2. "Found one pearl of great price" symbolic of the true church – an oyster in the sea – its growth is unseen by men (The leaven also unseen, is Satan's counterfeit for God's reality).
3. "And sowed in his field" i.e. this world, which is under Satan's control and authority.	3. "Sold" – (Strong - 4097) 'Piprasko', means "to carry across the sea as export to another country" – see No. 1 above "the travelling Merchant".

THE *EVIL SIDE* OF THE KINGDOM *(The result of sowing evil seed – tares)*	THE *GOOD SIDE* OF THE KINGDOM *(The result of sowing the good seed of the word of God)*
4. "When it is grown, it is the greatest among herbs and becomes a tree" – An *external* spectacular growth. (For the symbolism of tree, birds and boughs, refer Ezk. 31 & Dan. 4:20-22).	4. "All that he had". The word 'selleth' of v. 44, is a different word (Strong's No 4453, 'Peleo' which means "to trade or sell",) Our Lord sold Himself (Phil. 2:5-8.)
5. In the branches of which the Devil's accomplices lodge. (Birds of the air represent worldly powers of evil - compare prince of the power of the air, Gen 15:11; Luke 8:5, 12; Eph 2:2). Also these birds of the air took away the good seed, in the parable of the sower, and were therefore evil. *(No interpretation of this parable is given in the text.)*	5. "And bought it". By His precious blood, (Acts 20:28; Eph. 5:25-27; 1 Pet. 1:18, 19). *(No interpretation of this parable is given in the text.)*
III. The Leaven (v.33). **Hidden evil.**	**IV. The Treasure (v.44)** **Hidden *treasure*.**
1. This leaven (yeast) represents evil, and it puffs-up and has fast growth (compare it with the mustard seed) I Cor. 5:6-8 give an inspired commentary of leaven.	1. The 'treasure' *hidden* in the world (field) is Israel (Ex. 19:5; Ps. 135:4).
2. "Which a woman took" – this could represent leaders of the religious systems, such as Jezebel in Thyatira (Rev. 2:20), and in an extended sense 'mystery', "Babylon the great, the mother of harlots and abominations of the earth" (Rev. 17:5). Throughout the ages, His Holy Person and the sound doctrine have been adulterated by the woman with leaven; these abominable insinuations have spread (both in Judaism and Christendom), and only a very few on the narrow-way, have escaped from the pollutions of these evil doctrines.	2. "When a man hath found". – "I found Israel like grapes in the wilderness" (Hosea 9:10), is precious to Him. He hideth and for the joy (Matt. 25:21 & 23) thereof goeth and selleth *all that He hath* (Matt. 13:44). As for Matt. 13:45, where the pearl is symbolic of the church, the blood of Christ answers for Israel as well as for Gentiles.
3. "Three measures of meal" –The meal-offering (Lev 2:4-9), typifies the person of Christ as the sweet savour to God, and as the food of His people, of which they partook in communion with God. The woman is doing what the Word prohibits, and adds leaven into this meal, (Lev 2:11, 10:12).	3. "And buyeth that field" – Christ has secured that treasure through His precious blood, shed on the cross, (Jer. 31:11; John 11:51; Heb. 9:15).

THE *EVIL SIDE* OF THE KINGDOM *(The result of sowing evil seed – tares)*	THE *GOOD SIDE* OF THE KINGDOM *(The result of sowing the good seed of the word of God)*
4. It was *hidden*–suggestive of evil under handed dealing to abort the days of unleavened bread (Acts 12:3), when the Holy Spirit was at work. The hidden leaven speaks of the unseen corruption which works subtily. – The evil doctrine (Matt. 16:6, 12; 2 Tim. 2:16 - 18; 4:3, 4; 2 Pet. 2:1-3); wickedness (1 Cor. 5:8); hypocrisy (Luke 12:1); and mixing religion with politics (Mark 8:15).	4. "He *hideth*" - This will be the position until the King manifests Himself just before the Millennium. Then the 'field' will yield up its treasure.
5. The Words 'until' of *"until* the harvest" and 'till' of *"till* the whole was leavened", is the idea of completely becoming evil and corrupt, as grown into a huge organisation, puffed-up leaven. *(No interpretation of this parable is given in the text.)*	5. "For Joy". What joy He will have, when He takes His treasure to Himself! (Deut. 30:9; Isa. 49:13; Zep. 3:17). Ultimately, this joy will be exhibited during the feast of Tabernacles, which would be revealed at the commencement of the Millennial Kingdom (Zec. 14:16, 18, 19), and "Enter thou into the joy of the Lord" (Matt. 25:21, 23). *(No interpretation of this parable is given in the text).*

VII. The Man that is a House – holder (v 52)

1.   While this man does not fit into the development of either side of the kingdom of heaven, (good or evil) his house is *the repository* of all the treasures of the Kingdom of Heaven, that have been expressed in the above mentioned parables.

2.   "Things new and old" would remind us of the New Testament, confirming OT prophecies, such as:

"Things old"	"Things new"
"And in the days of these kings (the gentile kings as seen in their diminishing value in the image of Dan. 2) shall the God of Heaven set up a Kingdom which shall never be destroyed" (Dan. 2:44).	"And the Kingdom shall not be left to other people" (i.e. it will go to Abraham's seed Christ, Gal. 3:16) as promised in Gen. 22:17, 18 but it shall break in pieces and consume all these kingdoms and it shall stand for ever – because the King, no longer rejected, returns to rule in accordance with things both new and old.
Things known before are "Things Old".	Things revealed in these parables are "Things New".
"Son of Man" referred to in Dan. 7:13, and Matt. 13:37	The treasure – Israel (v.44).
The devil and his (fallen) angels (Matt. 13:39).	The pearl of great price – Church (v.46).

These parables cover the period between the Lord's first and second advents. The parables of the Sower and Wheat and Tares relate to the *proclamation* of the good and evil sides of the kingdom, Mustard seed and the Leaven the *development* of the evil side of the kingdom through evil seed – tares, while the parables of pearl and the treasure speak of the *worth* of the kingdom, of the Church and Israel, both being precious to Christ.

Item No 2, under 'Mustard seed':

"Which a man took" – Could this be 'the way of Cain' (Jude 11) as supported by Nimrod, who obliterates the way of God, by standing before the Lord, establishing the sun-worship, (Gen. 10:8-10).

Item No 2, under 'The Leaven':

"Which a woman took" – Could this be Semaramis "the queen of heaven" (Jer. 7:18), mother of Tammuz (Ezk. 8:14) – Nimrod's wife, who invented the mother and child-son worship the Cain-system of works with idolatry.

Are not the evil-principles of that mustard seed, "which a man took", – *the spectacular fast growth,* and that of the leaven, "which a woman took" – *unseen rapid evil growth* – very much evident in the present religious Christendom – a counterfeit of the true kingdom.

Conclusion

Our Lord Jesus Christ said: "The word that I have spoken, the same shall judge him in the last day" (John 12:48b). To this remarkable statement, He added "For had ye believed Moses, ye would have believed me, for he wrote of me" (John 5:46). "(The Scriptures) are they, which testify of me" (John 5:39).

In the parable of the sower, the sowing of the seed – the Word of God – actually commences with the preaching of John the Baptist (Matt. 3:2), and will continue until the rejected King returns in power and glory, as we find in Matthew 24:30, to set up the Kingdom of Heaven on earth, (Matt. 6:10,11). In Paper No: 04-02, we have referred to Daniel 2:44, concerning the "God of Heaven", setting up an indestructible Kingdom, bringing to an end the Gentile kingdoms represented by the metals used in the image. John's preaching (Matt. 3:2), concerning the Kingdom of Heaven, commenced during the Caesars of the Roman empire which corresponds to the iron of that image. John's preaching, and all the preachings thereafter, to date, have been the sowing of the *good* seed in all the terrains – wayside soil, shallow and rocky soil, thistle filled soil or good ground. At the same time, an enemy was sowing tares – *evil* seed, which developed into the evil side, or counterfeit of that true Kingdom.

In these parables of the kingdom, we have seen that there were evil enemy forces that came in from outside; which brought, a *dark side* to the preaching of the Kingdom of Heaven. In fact, there is a huge growth of hot (mustard) fleshly religion in which evil vultures lodge, and which has proved a clever deceptive counterfeit, with a rich and successful *appearance*. The truth is an evil-leaven is working unseen, in and through it all.

At the same time, as the growth of religious wickedness was enlarging in popularity and seeming success, the seed that was falling into the good soil, was springing up and bringing forth fruit, *precious* to God, which is the *bright side* of the kingdom. This would eventually be manifest in a small but very valuable pearl, the *Church*, which would be 'exported' to heaven - confirming John 14:3 – leaving the hidden treasure, even *Israel* to be taken up again, to receive her King back. She has so far rejected her King, who will return and save her through, and out of the great Tribulation (Matt. 24:29, 30) and will establish her in the Kingdom, fulfilling the promises given to Abraham.

153

"The Kingdom of Heaven" and "The Kingdom of God"

Differentiated

The expression "Kingdom of *Heaven*" which appears only in the Gospel of Matthew is not the same as that of the "Kingdom of *God*". There is a distinction between the two, as we find both the expressions appearing in one context, in Matthew 19:23, 24. This clearly reveals that the spirit of inspiration has *different intentions* for these two expressions.

It is God's will and purpose that the "Kingdom *of Heaven*" be established on earth by the King Himself, in due time after the collapse of the Gentile rule. *(Please refer to "The Times of the Gentiles", Paper No 04-02).* Then it will be manifested visibly and enjoyed worldwide, when the curse will be removed. It was heralded by the forerunner, John the Baptizer (Matt. 3:2) and proclaimed by its King, our Lord Jesus Christ Himself (Matt. 4:17). Its high moral principles were promulgated by its sovereign King Himself, as laid down in Matthew chapters 5 – 7. The Kingdom's Character during the absence of the King, good influence by God, and the bad influence by Satan, both are set forth in the seven parables of Matthew Chapter 13. *(See "The Seven Parables of the Kingdom", Paper No. 08-04).* It will be fully manifested on earth, at the appearing of the Son of Man (Matt. 24:30; 25:31), when He begins His Millennial reign.

The least in the Kingdom of Heaven, will be greater than John the Baptizer (Matt. 11:11), its first Herald, the forerunner of its King and the friend of the Bridegroom.

The "Kingdom of Heaven" is always in the *future* as to its complete realisation, "Thy Kingdom Come". Hence it has a *prophetic* sense. Its reigning power, even though manifested on earth, originates from heaven to which it belongs and has the heavenly purposes, "Thy *will* be done on earth as it is in Heaven". Hence it is called the Kingdom of Heaven. It is Heavenly in character, contrasting to the rule of human Kings on the earth. (See Dan. 2:44, 4:26 and Ps. 103:19).

The "Kingdom of *God*", on the other hand, is the sphere of salvation enjoyed by the *individual* and entered into, only by the new birth by the Holy Spirit (John 3:5-7). It is not just meat and drink (Rom. 14:17), or flesh and blood (I Cor. 15:50), but possessing its *spiritual nature* in the hidden man of the heart, enjoying its spiritual content and element. It is "righteousness, and peace, and joy in the Holy Ghost" (Rom. 14:17).

"The Kingdom of God is *within* you" (Luke 17:21). The same Greek root word here rendered as 'within' is given as "among you" in John 1:26. It should be "among you", or "in the midst". It is very difficult to believe that the Kingdom of God was 'within' the hearts of these Pharisees, who at the very time were thickening their plot to kill the King, who is in their midst. "Among you" would really mean, "it is really present", even though it is *unseen,* which of course is true of this *Spiritual Kingdom.* It was actually "in the midst" of the Pharisees in the person of the King.

The Kingdom of God "would not come with *observation"* (Luke 17:20-21). The Greek *'parateresis'* is only here in NT, and suggests a physician who closely watches the observable symptoms of his patient. However, the "Kingdom of Heaven" will have a visible manifestation of its heavenly character, through its subjects during His reign.

"The Kingdom of *God",* is so termed because it is the immediate result of God's reigning in the souls of men. "The Kingdom of *Heaven"* so called, because it is, in a way heaven opened over the Kingdom established by the King on the earth. The former is *inner* and *spiritual,* while the latter is the rule of heaven over earth, "The Kingdom of Heaven" has an *earthly sphere,* as it relates to things, "kept secret from the foundation of the world", (Matt. 13:35).

(Please refer to Paper No. 03-09).

The following tabulation highlights the salient features of these kingdoms:

The Kingdom of Heaven	The Kingdom of God
1. Appears only in Matthew's Gospel. (32 times)	Appears in all the Gospels and in 13 of the remaining N T books.
2. In its ultimate, it is heaven's rule *on this earth.*	It is the immediate result of God's reign over and in the *souls of men.*
3. Thy Kingdom come, Thy will be *done on earth,* as it is in heaven (Matt. 6:10)	Does not depend upon setting up a Kingdom on earth, but it is rather in the *hearts of men* - even in harlots as in Matt. 21:31, but rich men appear not to be able to enjoy this privilege (Luke 18:25).
4. Culminates upon the establishment of the Lord Jesus Christ as the Millennial King of the whole earth, as the Son of Man (Matt. 24:30; 25:31). *Has a visible and physical aspect.*	*"Seek ye first* the Kingdom of God and His righteousness" (Matt. 6:33), whereby the rule is in the hearts of men. *Has a moral and spiritual aspect.*
5. It is the rule of Heaven on the *earth.*	It is God's spiritual order governing the *individual men,* manifesting in his life of faith.
6. It is future as to its complete realisation and hence *has a prophetic sense.*	It describes the sphere of salvation, enjoyed by the individual and entered into by the new birth (John 3:5-7), and hence has a *moral and spiritual sense.*
7. *It will be observable,* and would manifest its heavenly character and order through its subjects and reign, in the Millennium.	*It is inner and spiritual,* (not observable) not just meat and drink (Rom. 14:17) or flesh and blood (I Cor. 15:50), but possessing spiritual content and element, the expression of righteousness and peace and joy in the Holy Ghost, (Rom. 14:17).

Numbers in the Word of God

Our Lord Jesus Christ, in Matthew 5, verses 17 & 18, mentions a 'jot', and a 'tittle' *Jod*, is the tenth letter of the Hebrew alphabet. – Please refer to the title appearing over verse 73 in Psalm 119 for this Hebrew character. A *'tittle'*, is a tiny protrusion at the top right hand side of the fourth letter *'Daleth'*, (ד) and this tiny tittle distinguishes this letter from *'Resh'*, (ר) the twentieth letter of the Hebrew alphabet. – Please refer to the Hebrew characters given as title over verse 25 and verse 153 of Psalm 119. The following would assist in grasping this significance:

Numbers 1:14 and 2:14 reads as:

Num. 1:14: "of Gad; Eliasaph the son of DEUEL"

– Hebrew letter 'Daleth' used in Deuel.

Num. 2:14: "of Gad shall be Eliasaph the son of REUEL"

– Hebrew letter 'Resh' used in Reuel.

1. It appears that in each of these verses, the same person is alluded to, but the translators were apparently unable to distinguish between 'Daleth' (ד) and 'Resh' (ר). The manuscript probably supported a mis-scribed 'Daleth', which was read as 'Resh'. If this, our observation is proved correct, the inspired Word of God depends for its correct translation into another language, not only upon spiritual considerations, but also upon scholarship. We consider that 'Deuel' should be the correct rendering in both the above verses quoted, considering the same name appearing in other passages (Num. 7:42, 47; 10:20). One will be able to appreciate the vital difference that a little tittle of a letter could make in the above quoted references. It may appear that this small error has only affected the pronunciation of a proper name, but considering the meaning of these two Hebrew words, Deuel (Strong - 1845) means "Known of God" and Reuel (Strong - 7467), "Friend of God", the spiritual implication could be inestimable.

2. Our Lord assesses greater importance to this tiny jot and tittle, which constitute the Word of God, than to heaven and earth, which will pass away. By so much does God value each letter of His inspired word with their tiny parts, even every letter of it is God-inspired. "I have given them the *words* (plural) which Thou gavest me". (John 17:8). On our part we are also called to be good and faithful stewards of God's Word.

3. Neither Hebrew nor Greek has a separate numerical system. Each letter or alphabet is also utilised to denote a number. There is no letter to denote 'cipher' (0), or for number '6' in Greek. Ten thousand is the highest number in Greek; hence, "Ten thousand times ten thousand and thousands of thousands" (Rev. 5:11). It appears as if the Greek

numerical system is insufficient, considering redemption's rich harvest.

4. This consideration could set the spiritual mind thinking along the lines, whereby, if each letter of the alphabet has its own numerical value, then each word or phrase may possibly have some common numerical pattern or factors, indicating the inspiration of Scripture and its Divine Authorship. (Please refer to Para No. 8 below and the tabulation given therein). One should be aware that modern versions of the Bible, being based on different texts, with their omissions and additions, would make such a consideration impossible. So, we could not use them. The King James Version is based on the most authoritative text, known as "Textus Receptus".

5. Before launching into this interesting and educative spiritual subject of numerics, we should not miss the simpler approach to the meanings of numbers. The meanings are set out, as follows, in simple manner, for easy remembrance. The suggested spiritual meanings and implications of a few numbers in God's Word are summarised as follows:

1. Unity – God-Head.

2. Separation – Division; and Witness.

3. Divine Perfection – Witness, the witness of Calvary.

4. Universality – The World and its winds.

5. Grace – Human dependence.

6. Man, under sin.

7. God's seal – Perfection of Divine persons and ways – Completeness.

8. Resurrection – A new beginning.

9. Finality and fruitfulness.

10. Testing to prove, for a purpose, to bring into order.

11. Disorganisation.

12. Governmental perfection.

13. Rebellion – Satan's number.

17. Perfection of spiritual order.

18. Bondage, 'Whom Satan hath bound' (Luke 13:6).

37. The Living Word of God.

40. Probation – Testing for testing's sake.

50. Jubilee – Freedom and Deliverance.

153. Perfection of number from a Heavenly point of view.

Memorising these meanings may help and prove our study of this subject more intelligible.

6. Given below, are the numerical equivalents of both Hebrew (22) and Greek (24) alphabet, along with the meanings of the Hebrew letters:

HEBREW ALPHABET			FINAL	ENGLISH EQUIVALENTS	SIGNIFICATION	NUMERICAL POWER
א	'Aleph	(aw'-lef)		a	Ox	1
ב	Bêyth	(bayth)		bh ב, b בּ	House	2
ג	Gîymel	(ghee'-mel)		g hard	Camel	3
ד	Dâleth	daw'-leth		d	Door	4
ה	Hê	(hay)		h	Window	5 (Lattice, Breath Hole)
ו	Vâv	(vawv)		v	Hook or Fore-arm	6
ז	Zayin	(zah'yin)		z	Weapon	7
ח	Chêyth	(khayth)		kh	Fence	8
ט	Têyth	(tayth)		t	Hand	9 (or Coiled Snake)
י	Yôwd or Jod	(yode)		y or j	Hand closed	10
כ	Kaph	(caf)	ך	Ch כ, c or k ךּ	Hand bent	20
ל	Lâmed	(law'-med)		l	Ox-goad	30
מ	Mêm	(mame)	ם	m	Water	40
נ	Nûwn	(noon)	ן	n	Fish	50
ס	Çâmek	(saw'mek)		s	Prop	60
ע	'Ayin	(ah'-Yin)		h aspirate, ng at end	Eye	70
פ	Phê	(fay)	ף	ph=ϕ, p = pê פּ (pay)	Mouth	80
צ	Tsâdêy	(tsaw-day')	ץ	ts or tz	Fish-hook	90
ק	Qôwph	(Cofe)		k or q	Hole of an axe	100
ר	Rêysh	(raysh)		r	Head	200
ש	Sîyn	(seen)		s שׂ, sh שׁ (sheen)	Tooth	300
ת	Thâv	(tawv)		t תּ, th ת (thawv),	Mark or Cross	400

158

GREEK ALPHABET		NAME	NUMERICAL VALUE
α	A	alpha	1
β	B	beta	*2*
γ	Γ	gamma	3
δ	Δ	delta	4
ε	E	epsilon	5
ζ	Z	zeta	7
η	H	eta	8
θ	Θ	theta	9
ι	I	iota	10
κ	K	kappa	*20*
λ	Λ	lambda	30
μ	M	mu	40
ν	N	nu	50
ξ	Ξ	xi	60
o	O	omicron	70
π	π	pi	80
ρ	P	rho	100
σ	Σ	sigma	200
τ	T	tau	300
υ	Y	upsilon	400
φ	Φ	phi	500
χ	Ξ	chi	600
ψ	Ψ	psi	700
ω	Ω	omega	800

NB: NO Greek alphabet is given to signify Number 6.

7. In both Hebrew and Greek alphabet if each letter stands for a number, and by substituting the relevant numbers for their letters, we would arrive at a *numeric value* of a word. For instance in Greek, the numeric value of the word 'Christ' will be **1480**, the working of which is shown here:

chi + rho + iota + sigma + tau + omicron + sigma = that is,

600 + 100 + 10 + 200 + 300 + 70 + 200 = 1,480.

8. In the accompanying tabulation, we have arrived at the numeric value for some of the names of God and of the Lord Jesus Christ, in Greek, in which the number 37 appears as a common basic factor for all these names. On this account, and also because man can know God only through Divine revelation, the meaning of this number 37 (an indivisible number in itself) appears to be pointing to the source of all revelations, that is, to the living Word of God. (Heb. 4:12, 13).

Titles	Numeric Value	The Living Word of God		Perfection	Resurrection
GODHEAD (Strong - 2322)	592	= 37	x 2		x 8
JESUS	888	= 37	x 3		x 8
CHRIST	1480	= 37	x 5		x 8
SON OF MAN	2960	= 37	x 10		x 8
IMAGE OF GOD	1369	= 37	x 37		
GODHEAD (Strong's 2305)	962	= 37	x 26		
LOGOS	373	= 37	x 10		+ 3
WORD	777	= 37	x 3	x 7	
TRUTH	64		8		x 8
LORD	800		100		x 8
MESSIAH	656		82		x 8

Godhead	592
Jesus	888
Christ	1,480
Son of Man	2,960
Total	5,920

This number 5920 is also the numeric value of the verse "Behold the bridegroom cometh: go ye out to meet Him." (Matt. 25:6).

9. The words 'Godhead', 'Jesus', 'Christ', and 'Son of Man' each have an underlying numeric meaning (i.e. 37 -- the living Word of God) and 8 = resurrection. Again the words 'Image of God', 'Godhead', 'Logos' and 'Word' are also united by the same

common factor 37 (the living Word of God). This should help us to appreciate the importance attached to the underlying unity of expression given to each of these divine titles. Is it not significant that the names of Deity are associated with resurrection, and the divine revealed Word of God! Therefore, any Bible translation that omits or alters these words, must be suspect, and such a translation should be rejected.

Symbolic Implications of Numbers

Some of the symbolic implications and significances of the various numbers are detailed below. For some numbers, we have clear scriptural explanations, while for others their significance is only implied. However, while attributing symbolic implications, straining and subtle trilling is to be avoided. In order to decide whether a figure mentioned in the Scripture is employed ordinarily only with an arithmetic value, or ordinarily as well as symbolically or even exclusively in a symbolical sense, we have to examine its general sense, its history and the context, with that of the general analogy of the scriptural scheme as a whole.

In considering these numerical significances, we are to be clear of all superstitions attaching to numbers, as the Godless worldly people do, under the influence of Satan and his angels. Let us remember that the Devil also uses numbers together with the twelve signs of the Zodiac, and his other favourite symbols, to control the lives of thousands of millions through astrology and numerology. Was not Satan defeated at Calvary by the "Alpha and Omega", "The First and the Last", (Rev. 1:8,17), which titles are highly suggestive of letters and numbers, characterising the Conqueror, having the final word as King of kings and as Lord of lords: "He spake and it stood fast", and "it was so from the beginning."

ONE denotes Unity:

"One body, one Spirit, one hope, one Lord, one faith, one baptism, one God." (Eph 4:4-6). ('one' used 7 times)

"That they may be one", the prayer of our Lord in John 17:11-23.

TWO denotes Division, Separation or Contrast and Testimony:

"God divided the light from the darkness. And God called the light Day, and the darkness He called Night." (Gen. 1:4, 5).

Two also symbolises testimony even witness (Zech. 4:11; 11:7; Isa. 8:2; Rev. 11:3).

Two tables of the testimony, tables of stone (Ex. 31:18)

Two cherubim over the ark of the testimony. (Ex. 25:18)

The dimensions of the Temple are two times that of the Tabernacle.

A testimony to God's faithfulness, (Job 42:10; Isa .61:7; Jer. 16:18)

Double honour to elders who labour in the Word and doctrine (1 Tim. 5:17)

God is His own witness; but that witness is twofold, His own word and His oath (Heb. 6:13.17), Himself and His Son, (John 8:18)

In Matthew ch. 7, we find *seven* pairs – each are contrasts – mote & beam, straight & wide, narrow & broad, good & corrupt, wise & foolish, rock & sand and stood & fell, meaning separation and contrast.

THREE like seven, signifies Divine Perfection and Completeness:

The Trinity (Rev 1:4; 4:8); (2 Cor 13:14) the thrice Holy God, (Isa. 6:3).

Man = Body, Soul and Spirit. "In His own image" (Gen. 1: 26, 27 & 2:7). Order reversed in 1 Thess. 5:23.

Three great feasts (Ex. 23:14-17; Deut. 16:16).

The three-fold blessing (Num. 6:24-26)

The three times prayer (Ps. 55:17; Dan. 6:10).

The third heaven (2 Cor. 12:2).

Christ "the way, the truth, and the life";

Christ Prophet, Priest and King.

The three-fold theophany – visible manifestation of God (Gen. 18:2; I Sam. 3:4, 6, 8; Acts 10:16)

Three-fold witness (Deut. 17:6; Hosea 6:2; 2 Cor. 13:1)

THREE AND A HALF (3 ½), is seven broken in two:

Three years and a half, drought in Israel (Luke 4:25; Rev. 11:2, 3, 9; 12:6; James 5:17).

The Great Tribulation, a period of evil, shortened for the elect's sake, (Matt. 24:22).

In the midst of the week (42 months or $3^1/_2$ years), he shall cause the sacrifice and oblation to cease (Dan. 9:27).

"Time, times and a half", "1260 days", "Three days and a half, "Forty and two months" (Dan. 7:25; 12:7; Rev. 11:9; 12:6; 13:5).

FOUR symbolises Universality and World Wide extension:

"The four winds of heaven" and "Four corners of the earth" (Dan. 7:2; Matt. 24:31; Rev. 7:1). Eden's four streams (Gen. 2:10).

The four living creatures or cherubim with four wings and four faces (Ezk.

1:5; Rev. 4:6), in contrast to the four great beasts (Dan. 7:3) of evil, dreadful and terrible character.

'"Knit at the four corners" (Acts 10:11) Four winds (Rev. 7:1).

FIVE denotes Human-dependence and Grace:

Five cubits square brazen altar (Ex. 27:1).

Five water-washed stones of David, dependent on divine direction (1 Sam. 17:40).

Five porches of Bethesda – Dependent on the moving of the waters (John 5:2).

Five words with my understanding than ten-thousand. – words of grace. (1 Cor. 14:19).

As 3½ is related to 7, so is 5 to 10: Five is the penal number (Ex. 22:1; Lev. 5:16).

SIX is twelve divided into two:

Six is man's number, created on the sixth day, always one short of perfection, the number seven.

In Hebrew, there are *six* words for 'man', namely: Adam, Ish, Enosh, Anashim, Geber and Methim.

Nebuchadnezzar's image of gold, stood 60 (6 x 10) cubits high and six cubits broad (Dan. 3:1); and the orchestra used six different types of musical instruments, for its human service and worship (Dan. 3:4, 9, 14).

Goliath had six pieces of armour (1 Sam. 17:5-7), and his spear weighed 600 (6 x 100) shekels of Iron. All his brothers had six fingers and six toes, in each hand and foot, (2 Sam. 21:20-22; 1 Chron. 20:6).

Six symbolises the world given over to judgement – 600 (6 x 100) years of

Noah when he completed and entered the ark (Gen. 7:6).

Six – the world number, is one short of the sacred seven, which it mimics (Rev. 13:1), but can never reach that fullness of seven.

There is a pause between the sixth and seventh seals, and the sixth and seventh trumpets and the sixth and seventh vials, – So the judgements on the world are complete in the sixth by the fulfilment of the seventh – the world's Kingdoms become Christ's. (Rev. 6:12 to 8:1; 9:13 to 11:15; 16:12 to 17).

As twelve is the Church's number, so six its half, symbolises world-kingdom.

SEVEN represents Divine Perfection, God's seal:

The Bible alphas (begins) with seven days in Genesis, and omegas (ends) with a succession of sevens in Revelation.

Seven is also a divine work, in judgement, or mercy, or revelation (Gen. 4:24; 41:3, 7; Ex. 7:25; Matt. 18:22).

"I will punish you seven times more for your sins" (Lev. 26:18, 21, 24, 28; Isa. 4:1; 11:15; 2 Sam. 24:13).

"Seven times shall pass over thee" – Nebuchadnezzar. (Dan. 4:16, 25).

"Seven last plagues" (Rev. 15:1)

Divine fullness and completeness is signified by number seven:

"The seven Spirits" belonging to God (Rev. 1:4; 3:1). There are seven burning lamps, which are the seven spirits of God. (Rev. 4:5).

Seven dominates the offerings and divine rites. (Lev. 12:2, 5; 13:4, 6, 21, 26, 31, 33, 50, 54; 14:7, 8, 9, 16, 27, 38, 51; 15:13,19,28; 16:14,19; Num. 12:14; 2 Kings 5:10,14).

The seven day's of grace (Gen. 7:1-10); also at the taking of Jericho (Josh. 5:13 to 6:20). And its antitype, spiritual Babylon, shall fall at the sounding of the seventh trumpet (Rev. 11:13, 15; 14:8).

The seven branched candlestick (Ex. 25:37), and the seven lampstands – correspond to the seven churches (Rev. 1:12, 20).

The seven deacons (Acts 6), and the seven-fold gifts in Rom. 12:6-8; 1 Cor. 12:29.

Seven times a day "Do I praise Thee" (Ps. 119:164)

Seven petitions of the Lord's Prayer in John 17

Seven Beatitudes (Matt. 5)

Seven qualities of love (1 Cor. 13:4-7)

Seven qualifications of an elder (1 Tim. 3:2-4)

Seventy-times-seven – total forgiveness (Matt. 18:22)

"The words of the Lord are pure words. . . purified seven times" (Ps. 12:6).

Seven colours of the rainbow; and seven musical notes

Satan mimics the Divine seven (Pro. 6:16; 26:25)

Balak preparing seven altars, seven oxen and seven rams, as instructed by Balaam (Num. 23:1).

Mary Magdalene's seven devils (Mark 16:9; Luke 8:2)

The unclean spirit returning with seven other spirits more wicked than himself (Matt. 12:45).

The seven Canaanite nations subdued by Israel (Deut. 7:1; Acts 13:19)

The dragon with seven heads and seven crowns (Rev. 12:3)

The Beast with seven heads (Rev. 13:1).

The whore with seven heads (Rev. 17:3).

EIGHT introduces a New Series or Era, and denotes Resurrection:

Circumcision on the eighth day begins a new life in the covenant (Gen. 17:12).

In Genesis 24, the name of Isaac appears 8 times, and after Rebekah's betrothal is affirmed, from verse 53 onwards, her name also appears 8 times, and who brought resurrection to the lineage of Jacob / Israel.

Lepers are reinstated on the eighth day (Lev. 14:10; 15:14, 29).

The eight souls saved, Noah's family, left the ark on the eighth day, after staying a further seven days. (Gen. 8:12).

David was eighth and brought regeneration to Israel, (I Sam. 16:10, 11; 17:51, 52).

After the seven has been completed, the eighth day. (Ex. 22:30; Lev. 9:1; 22:27). Harvest: numerical value is 704 = 8 x 88.

Christ's resurrection was on the eighth day.

The Lord's Day, the eighth after the seventh (Sabbath day), brings to an end the Sabbath days system, and ushers in a new era of grace, based on resurrection (2 Tim. 1:10). The first of the weeks (Matt. 28:1 Margin)

There are eight individuals raised from the dead in the Word of God:

The son of the widow of Zarephath (1 Kings 17:17-24); Shunemite's son (2 Kings 4: 32-35); Unnamed man (2 Kings 13:20,21); Jairus the ruler's daughter (Matt. 9:23-25; Mark 5:22,42; Luke 8:41, 54 & 55); Widow's son (Luke 7:14,15); Lazarus (John 11:43); Dorcas (Acts 9:40,41); and Eutychus (Acts 20:10).

NINE is the last digit, and brings Finality and Fruitfulness:

Abraham was 99 when he was circumcised and received the promise of fruit—Isaac (Gen. 17).

Jubilee-year: Eat of the old fruit until the 9th year, (Lev. 25:19-22).

The fruit of the Spirit is nine-fold, (Gal. 5:22, 23).

The gifts of the Spirit are nine, (1 Cor. 12:8-10).

At the ninth-hour - It is finished, (Luke 23:44-46).

The numeric value of:

'In the beginning God'	- 999
'Created the heaven'	- 999
'My wrath' (Heb 3:11)	- 999
'Blood'	- 99
'Amen'	- 99

'Verily' is used 99 times in NT. 'Bottomless Pit' and 'Rest' used 9 times each in NT.

TEN represents Perfection of Order, and Testing to Produce a Result for a Purpose:

Ten Commandments contain God's basic moral and spiritual requirements, proved that the flesh was weak – the test ended in failure (Rom. 8:3).

The tithe indicates that the whole property belonged to God (Gen. 14:20).

The ten plagues were the entire round of judgement from God's hand, its purpose was that God would be magnified in His dealings with Pharaoh (Ex. 9:13-16).

The Tabernacle, Temple, and New Jerusalem have ten as a multiple figure in all their measurements, (but the Temple ended with not one stone left upon another).

In the NT the ten lepers, ten virgins, ten talents, ten cities in reward for ten pounds gained – are all various tests of faith, testimony, or stewardship, – some ended in success and others in failure.

The 'thousand' years (Rev. 20:2), is ten raised to the third power (10^3).

Satan's final rebellion after 1000 (10 x 10 x 10) years. (Rev. 20:2, 7, 8).

Antichrist too has his use for number ten, comprising the whole cycle of world power:

Ten nations opposed to Abraham's seed (Gen 15:19, 20).

Ten toes on the image in Nebuchadnezzar's dream to be smitten by the stone (Dan. 2:34).

Ten horns on the fourth beast (Dan. 7:7, 20, 24; Rev. 12:3; 13:1; 17:3, 7, 12) are the 'ten kings'.

The ten days of Smyrna's tribulation (Rev. 2:10), the completion of the world's powers persecuting the church.

TWELVE represents Governmental Perfection:

"12 years they served" (Gen. 14:4) - first mention.

12 tribes of Israel; 12 Elim wells (Ex. 15:27); 12 stones in the high-priest's breastplate, and 12 names on his shoulders.

12 patriarchs.

12 Shewbread loaves.

12 gates for the 12 tribes (Rev. 21:12); 12 angels (Rev. 21:12); 12 apostles (Rev.

21:14); 12 foundation stones (Rev. 21:19-20).

12 Stars (the women is Israel, Rev. 12:1).

12 manner of fruits (Rev. 22:2).

Twelve squared (12 x 12) and multiplied by 1000, gives 144,000, of the sealed Israelites under divine protection taken from the 12 tribes (Rev. 7:4).

The 24 elders (12 x 2) mentioned *seven* times in Revelation (Rev. 4:4 twice, 4:10; 5:8, 14; 11:16; 19:4) are symbolic of the church, and Israel.

THIRTEEN is the number for Rebellion and for Satan.

"In the thirteenth year they rebelled . . ." (Gen. 14:4).

Israel's rebellious nature and their protests to God were revealed through His prophet Malachi, pointing out 13 times, by the expressions "Yet ye say...", "But ye say ..." etc. (Mal. 1:2, 6, 7 twice, 1:12, 13; 2:14, 17 twice 3:7, 8, 13 & 14).

Thirteen evils in man's heart are mentioned in Mark 7:21, 22.

The name 'dragon' occurs thirteen times in Revelation.

Thirteen is a number associated with Satan and Idolatry exemplified in the numeric value of:

Satan in Hebrew is 364 = 13 x 7 x 4.

Satan in Greek is 2197 = 13 x 13 x 13.

Devil (Gr. *Diabolos*) 247 = 13 x 19 (Rev. 20:2)

Serpent 780 = 13 x 60.

Dragon (Rev 12:3) 975 = 13 x 75.

SEVENTEEN denotes Perfection of the Spiritual Order:

Number 17 is ten added to seven (10+7), a prime number.

In Genesis chapter one, the expression "And God said" appears 10 times + "And it was so" appears 7 times = 17, a prime creation of perfection.

The ark rested on the 17th day (on the 7th month, which became the first month in Ex. 12:1).

17 Singers and 17 musicians were appointed (1 Chron. 15:17-21).

17th day in that first month is the day of Christ's resurrection; crucified on the 14th day and resurrected on the 3rd day after the 14th.

Jerusalem occurs 17 times in the Psalms.

Jeremiah prays 17 times in the book of Jeremiah.

Jeremiah buying a field for 17 shekels of silver, indicating building of houses etc., in the land of Israel, their restoration after captivity.

'Agape' – Divine Love appears 17 times in John's Gospel.

'Aphesis' – Remission appears 17 times in NT.

17 x 9 = 153. [Finality (9) x Spiritual perfection (17) =153]. Perfection from the heavenly point of view. The only mention is in John 21:11. 153 "great fishes" safely landed, without breaking the net – the final catch. Hence forth it will be counting sheep "shepherd my sheep" (John 21:16 Marg.).

FORTY symbolises Probation; Testing for Testing's sake, involving chastisement, humiliation and punishment:

Rain upon the earth for 40 days and 40 nights (Gen. 7:4).

Moses spent 40 years in Egypt, 40 years in Midian, and 40 years in the wilderness journey of Israel.

40 days on the mount (Ex. 24:18), and a second 40 days after Israel's sin of idolatry – golden-calf (Deut. 9:18, 25).

40 years of wilderness wanderings of Israel:

- a period of God's chastisement (Num. 14:33)

- a period of testing (Deut. 8:2)

- a period of Israel's grieving the Lord proving as "a people that do err in their heart" (Ps. 95:10).

The penal issue of the 40 days' probation in searching Canaan (Num. 13:25; 14:34).

Israel's 40 years of chastisement under Philistines (Jud 13:1).

40 days and 40 nights of Elijah (1 Kings 19:8).

Jonah's 40 days warning to Ninevites (Jonah 3:4).

40 days of Christ's temptation (Matt 4:2). Testing for testing's sake, to prove Who He was – The Son of God.

40 is also a time of probation for Israel by tranquil prosperity, (Jude 3:11; 5:31; 8:28), under certain Judges of Israel.

Saul, David and Solomon each reigned 40 years.

Ezekiel (4:4-6) lay on his right side 40 days, a day for a year which with the 390 on his left side, makes the 430 of Israel's sojourn in Egypt, (Ex. 12:40,41; Gal. 3:17).

FIFTY represents Jubilee, Liberty and Joy (Lev. 25:8-12):

From the eighth day (Sunday) when the first fruit sheaf was waved, the seven

Sabbaths were counted; and the day following, that is, on the 50th or Pentecost a new era began (Lev. 23:11, 15, 16; Acts 2:1).

Lev. 25:8, 9 is a type of the continual Sabbath, the new era of a regenerated world, (Isa. 61:1; Acts 3:21; Rom. 8:21).

SEVENTY in combination with seven (7) Divine perfection, and ten (10): Perfection of order:

70 nations of Genesis 10.

The 70 who went down to Egypt (Gen. 46:27).

The 70 palm trees at Elim, (Ex. 15:27; Num. 33:9).

The 70 elders of Israel (Ex. 24:1, 9; Num. 11:16).

The 70 years of captivity (Jer. 25:11).

Daniel's 70 weeks of sevens – prophecy (Dan. 9:24).

The 70 disciples of our Lord (Lk. 10:1).

Seventy and seven fold (Gen. 4:24).

Seventy-fold (Matt. 18:22).

SIX, SIX, SIX (666), the raising of the six from units to tens, and from tens to hundreds:

666 is a number attributed to the Beast, (Rev. 13:1,18) notwithstanding his progression to higher (evil) powers, can only rise to greater ripeness for eternal damnation and judgement.

The children of Adonikam (Lord of Rebellion) were 666 (Ezra 2:13).

Numerical Value of:

Greek word 'Euporia' for 'wealth' in Acts 19:25 – wealth from the worship and Grafting of the goddess Diana = 666.

Greek word 'Paradosis' for 'tradition' in Matt. 15:6 (the traditions of man) = 666.

The sun-god 'Teitar' (for whom December 25th is the birthday) = 666.

"Pope" – "The Vicar of Christ", in Latin (*Vicarius Filii Dei*) = 666.

"Saturnia" is the city of Saturn – Rome = 666.

(S = 60 + T = 400 + U = 6 + R = 200 i.e. 666).

"Satan" in Chaldea = 666.

Appendix

The Hebrew Alphabet Letters As Employed In the Old Testament.

The following information, concerning the Hebrew alphabet, will be of interest to the readers:

Hebrew is the language of the Old Testament, with the exception of Daniel 2:4b to 7:28, and Ezra 4:8 to 6:18; 7:12 to 26 which were written in Aramaic, the ancient language of Syria, and substantially identical with Chaldaic, the language of ancient Babylonia.

Hebrew was "the language of Canaan" (Isa. 19:18) - not the language of the Canaanites, but the language of the Israelites, who came to Egypt from Canaan as distinguished from that of Egypt. It is known as the "Jewish language" (2 Kings 18:26, 28) as distinguished from Aramaean.

Psalm 119 is an acrostic, and is the most elaborate of the *seven* Hebrew alphabetical Psalms (other Psalms are: 25, 34, 37, 111, 112 and 145). It is divided into twenty two sections corresponding to the twenty-two letters of the Hebrew alphabet. The eight stanzas of each section begin with the same letter, in the proper sequence of the alphabet as designated to each section. In Psalms 25,

34, each verse, and in Psalms 37, 111, 112, and 145 each stanza commences with a letter of the Hebrew alphabet consecutively. (In this connection, please see the marginal notes given by Newberry in his "Englishman's Bible").

The last chapter of Proverbs, attributed as the words of King Lemuel, includes an acrostic of twenty-two verses, portraying a virtuous wife. (Pro. 31:10-31).

Similar acrostics are also found in each of the 1st, 2nd and 4th chapters of Lamentations:

While in the third chapter, the first three verses begin with the first letter of Hebrew alphabet, the next three verses with the second letter and so on, until all the 22 letters are covered in the 66 verses of this chapter. This Alphabetic acrostic of formulated structure will facilitate memory. This method of writing with no letter of the alphabet missed, seems to be of Divine origin, and ensures that the burden of the subject has been fully expressed, implying the subject is thoroughly dealt with.

A Comparison between Moses and Samuel
Two Mighty Intercessors

"Though Moses and Samuel stood before me, yet My mind could not be toward this people" (Jer. 15:1). Moses and Samuel are linked together in Jeremiah 15:1 and also in Psalm 99:6, as having great power with God in prayer and intercession. "They called upon the Lord, and He answered them":

> Moses: Ex, 17:4; 32:30-32; 34:5-9 with Deut. 9:18, 19; Num. 12:13; 16:22 & 21:7.
>
> Samuel: 1 Sam. 7:8, 9; 12:23.

"God forbid that I should sin against the Lord in ceasing to pray for you" (1 Sam. 12:23). There are at least seven similarities between them:

1. They were alike in standing before God (Jer. 15:1; Ps. 99:6).

2. Both had Godly parents (Ex. 2:1-4; 1 Sam. 1:1-8).

3. Both had a direct call from the Lord. (Ex. chs. 3, 4; 1 Sam. ch 3).

4. Both delivered Israelites from oppression; Moses from Pharaoh and Samuel from the Philistines. (Ex ch 12; 1 Sam. 7:8-13).

5. Both had singular miracles wrought for them in proof of their approval by the Lord. (Moses Ex. 4:1-9 and Samuel: 1 Sam. 6:19).

6. Both were vindicated by and before the Lord as unselfish men before their relatives and before the people they served:

   Moses: Num chs. 12, 16, 17
   Samuel: 1 Sam 12:1-5

7. Both threw out the challenge concerning testimony as judges and leaders of God's people, bearing the weight themselves, as true servants:

   Moses: "I have not taken one ass from any of them" (Num 16:15).

   Samuel: "Whose ass have I taken" (1 Sam 12:3).

They left others to enjoy the comfort that they denied themselves. What an example to follow!!

Linking these two men of God together emphasises *to us* the need and the importance of faithful prayer as found in James 5:17, 18 where Elias is shown as our example, although a man of like passions.

The Comparison between the Two Jonahs
Jonah the Son of Amittai and Simon Bar Jonas

Not only did these two preachers (Jonah 1:1 and John 21:15) have the same appellation, but there are at least twelve similarities between them. This should lead believers to appreciate God's design found in His Word. The divine Author stamps the impress of His person and His own divine intentions upon the book of Jonah and the Gospel narrations — God speaking once, yea twice, and even so, man perceives it not (Job 33:14). Nineveh repented, but was eventually overthrown (Nahum 1:1, 2). Israel showed partial repentance at Pentecost (Acts 2:37 & 41), but was ultimately set aside and scattered in AD 70, as the Lord Jesus foretold in Matthew 23:37 to 24:2.

The similarities are set out as follows:

1. Both had the same appellation. Jonah: which means 'a dove', which in the context is that of a messenger, like a message carrying pigeon.

2. Both were Jews.

3. Both were Galileans (2 Kings 14:25 Gath-hepher is a town of Zebulun, in lower Galilee; Matt. 4:18).

4. Both were in unclean places, before they were sent to the Gentiles:

– Jonah from the fish's belly (Jonah 1:17)

– Simon from the house of one Simon a Tanner (Acts 10:6) – Tanners are an aversion to the Jews.

5. Both were unwilling to preach to the Gentiles (Jonah 1:13; Act 10:14).

6. Both were from Joppa (Jonah 1:3; Acts 10:8).

7. Both were mentioned in chapter 16 of Matthew's Gospel (vv.4 & 17).

– Sign of Jonas the prophet (v 4)

– Blessed art thou Simon Bar Jona (v 17)

8. Both were found sleeping (Jonah 1:5; Acts 12:6).

9. Both were emotionally variable:

Jonah: Glad and Angry (Jonah 4:6,9).

Peter: Rightly declares 'Thou art the Christ', but immediately "began to rebuke Him" (Matt. 16:16 & 22).

10. Both preached and declared the resurrection from Psalm 16.

Peter: Acts 2:25-27 with Ps. 16:10.

Jonah: Cried from the belly of the fish "Thou hast brought up my life from corruption" (Jonah 2:2-10), and came out uncorrupted as a sign to Christ's death and resurrection (Matt. 12:40).

11. Both were subjected to close questioning (Jonah 1:8; John 18:17, 25-26).

12. Both acted contrary to the mind of God (Jonah 4:2; Matt. 16:22, 23).

BIBLE STUDY

STUDY PAPER : 08 - 09

The Tenth to the Fourteenth Day of Christ as the Passover Lamb

Israel was commanded of God, through Moses, to take a lamb, a male of the first year, without spot or blemish on the *tenth day* of the first month Nisan, every man a lamb according to their household. This lamb was to be kept up until the *fourteenth* day of that month and the whole assembly of the congregation of Israel was to kill it in the evening; it is the Lord's Passover (Exodus ch. 12). The blood of the Passover Lamb protected Israel, but particularly the first born, of men and the cattle - the blood made them safe and the word of Moses and of God made them sure. In the New Testament it is now "Christ our Passover" (1 Cor. 5:7), the substance of that type in the Passover Lamb. This paper seeks to outline the events that took place from that tenth to the fourteenth day of Nisan, the first month, as fulfilled by the Lord Jesus Christ.

Problems arise when harmonising these details, as given in the four Gospels, into one continuous narrative, giving rise to varying solutions. The sequence of some passages is clear, but others are not easy to arrange chronologically, but which we seek to unravel. Bearing in mind that John wrote much later than the other Gospel writers, a searching reader will notice that John led of the Holy Spirit, gives additional information confirming, amplifying and clarifying the details given in the other Gospels.

The following background information will enable us to widen our understanding of this subject:

The observance of the weekly Sabbath of rest (our Saturday) when no servile work was to be carried out, was a commandment of the Lord (Ex. 20:8-11) and was regarded as a "holy convocation" as in Leviticus 23:3; but as verse 4 states "these are the feasts of the Lord, even holy convocations", indicating that least days were also Sabbaths.

The first day of the Passover week, no matter upon what day of the week it fell, was therefore, always a Sabbath (Lev. 23:7 & Num. 28:16-18). This distinction is essential in the understanding of the Gospel narratives, enabling us to differentiate the *'weekly sabbath'* and the *'feast sabbath'*. A plain reading of the Gospels reveals, that the "preparation day", mentioned in Matt. 27:62; Mark 15:42; Luke 23:54; and John 19:14, 31, 42 would only mean the 13th day, and of course the following day was the 14th the Passover day, an high day and a Sabbath day (John 19:31). The following will be a guide in this respect.

The Passover Sabbath, The Weekly Sabbath and the Preparation Day Distinguished.

After the crucifixion and burial of our Lord Jesus, we read in Luke 23:54, "and that

171

day was the *preparation* and the *sabbath* drew on". The 'preparation' here means the removal of all leaven from the house for the feast of unleavened bread, which took place on the 13th day. Therefore the Sabbath mentioned in Luke 23:54 must indicate the PASSOVER SABBATH of John 19:31, even the 14th Nisan. However, having prepared the spices and ointments on the 15th day, as in Luke 23:56, they "rested on the sabbath day, according to the commandment", indicating this was the weekly Saturday Sabbath, that is the 16th day of Nisan. The following is quoted from a Bible Dictionary:

> "On the evening of the 13th as it began, the head of the family searched the house with a lighted candle that he might seek out all leaven. The hour on the 14th at which one must refrain from eating leavened-cakes was variously fixed... Work ceased on the 14th ... The time of the Passover sacrifice is defined by the law as "between the two evenings" (see Newberry margin). This was interpreted by the Pharisees and Talmudists to mean from the hour of the sun's decline until its setting; and this was later the temple practice.

"Between the evenings"

At the beginning of the 14th day, the Passover lamb is to be killed, "between the evenings" (Ex. 12:6 Newberry Margin), which is understood as the hour of "the sun's decline until its setting", and not "between two evenings". This may be confirmed from the 10th verse of the same chapter which says: "Ye shall let nothing of it remain until the morning". This means "from the evening to the following morning". Therefore, "between the even (evening)" cannot mean the evenings of two days. Besides this, the other passages also, where the same Hebrew word for 'even' occurs, confirm this, as in Ex. 29:39, "The one lamb thou shall offer in the *morning* and

the other thou shall offer at *even*", is effectively 'between the evenings' as mentioned above. Again the lamps were also to be lit "*at even*" (Ex. 30:8). However, in Leviticus 23:27-32 a quite different Hebrew phrase is used, in referring to the "day of atonement", which covers one full day from "*even to even*", in contrast to The phrase "between the evenings". Therefore, the phrase "between the evenings", does not cover the evenings of two days.

The Feast of Unleavened Bread

The feast of unleavened bread had to begin on the fifteenth day, after the 14th - the Passover Sabbath (Lev. 23:6). It was not a feast in the same sense as that of the Passover feast, but a daily abstaining from leaven only – fulfilled spiritually by us believers as in 1 Cor. 5:8. So, cleaning the house from leaven, could only take place on the *13th Nisan*, which therefore, became known as "the day of preparation". In this way the 'Passover' and 'unleavened bread' became synchronized in the minds of the Jews, as Mark 14:1 and Luke 22:1 state "After two days was the feast of the Passover and of unleavened bread", "Now the feast of the unleavened bread drew nigh which is called the Passover". Typically, the Passover had to be part of unleavened bread, since there was no sin in Christ. He offered Himself without spot. Though the crucifying of the Lord took place on the 13th, that is, on the *preparation day,* the Lord actually took hold of death at the beginning of the 14th day, as the day commenced at even i.e. "between the evenings". According to Genesis 1:5 the day commences with the evening.

Passover Day

"Ye know that *after two days* is the feast of Passover, and the Son of Man is betrayed to be crucified" (Matt. 26:2). Thus Christ indicated that after the following two days, He would be crucified. This would bring out the following:

1. The commencement of the 11th day is given in Matthew 21:18, at the end of which Christ made the above pronouncement, indicating the two days, i.e. the 12th and the 13th day of Nisan, 14th being the *Passover day* (Lev. 23:5).

2. "The Son of Man *is* betrayed to be crucified", indicates the immutability of His counsel, as if it has already been effectively enacted. This is qualified by His statement "after two days is the Passover", when the Passover lamb has to be killed. The Passover day was marked by the killing of the Passover lamb.

Passover Feast

This observance was a custom of the Jews. In fact 'feast' in Matt. 26:2 and Mark 14:1 is an *italicised* word, indicating that it is not in the original text In Matt. 26:2, this word simply means to eat the Passover. However, it was an essential observance and it is on this very occasion, that our Lord Jesus instituted the "Lord's Supper". The institution of the LORD'S SUPPER is narrated from verse 19, after the Passover had been eaten, and the cup mentioned in Luke 22:17 is related to the Jewish Passover.

One of the implications that the Apostle John so helpfully provides, through the Holy Spirit, is found in John 13:1 and onwards. John's narration also stresses that the Passover feast was ended, before the Lord instituted His own supper, as confirmed by Luke, in Luke 22:19. Further, John's narration says, "Now, *before* the feast of the Passover" (John 13:1), the word 'feast' not being *italicised* here. All these were *"before* the feast of the Passover", that is before the actual Passover day.

This should clear away any misunderstanding one may have, that the Lord ate the Passover at the very hour on the Passover day. He ate it in the evening, that is, the beginning of the 13th Nisan and went on to take hold of death at the beginning of the 14th day, at the very moment the Passover Lamb had to be slain.

The Lord Jesus Christ Fulfilled Every Detail Concerning the Passover-Lamb

Although, to the casual reader of the Gospel, Jesus Christ appears to be a victim of circumstances, in fact, on close scrutiny, it will be found that He controlled the circumstances, the events and the timings of those days as He did always.

He was the *last Passover-Lamb,* without spot or blemish. "Jesus therefore, knowing all things that should come upon Him, went forth" (John 18:4).

"In knowing all things" He fulfilled *everything* concerning the Passover Lamb:

1. He was a Lamb without blemish and without spot (Ex 12:5)

The purpose of keeping the Passover-lamb *for five days* from the tenth to the fourteenth day of the first month, gave opportunity to ensure that it was "without blemish". The Lord Jesus Christ, as the *Passover-Lamb,* fulfilled this demand in Himself, (1 Cor. 5:7), *primarily* in the sight of God, to fulfil the Scriptures (Ex. 12:5), as tested and examined by the events of those five days. (Matt. chs. 21 to 27)

2. The 10th to the 14th day (Ex 12:3, 6)

The Lord Jesus Christ returned from Jericho to Bethany, *six days* before the Passover (John 12:1) that is, six days before the 14th

173

Nisan; which would be the 8th, a Friday. They rested on the next day, the 9th a Saturday.

Concerning the following Sabbath (16th Nisan), we read in Luke 23:56, that the disciples and the women "rested on the sabbath day". Therefore, we may conclude that they necessarily rested on this Sabbath 9th also, though not specifically stated in the Gospels. This day lasted till about 6 p.m. That night, that is the next day according to Jews, the supper was arranged when Martha served and Lazarus, who was raised from the dead, was also present (John 12:2). After about 12 hours, and during the following morning (John 12:12), the triumphant entry into Jerusalem was made, that is on Sunday the 10th Nisan (Matt. 21:1-10). On that 10th day of Nisan, the Lord Jesus Christ, chosen to be the Passover Lamb, fulfilled Exodus 12:3, also "the law or the prophets" (Matt. 5:17). According to Matthew's narration, it was *after the feast* in Bethany (Matt. 26:6), that Judas went to the chief Priests and offered to betray Jesus for thirty pieces of silver (Matt. 26:6,14; Mark 14:10), being the price set on Him, fulfilling the OT prophecy given in Zech. 11:12, and as seen in Matt. 26:15. This took place after the supper in the house of Simon the leper (Mark 14:3), which happened, early on the 10th of Nisan, after the completion of that Jewish Sabbath.

(Incidentally, this also affirms that the woman anointing Jesus Christ in the house of Simon the leper at Bethany (Matt. 26:6-13; Mark 14:3-11) and Mary who anointed Jesus' feet (John 12:2-8) at the supper arranged at Bethany by Martha, are identical, but recorded differently. Both narrations confirm that it was in Bethany.)

3. As the Lamb of God, Christ took hold of death on the 14th Nisan

The Lord Jesus Christ gave Himself "between the evenings", at sundown, just at the beginning of the 14th Nisan (Ex. 12:6 Newberry Margin). As seen earlier, He with His disciples ate the Passover in the evening of the previous day, and He Himself took hold of death at the very moment the Passover Lamb had to be slain.

4. Not a bone of Him was broken (John 19:36)

When Christ was crucified on the cross and died, not a bone of Him was broken. The soldiers not knowing what they were doing fulfilled God's Word, which was prophesied some 1,500 years before. Both in shadow and type, it was true, "neither shall ye break a bone thereof" (Ex. 12:46. Compare John 19:36 with Num. 9:12 & Ps. 34:20).

Crucifixion was not on a Friday

The heathen feast day, which was always a Friday before the spring, commemorating the end of the winter and the annual resurrection of nature, *vernal equinox,* (the times when the sun crosses the equator, making night and day of approximately equal length all over the earth, occurring about March 21). This is marking the end of 40 days of weeping for Tammuz (refer Ezek. 8:10-14), – Christianised as LENT – was one of many heathen festivals that the Emperor Constantine adapted as a Christian festival, to which was added 'good' i.e. 'Good Friday'. Thus the traditional theory that Jesus was crucified on a Friday came into being, which necessarily contradicts the various details given in the Gospels. This traditional view that Jesus was crucified on a Friday, and that He ate the Passover on the regular day of the Passover, would place His journey from Jericho to Bethany, as recorded in John 12:1, *on a Jewish weekly Sabbath* (Saturday), which occurred *six days* before the Passover. Such a journey would be quite contrary to the OT law, and it would be impossible for our Lord to undertake on a Sabbath day.

It may be objected that our Lord Jesus Christ died on Wednesday evening, (the beginning of the Jewish Thursday), by pointing out that the two disciples on the way to Emmaus on the first day of the week (Sunday) said to our Lord, in speaking of the crucifixion and the events accompanying it, "Besides all this, today is the *third day since* these things were done" (Luke 24:21). If crucifixion took place on Wednesday, would not Sunday be the fourth day? But the answer is simple. The crucifixion and the burial were completed just as the Jewish Thursday was beginning, that is the 14th Nisan, at *sunset of our Wednesday.* Thus the first day after Thursday would be Friday; the second day after Thursday would be Saturday and the 'third day *since'* would be Sunday, the first day of the week. So the supposed objection, in reality, supports the facts. On the other hand, placing the crucifixion on a Friday makes God's word given in Luke 24:21 void: "Today (Sunday the resurrection day) is the third day *since* these things were done".

The Days from 10th to 17th Nisan

The days from the 10th to 14th Nisan, during which the Lord Jesus, as the Passover-Lamb was kept up for examination, together with the subsequent three days up to the 17th are set out as follows.

> *Note:* Please take note that all days referred to below, are *Jewish days* being reckoned from evening 6 p.m. our time. The Chart annexed, will show clearly the comparison between the Jewish day and ours (Roman), indicating the major events that occurred from the 10th to 17th Nisan, as found in the Gospels.

Tenth Nisan (The first day of the week)

(Our Saturday – Sunday)

The Lord Jesus enters Jerusalem on the colt of an ass, (Matt. 21:1-17), and the multitude received Him saying "Hosanna (Hebrew 'Hoshiahnah' meaning 'save now') to the Son of David". This was followed by the cleansing of the Temple.

Eleventh Nisan

(Our Sunday – Monday)

The narration about this day starts, as we read "Now in the morning, as He returned into the City He hungered" (Matt. 21:18). The activities of this eleventh day commenced, with the Lord being hungry and finding no fruit on the fig tree, and cursing it. The further activities of that day are described in great detail up to Matthew 26:2. Incidentally, such elaborate detail is not given about any other day of the Lord's glorious ministry.

Twelfth Nisan

(Our Monday – Tuesday)

Christ said: "Ye know that *after two days* (i.e. the 12th and the 13th day), is the feast of the Passover and the Son of man is betrayed to be crucified" (Matt. 26:2). It was on this day, the 12th that the Lord arranged for the preparation of the Passover-feast (Matt. 26:17).

Thirteenth Nisan

(Our Tuesday – Wednesday)

This day began, our Lord sitting with the twelve, "when the hour was come" (Luke 22:14; John 13:1,2) for eating of the Passover and also the institution of the Lord's Supper, followed by His agony in the garden of Gethsemane. After this the Lord allows Himself to be arrested and taken before Caiaphas and the Sanhedrin, where He was tried and mocked (Matt. 26:57-58). He was then hurried to Pilate (Mark 15:1) at sunrise, who eventually tried Him and found Him faultless, nevertheless, gave Him over to be crucified. It may appear that men were acting against Christ, but it was God Himself working as fore-ordained and as foretold; "The Lord hath laid on Him the iniquity of us all", "for the transgression of my people was he stricken", "He shall bear their iniquities", and "He bare the sin of many" (Isa. 53:6, 8, 11, 12). He thus finished the work of salvation on the cross at Calvary by the ninth hour (3 p.m. our time). This is the "preparation of the Passover" day (John 19:14). This crucifixion day is otherwise described as "the Jew's preparation day" (John 19:31 & 42).

Fourteenth Nisan

(Our Wednesday – Thursday)

Jesus Christ took hold of death on the 14th Nisan as the Lamb of God, 'between the evenings' as explained earlier, (Ex. 12:6) - that is the hour of the sun's decline until its setting, at the beginning of the 14th, as the 13th day closes by about 6 p.m. The Passover Sabbath was a 'high day' (John 19:31), Joseph of Arimathaea and Nicodemus completed the burial by the sun set (Mark 15:42; Luke 23:53, 54), so that effectively, no work was done on the 14th day. The Scriptures were fulfilled, and therefore *this* Passover Lamb took hold of death as the 14th day commenced with the evening at the end of the 13th day. "In the fourteenth day of the first month, at even is the Lord's Passover" (Lev. 23:5).

The Lord's body rested in the tomb for the whole of this day – first day in the tomb.

Fifteenth Nisan

(Our Thursday – Friday)

"On the fifteenth day of the same month is the feast of unleavened bread unto the Lord" (Lev. 23:6).

The women prepared spices and ointment as found in Luke 23:56.

The Lord's body rested in the tomb for the whole of this day – second day in the tomb.

Sixteenth Nisan
(The weekly Sabbath)

(Our Friday – Saturday)

This is the mandatory weekly - Sabbath-rest day. Luke is helpful here: "and *rested* the Sabbath day, according to the commandment", after having prepared spices and ointments on the previous day (Luke 23:56; Ex. 20:10).

The Lord's body rested in the tomb for the whole of this day – third day in the tomb.

Seventeenth Nisan
(The first day of the week)

(Our Saturday – Sunday)

Mary Magdalene came while it was *yet dark,* on the first of the *weeks* (The Greek text is in plural, being the seven weeks to Pentecost). But the Lord Jesus had risen before that, even in the early hours of the 17th day (Matt. 28:1; Luke 24:1; John 20:1), which is the first day of the week. "Now when Jesus was risen early, the first day of the week(s)" (Mark 16:9). "The first day of the week(s) cometh Mary Magdalene early, when *it was dark,* unto the sepulchre and seeth the stone taken away from the sepulchre" (John 20:1). She came also later as we read in Mark 16:1, with others, at the rising of the sun (Mark 16:2). The risen Lord joined the two on the Emmaus road and revealed Himself to them. (Luke 24:13-32).

Our Lord's body rested *"in the heart of the earth"* for three full days

"For *as* Jonah was three days and three nights in the whale's belly; *so* shall the Son of Man be *three days and three nights* in the heart of the earth" (Matt. 12:40). Only the Lord

176

Jesus has this information as to the length of this period of *three days,* up to the 17th day (After 6 p.m. on the Saturday – our time) in order to fulfil exactly the period in which Jonah was in the belly of the great fish. The great fish had to be told when to vomit up Jonah, by the same One who Himself knew exactly when to rise from the dead.

"Destroy this temple and *in three days* I will raise it up" was again a *sign* given by our Lord to the Jews, and He spoke this of the temple of His body. John says that the disciples particularly remembered this "after He was risen from the dead" (John 2:18-22).

"Today is the *third day* since these things were done" (Luke 24:21). That is, the 17th day is 'third day since', which left no doubt in their minds, that the Lord Jesus took hold of death early on the 14th day. The incident of the Pharisees repeating our Lord's word "after *three days* I will rise again" Matt. 27: 62-65 and thus demanding the sepulchre to be sealed, also confirms that our Lord's body rested for three full days in the heart of the earth. For this sealing of the tomb, they allowed 'servile work' on a Sabbath high day!

Christ's Glorious Resurrection

The day of Christ's resurrection was the anniversary of the crossing of the Red Sea as seen below:

14th day – "The self same day" Israel was brought out of Egypt (Ex. 12:51).

15th day – The day Pharaoh chased Israel (Ex. 14:7-9)

16th day – "All the night" (to dark), darkness to Egyptians and light for Israelites (Ex. 14:20)

17th day – "In the morning watch" and "when the morning appeared." Thus the Lord saved Israel *that day* out of the hand of the Egyptians" (Ex. 14:24, 27 & 30).

This day was also the day when the Ark rested on mount Ararat (Gen. 8:4), even the 17th day of Nisan, the first month, which before the Exodus was the seventh month (Ex. 12:1), "But saved Noah the eighth" (2 Pet 2:5), who typically came forth from the waters, indicating that it must be on this same day that our Ark, the Lord Jesus Christ, must and would rise from the dead.

Well might we ask, as with the Jewish people of those days at Jerusalem, "Who is this?" (Matt. 21:10).

"Is this the Man? Can this be He
The prophets have foretold?
Should with transgressors numbered be,
And for my sins be sold ! !"

The Hours of Trial and Crucifixion of the Lord Jesus

Closely associated with the above mentioned dates, are also the hours of the trial of the Lord Jesus, and the way they were conducted. All the four Gospels record these hours and the various details, none without significance. Many OT prophecies relating to the Messiah were fulfilled during these hours.

Roman time is used only in John's Gospel, which is the same as we employ now, but in all the other Gospels and also in Acts, time is reckoned after the *Jewish* custom. The Jewish day commenced from evening: "And the evening and the morning were the first day" (Gen. 1:5), that is, they calculate the time from sundown to sunrise and from sunrise to sundown. John wrote his Gospel much later than the other Gospel writers, perhaps after Jerusalem was destroyed, and so he uses Roman time, which was then in vogue.

The Lord and His disciples had eaten the Passover in the evening, after which they went out to the garden of Gethsemane. There

177

He was betrayed by Judas, seized by the officers from the chief priests and Pharisees, and forsaken by His own disciples. He was then taken to the high priest. The order of events following the arrest of the Lord Jesus appears to be:

1. The *Jewish trial* of Jesus was in three stages:

(a) Brought before Annas (John 18:12-14 & 19-23).

Caiaphas was appointed as high priest by Rome, for political reasons, when his father-in-law Annas, was the high priest. Scripture names them both as high priests (Matt. 26:3, 57; Luke 3:2; John 18:13; Acts 4:6).

(b) The trial before Caiaphas the high priest and the Sanhedrin at the high Priest's palace (Matt. 26:57-68; Mark 14:53-65; Luke 22:54-62; John 18: 24, 28), both trials, being at night, were illegal.

(c) Finally in the morning the chief priests, scribes, elders and the whole council gathered and decided to take Him to Pilate for the implementing of their death sentence (Matt. 27:1; Mark 15:1; Luke 22:66-71).

2. Associated with 1. (b) above is Peter's denial (Matt. 26:58, 69-75; Mark 14:54, 66-72; Luke 22:54-62; John 18:15-18,25-27), and Judas' suicide (Matt 27:3-10; Acts 1:18-19).

3. The *Gentile trial* foretold by our Lord in Luke 18:32, was in three stages:

(a) Jesus was questioned by Pilate for the first time (Matt. 27:2, 11-14; Mark 15:1-5; Luke 23:1-5; John 18:28-38);

(b) Pilate sent Jesus to Herod (Luke 23:6-12); and

(c) Herod sent Jesus back to Pilate, who released Barabbas (meaning "son of a father") and delivered Jesus (the Son of God) to be crucified. (Matt. 27:15-26; Mark 15:6-15; Luke 23:13-25; John 18:39-40).

The Jews were busy all night to accomplish their evil designs and finally Pilate gave his sentence at the *"sixth hour"* (John 19:14), that is, 6 o'clock Roman time, in the morning. Mark 15:25 says, "And it was the *third hour*, and they crucified Him". This is in perfect accord with John's Gospel, as above, when He was still on trial at 6 a.m. Here, according to Jewish time, He was crucified at the *third hour*, or 9 a.m. our time. After the death sentence by Pilate, He was led forth in a procession out of the city to Golgotha, the cross had been laid on Simon of Cyrene (Matt. 27:31, 32; Mark 15:20, 21; Luke 23:26). In fact, the Lord Himself was in divine control of all these proceedings, through and through, from His arrest, trial, crucifixion, and finally gave up His spirit.

Thus there elapsed a time of *three hours* from the time of judgment to the actual crucifixion at 9 a.m. our time.

Matthew, Mark and Luke tell of the darkness that settled over the land from "the *sixth hour* . . . until the *ninth hour*" (Matt. 27:45, 46; Mark 15:33, 34; Luke 23:44), that is from 12 noon until 3 p.m. our time. He was on the cross from 9 a.m. till noon suffering at the hands of sinful men (Acts 2:23). From then on, the scene changed to one of darkness when He was made "an offering for sin". During the second three hours, He was there "to put away sin by the sacrifice of Himself" (Heb 9:26) and darkness shrouded the scene, for man was shut out, when it became a matter of God's dealing with sin in the Person of Christ the sinless Substitute.

Consider also, how at the "third hour" (9 a.m.) the Lord Jesus was crucified, when the lamb of the *morning sacrifice* was to be offered upon the altar, and He gave up the ghost, when the lamb of the *evening sacrifice* (between the evenings) was offered (Ex. 29: 38, 39). These are the very hours during which Aaron was instructed of the Lord to burn on the altar "sweet incense every *morning*" and light "the lamps at *even* (between the evenings) and burn incense upon it" (Ex. 30:7, 8).

As soon as the Lord Jesus delivered up His Spirit, after the ninth hour, (3 p.m.) between sun-down and sun-set, the veil of the temple was rent from the top to bottom (Matt. 27:51; Mark 15:38), indicating that it was not by *human hand.*

Acts 3:1 tells us that the *ninth hour* was the "hour of prayer", that is, 3 p.m. We are also told according to Ex. 29:38, 39 and 30:7, 8 that during this hour of prayer, at even, when lighting the lamps, the priest was in the holy place of the temple, burning incense, just outside this veil. Thus the priest was there in the Holy place to witness the rending of the veil from top to bottom. What a fearful sight it must have been for the priest to see the veil rent. This means that the pattern given of heavenly things (Heb. 9:23), *was rent,* giving access into the sanctuary - in heaven itself - for all His people who keep on coming to Him, our Lord Jesus Christ, seeing He ever liveth to make intercession for us (Heb. 7:25) – that we may with boldness "enter into the holiest, by the blood of Jesus . . . through the veil that is to say His flesh" (Heb. 10:19, 20). What a testimony as to the efficacy of the work of Him who had just died!!

Neither before nor since, has not only the year of a man's death but also the month and the day, even the very hour, ever been recorded beforehand. This timing of our Lord's death was not accidental or coincidental – it was truly divinely planned. "The *hour* is come that the Son of Man should be glorified" (John 12:23, 27; 13:1).

Christ is however not only unique in respect of the timing of His death, it is His resurrection that crowns Him, the unassailable, invincible, vanquisher of death and hell, and the eternal hope of all who are in Christ, even of their own glorious resurrection.

Note: The following chart will help to fix the events and the days in their proper order.

THE TENTH TO THE SEVENTEENTH DAY CONCERNING CHRIST AS PASSOVER LAMB AND HIS RESURRECTION
(Jewish and Gentile Days Distinguished)

JEWISH DAY NISAN 32 AD				GENTILE DAY APRIL 32 AD
10th Nisan First day of the week	Enters Jerusalem (Matt. 21:7-17)	Night	Night	Saturday
		Day	Day	Sunday
11th Nisan	Night stay at Bethany (Matt. 21:17) Cursing of the fig tree (Matt. 21:18,19)	Night	Night	Monday
		Day	Day	
12th Nisan	"After *two* days is the feast of the Passover" (Matt. 26:2)	Night	Night	Tuesday
		Day	Day	
13th Nisan Preparation Day (John 19:42)	Passover-Feast Gethsemane Jewish and Gentile Trials *before* 6 a.m. Crucifixion 9 a.m. Death after 3 p.m. "between the evenings"	Night	Night	Wednesday
		Day	Day	
14th Nisan	Passover Sabbath High - Day (John 19:31)	Night	Night	Thursday
		Day	Day	
15th Nisan	Feast of Unleavened Bread	Night	Night	Friday
		Day	Day	
16th Nisan	Weekly Mandatory Sabbath (Ex. 20:8-11)	Night	Night	Saturday
		Day	Day	
17th Nisan First Day of the week	First Fruits of Resurrection When it was yet dark (John 20:1) The risen Christ with the two on Emmaus Road (Luke 24:13-32)	Night	Night	Sunday
		Day	Day	
		Night	Night	Monday